John Light

Visual Langua

Robert E. Horn

Throughout history words and images have occupied separate domains. We have been forced to think of ourselves as either word people or visual people. In this provocative and pathfinding book, Robert Horn shows how that wide gulf is at last being bridged. He makes a compelling case for considering visual language—the tight integration of words and visual elements—a truly new language with the distinct syntax and semantics expected of a language.

Horn argues that this new language growing up around us is a prelude to far-reaching changes in the very manner in which we will communicate in the next century. He notes that the creation of visual language emerges from people around the world inventing components out of necessity to communicate about the ever-increasing complexity of our lives. Visual language is being synthesized from previously separate vocabularies as diverse as computer flow charts, business process diagrams, and cartoons and animation. It has grown and spread organically and globally in ways that artificially created international languages—like Esperanto, which was invented by a single person—have never done. In a significant sense, it is already an international language of technology, science, and business.

This is several books in one: a lively introduction to the basic concepts of visual language; a splendid, concise history of some 70 major innovations that form the core history of the language; a closely reasoned survey of the research on the emerging syntax and semantics of the language; and an immensely practical guide to the applications of visual language.

But this book is not only a pathfinding and provocative treatise, *it is the first to use visual language itself to describe and analyze that language.* By his use of visual language on every page, Horn demonstrates that it is an immensely flexible and effective communication tool and one that invites and delights us. Readers will not only learn about visual language, but will have the full experience of total immersion. They will experience what Horn calls a new multi-modal process of reading, simultaneously demanding and rewarding.

Horn shows how visual language is the best tool we have for managing the world's ever-increasing complexity and the augmented speed at which our civilization moves. He doesn't merely make these claims, but lays out clearly how this new language can be useful in visualizing complex issues, exploring deeper connections and feelings, facilitating creative problem solving, making group process visible, presenting multiple points of view, and facilitating cross-cultural and international communication.

Bob Horn's book is not only fundamental to the rapidly expanding worlds of visual language, but, by its synthesis of the best of visual and verbal components, it is a major contribution to understanding human communication in general.

Visual Language

Global Communication for the 21st Century

Robert E. Horn

MacroVU, Inc. • Bainbridge Island, Washington

© 1998 by Robert E. Horn.

All rights reserved. No part of this book may be reproduced or transmitted in any form or by any means, electronic or mechanical, including photocopying, recording, or any information storage and retrieval system, without permission in writing from the publisher.

Creation of derivative works, such as information abstracts, unless agreed to in writing by the copyright owner, is forbidden. Copying of authorized derivative works by any means, including electronic recordings, is prohibited.

Trademark Information
Macintosh is a registered trademark of Apple Computer. Inc.
MacroVU is a registered trademark of Robert E. Horn, and VLicon is trademark of Robert E. Horn.
Information Mapping and InfoMap are registered trademarks of Information Mapping, Inc., Waltham, MA.
All other marks are the property of their respective owners.

ISBN 1-892637-09-X
Library of Congress Catalog Card Number 98-96408

Printed on acid-free paper.

To Order This Book
Call
(206) 780–9612
Fax
(206) 842–0296
or Write
MacroVU, Inc
Box 366
321 High School Rd. NE
Bainbridge Island, WA 98110

For More Information
macrovu.com

For all of my mentors, teachers, collaborators, and friends

The dream of a perfect language did not only obsess European culture. The story of the confusion of tongues, and of the attempt to redeem its loss through the rediscovery or invention of a language common to all humanity, can be found in every culture.

Umberto Eco, *The Search for the Perfect Language*

Each language constitutes a certain model of the universe, a semiotic system of understanding the world, and if we have 4,000 different ways to describe the world, this makes us rich.

V. V. Ivanov, "Reconstructing the Past"

Words and pictures are sometimes jurisdictional enemies, as artists feud with writers for scarce space. An unfortunate legacy of these craft-union differences is the artificial separation of words and pictures; a few style sheets even forbid printing on graphics. ... Words and pictures belong together.

Edward Tufte, *The Visual Display of Quantitative Information*

Contents

Preface and Acknowledgements

Origins of the ideas

The ideas for this book initially arose on the day, in 1984, that I first saw a Macintosh computer. I realized that easy access to computerized drawing programs would bring into being a whole new world of communication possibilities. For the first time, nonartists could use the computer to draw and could endlessly modify and reuse drawings once they were created. I immediately began to use some clip art in my ordinary business and personal communications. At that time I was CEO of Information Mapping, Inc., now one of the world's premier information management companies, and I thought of the graphic computer as simply a way to add graphics to our existing method of analyzing and organizing business communication documents.

Why this book now?

Not until a couple of years later did I come to understand that, in fact, people all over the world were using the capabilities of the graphic computer to create the fundamentals of a new communication tool—a language based on the tight integration of words and visual elements, which in this book I call visual language. I saw this book as necessary to establish visual language as a *language*. After some research, I realized that no framework existed for analyzing and understanding the new types of communication units that are created when text and visuals are combined. Neither was there a linguistics of visual language. Borrowing the approaches of natural language linguistics is an insufficient way to analyze the systematics of visual language. Nor is the simple addition of concepts from art theory sufficient. For this new communication tool to flourish, I identified a need for the kind of deeper understanding that can come from an analysis based on the integration of linguistic and visual elements. Finally, I saw this book as a way to encourage people to begin using more visual language in their communications, to integrate text and graphics to communicate more effectively.

Style of the book

An analysis of visual language must, of course, be written in visual language. (I hardly ever write otherwise these days.) This book could have been rendered in a variety of aesthetic styles, but I decided to use clip art, to further demonstrate how much one can communicate with this medium without original artwork. I also wanted to encourage others to use visual language, and the 1st hurdle often seems to be fear of drawing. I believe that clip art is going to be the primary tool that will facilitate most people's use of visual language in their everyday jobs. I recognize that using clip art gives this book a particular look that may be dismissed by some critics, which is often the fate of clip art. It is my belief, however, that clip art is yet evolving, and that different styles will soon become available that will make it an increasingly graceful and aesthetically pleasing communications tool.

A focus on 2 dimensions and static media

The two-dimensional page and screen are foundational for other media. Most of the semantic constructs discussed here transfer easily to the 3rd dimension and to motion. Thus, media such as virtual reality, multimedia, and animation are not heavily emphasized in this book. During their development, films are broken down into scenes and then into shots. This is why storyboards work in filmmaking. And it is why films can be analyzed using the techniques developed here for static media. As regards three-dimensional media like virtual reality, as such media develop enough complexity to be truly useful and interesting, they require the kinds of maps and navigational tools that are analyzed in this book.

Acknowledgements

I have been at work on this book off and on for 10 years. I want to thank many people who have made such a long-term commitment possible, productive, and a pleasure.

Many people have read all or part of the manuscript. I would like to acknowledge my appreciation to Terry Winograd of the Program on People, Computers, and Design at Stanford University's Center for the Study of Language and Information, for affording me the opportunity to share the collegiality of that center for several years as a visiting scholar while I was finishing this book. I would also like to express my appreciation to Tom Furness of the Human-Computer Interface Laboratory at the University of Washington in Seattle for the wonderful opportunity to be a visiting scholar there. I also thank William and Meredith Bricken for their enthusiastic discussions.

Many dear friends kept encouraging me throughout the project, including Bob Weber, Don Michael, John Garret, and David Sibbet. They also at times functioned as insightful reviewers and critics. I also want to thank Carl Binder for giving me the chance to teach early versions of my visual language workshops to his staff. That experience and many subsequent courses have sharpened my understanding of visual language and its place in the broader communications spectrum.

I thank Doug Gorman and Elizabeth Shaw, who read early versions of the book and made helpful suggestions. And I thank in particular 2 instructors, Mike Learned and Angelo Presicci, for many discussions about teaching my visual language courses for business communicators. I also spent many helpful hours with a seminar group at Stanford University in the fall of 1994, which is when I first taught visual language concepts.

A project of this size and complexity is a team effort, and, of course, many members of the team contributed in different roles. I want to thank my publishing consultant and book doctor Rebecca Salome of Entrepreneurial Authors®, who is also a dear friend. She helped me through the hard places in developing the book. I also want to acknowledge the role of my editor, Jennifer Wedel, production consultant Harrison Shaffer, and production assistance from Karen Alfke, Gail Sheehan, Noel Black, Padu Bergamo, Katherina Audley, Thierry DiDonna, copy editor Maureen Klier, proofreader Wendy Smith, and indexer Linda Gregonis.

Robert E. Horn
San Francisco, California
February 1998

Visual Language

Global Communication for the 21st Century

Chapter 1
A New Language Emerges

Contents of Chapter 1

History—personal and otherwise

I grew up in a little Iowa town and was educated much like everybody else of my generation. When I was a little boy, I liked to draw. In kindergarten, all my friends were busy artists, filling page upon page with brightly colored crayon drawings of houses and airplanes and trucks and dolls. For a few years, Mrs. Roberts, the art teacher, came to our classroom once a week to teach us a few things about how to draw. Mostly she just encouraged us by smiling and praising us. In grammar school, I never learned to draw very well, but I loved doing it. Then, one year, Mrs. Roberts stopped coming. We had more important things to do: learn our grammar and punctuation and, above all, improve our writing skills.

This split between using words and using images parallels a historical split. Just after the invention of the Phoenician alphabet (➔24)*, words and images (artistic pictures, sculpture, drawings) began to take separate routes. It is true that for at least one early period of time, in ancient Egypt (➔25–26), the two forms were combined. And in their way, Chinese and related languages have retained elements of their pictographic origins. (➔24). In the West, there were periods, too, during which visual elements were used as marginalia in otherwise completely textual documents. A diagram or picture occasionally accompanied text in medieval manuscripts. And from time to time a word or a phrase appeared on a painting. But, by and large, the visual and the verbal went their separate ways, becoming separate forms of communication. Each had its own vocabulary and syntax, each its own tools and concepts. Each had its own master craftsmen and teachers, each its own department in the university. Even in the elementary grades, teachers specialized in one subject or the other, not both. By the time I was in school, that was the way it was supposed to be. Everybody knew that you were either a word person (which was most of us) or a picture person (i.e., the artists). It was all part of a great either/or division that we have relied upon for millennia.

If you were a writer, and if for some reason you needed to explain something with an illustration, you got a graphic artist to work for you. For the most part, texts of entire books, indeed whole sets of encyclopedias, were written before an art director was called in to add the pictures. Similarly for magazines and newspapers. Real journalists were writers. Photographers added a little visual interest but weren't part of the critical core of a publication. Sometimes words and images needed to be tightly integrated, but that was an exception.

*Arrows with numbers in parentheses (➔   ) indicate page numbers in the book.

By the time I reached high school, my classmates and I were focused on getting into college. That meant more writing. Luckily, I had a series of wonderful teachers who did their best to prepare me to write essays, short stories, research papers, and dissertations.

In college, not a word was said about drawing. Well, there was one science teacher who drew diagrams on the board, and once in a while there were photographs in the textbooks. But in the normal course of studying the humanities and social sciences, visual communication of any kind was absent. During my undergraduate years, my vocational interests began to head in the direction of journalism. It just seemed natural to become a writer. I wrote a weekly op-ed column as an associate editor for the college newspaper. I also kept sketching, for the pleasure of it. A few of my pen-and-ink drawings were published in the college magazine. But I did not take a single art course in undergraduate or graduate school. Right after college, during the Korean War, I was drafted into the army, where I was made a clerk-typist. The army used maps a great deal, but at that time everything else was communicated with words. A lot of words. Army regulations filled many volumes. There was a standard procedure for everything, and as a clerk-typist I was in charge of reading them all.

And so it was when I attended graduate school in political science as well. I could go for months without encountering any kind of visual communication. When I did, it was usually a diagram—organization charts of the federal government, for example. Neither was there much drawing in my first job as a management intern for the government. During my time with the government, I spent a month in one agency's new computer department. I became so interested in the early computers that I decided to learn more. At that time, universities didn't have computer science departments, so I applied for and got a job at Univac, which was one of the 2 major companies early in the history of computing. At Univac, I began to observe the increasingly urgent need for new ways to manage the complexity of the modern world. We needed to be able to quickly and efficiently glean pertinent information about systems that had hundreds or thousands of elements; I learned from poring through the five-foot-tall stacks of computer manuals that prose had severe limitations.

But I still wanted to be a writer. I quit my job at Univac and spent a year in Paris trying to write a novel. I found out from that experience that I was not going to be a novelist, so I came back to the United States and began working as an editor. Through that occupation, I found myself working at Columbia University during an exciting period of social sciences and educational rethinking. Researchers had begun to use modern psychology and the systems approach that had been worked out during the cybernetics revolution to open up a great many questions about how people learn and about how best to teach. I found that I could use my background as a computer programmer, social scientist, writer, and editor to contribute to the work being done. I spent a couple of very productive years at the Institute of Educational Technology at Columbia University, teaching graduate courses, writing my first 2 books, and beginning to consult on various educational problems.

In the communications world, I began to notice some important changes. At the office and in the scientific presentations I attended, people were increasingly using 35mm slide projectors, particularly to display quantitative graphs and charts.

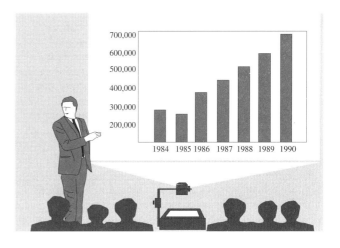

And I couldn't help noticing how television, as many observers have pointed out, had moved us into what was now being called a visual culture. Many critics were beginning to identify the far-reaching consequences of such a major shift in how we get our information, from print media to the tube.

It was first the camera and its various projection devices and then television that have made the big difference. "There is little doubt that contemporary lifestyle has been influenced, and crucially, by the changes enacted on it by the fact of the photograph. In print, language is the primary element, while visual factors such as physical setting or design format and illustration, are secondary or supportive. In the modern media, just the reverse is true. The visual dominates; the verbal augments. Print is not dead yet, nor will it ever be, but nevertheless, our language-dominated culture has moved perceptibly toward the iconic," says Donis Dondis in her 1973 book, *A Primer of Visual Literacy.*

"Man has functioned as a seer and embraced vastness for millennia," says Caleb Gattegno in his 1969 book *Toward A Visual Culture.* "But only recently, through television (and film and photography, the modern media) has he been able to shift from the clumsiness of speech (however miraculous and far-reaching) as a means of expression and therefore of communication, to the powers of infinite visual expression, thus enabling him to share with everybody immense dynamic wholes in no time." When I read his book, I thought that clearly something new was emerging here. We needed to explore and examine the phenomenon.

As visionary as Gattegno and Dondis were in predicting the emergence of a visual culture, they were still to some degree victims of the either/or mindset I described earlier. They saw the visual triumphing over the verbal. There is no doubt in my mind that we are afloat in a sea of visual images, which is transforming us into what can be called a visual culture. But is this all there is to it? No. Something more is going on. The phenomena are more complex than that.

A New Language Is Emerging

A larger synthesis in how people communicate is occurring. A wide variety of visual and verbal representation systems are coming together. The process is occurring in much the same natural way that other Creole and pidgin languages arise: where people speaking different languages come together and invent a new language that combines their original tongues.

Dialects converging

Boundaries are disintegrating between smaller sublanguages—diagramming, cartooning, advertising, graphical computer interfaces, and countless others. These "dialects" or "vocabularies" have begun to encounter one another and integrate into a larger, more inclusive language. As millions of such encounters occur, we find ourselves in the midst of the emergence of a new language: *visual language.*

Dynamic growth

Visual language is emerging as any other language does—by people creating it and speaking it. Already, visual language is growing and spreading in ways that artificial international languages—like Esperanto, which was invented by a single person—have never done. It is being born of people's need, worldwide, to deal with complex ideas that are difficult to express in text alone. The rapid increase in visual language's use in the last decade has been further fueled by the development of the personal computer, which has facilitated graphical communication via clip art and drawing programs without requiring much innate talent or long periods of training.

Goal of this book

The primary goal of this book is to investigate the properties of visual language that make it a language, as opposed to another in the multitude of communications methodologies. The different "dialects" and "vocabularies" mentioned above are contributing "word-like" units and "grammar-like" structures to visual language as it enters an important new phase in its development—a time of synthesis and more and more mainstream usage.

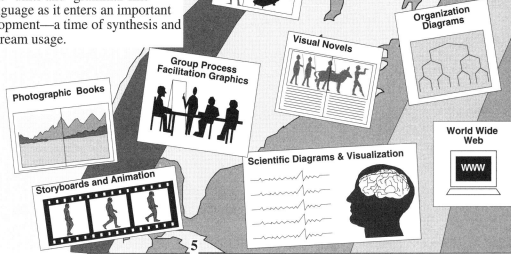

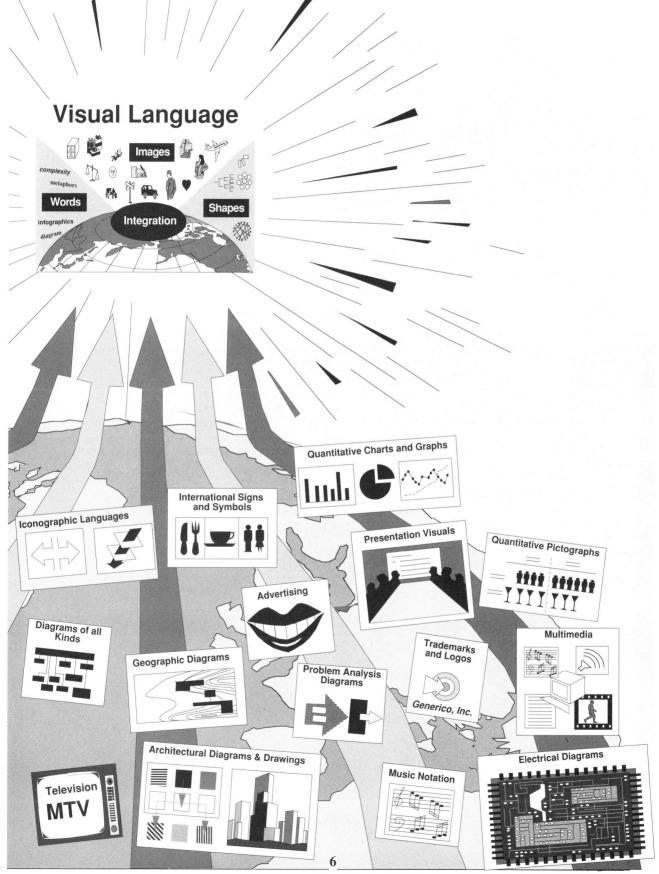

Visual Language

Images

complexity

metaphors

Words

Integration

Shapes

infographics

diagram

Quantitative Charts and Graphs

International Signs and Symbols

Iconographic Languages

Presentation Visuals

Quantitative Pictographs

Advertising

Diagrams of all Kinds

Geographic Diagrams

Problem Analysis Diagrams

Trademarks and Logos

Generico, Inc.

Multimedia

Architectural Diagrams & Drawings

Television MTV

Music Notation

Electrical Diagrams

What Is Visual Language?

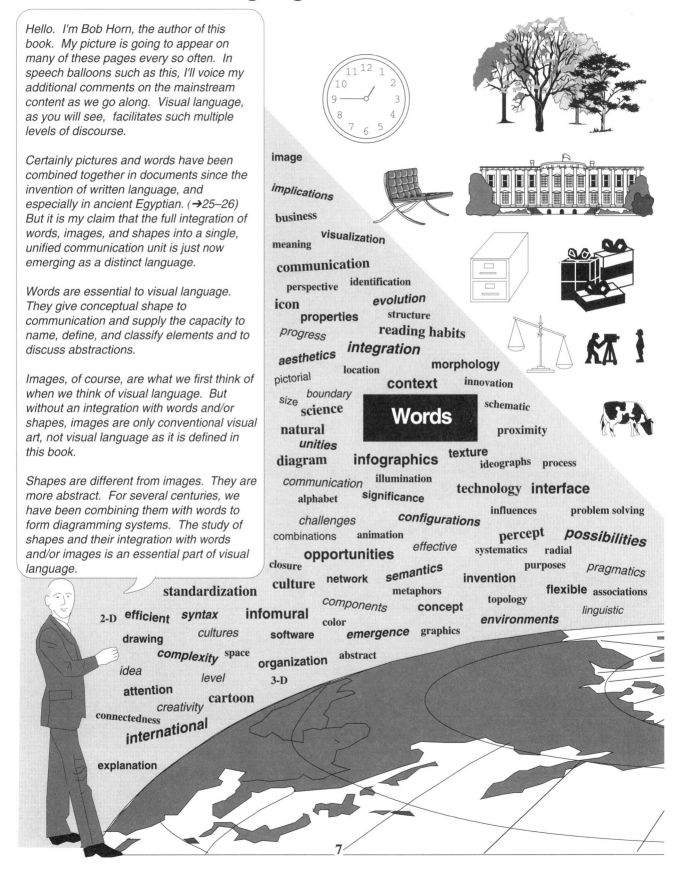

Hello. I'm Bob Horn, the author of this book. My picture is going to appear on many of these pages every so often. In speech balloons such as this, I'll voice my additional comments on the mainstream content as we go along. Visual language, as you will see, facilitates such multiple levels of discourse.

Certainly pictures and words have been combined together in documents since the invention of written language, and especially in ancient Egyptian. (→25–26) But it is my claim that the full integration of words, images, and shapes into a single, unified communication unit is just now emerging as a distinct language.

Words are essential to visual language. They give conceptual shape to communication and supply the capacity to name, define, and classify elements and to discuss abstractions.

Images, of course, are what we first think of when we think of visual language. But without an integration with words and/or shapes, images are only conventional visual art, not visual language as it is defined in this book.

Shapes are different from images. They are more abstract. For several centuries, we have been combining them with words to form diagramming systems. The study of shapes and their integration with words and/or images is an essential part of visual language.

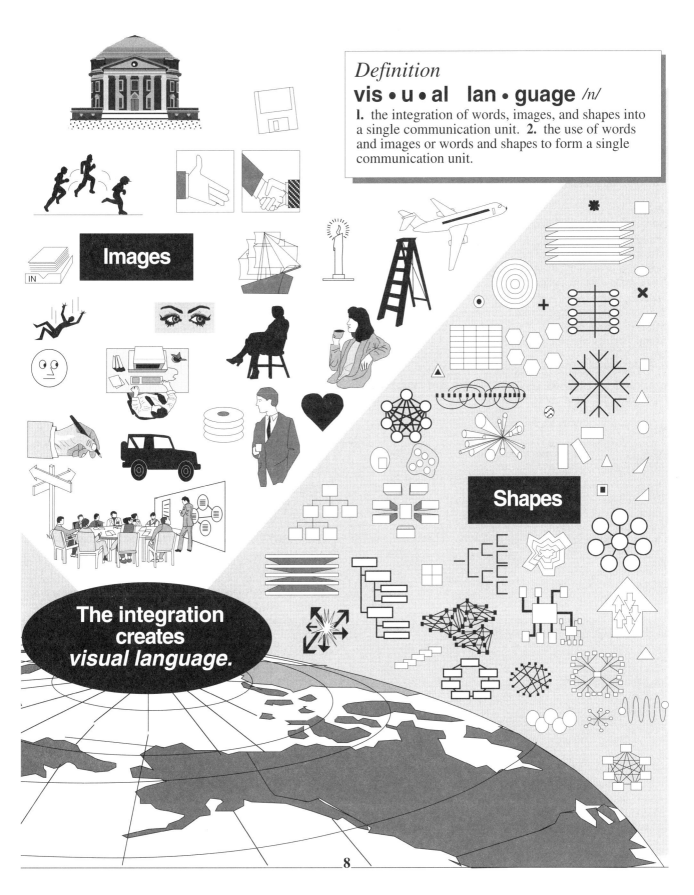

Definition
vis • u • al   lan • guage /n/
1. the integration of words, images, and shapes into a single communication unit. **2.** the use of words and images or words and shapes to form a single communication unit.

Images

Shapes

The integration creates *visual language.*

8

Text, Images, or Shapes Alone
Are Not Visual Language

When used separately, the individual components of visual language—words, images, and shapes—do not provide us with a truly "visual" language. I do not dispute that each visual language component can have great value when it is used alone. The major question this book will examine, however, is what happens when words, images, and shapes are *integrated*.

Right off I need to clear up a potential misunderstanding: Visual language is not about images by themselves, or shapes by themselves. The study of images alone or shapes alone has been the province of art critics and theorists. They have followed the lead of artists who only rarely include a few words in their visual pieces. Neither does visual language consist of what literary critics often call purple prose. Even the most vivid image-words are not visual language.

It is easy to mistake the notion of visual language proposed in this book for these artistic and literary "mixtures" of visuals and words.

Words alone

Here are two definitions, expressed verbally:

1. Transport: To carry or convey from one place to another.

2. Transportation: The act or state of being transported.

These examples are obviously not visual language, because there are no images or shapes associated with the words.

What about the following passage, which is heavy with visual words?

Down the foggy road the ancient yellow bus crept. Its tired pink fog lights barely cut a few inches through the fog. Its driver leaned forward, stretching his tight blue uniform. He held his hand over his eyes as if that would help him see through the fog. But not even that helped when a small child ran out across the road right in front of the bus …

No matter how many words are used, or how vividly words refer to visible attributes, words by themselves are not visual language.

Shapes alone

The shapes in these examples are obviously visual, but they are not visual language. In the absence of accompanying words or images, they do not communicate any kind of complete meaning. True, they are suggestive of classificatory distinctions, but they are incomplete.

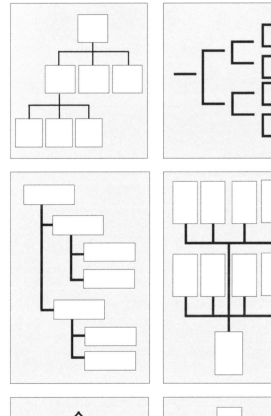

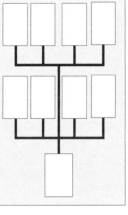

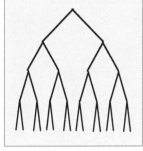

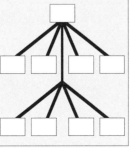

Images alone

These pictures are obviously visual, but they are not visual language. They lack words or shapes to provide the context and structure that are required in a meaningful, integrated unit of communication.

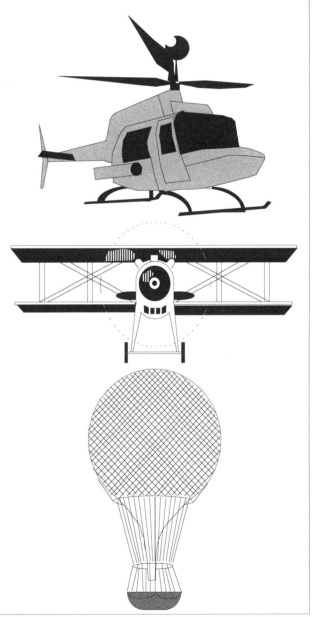

10

Integration of Words, Images, and Shapes Is Visual Language

in • te • gra • tion */n/*
The act of forming, coordinating, or blending into a functional or unified whole.

These pages illustrate some possible combinations of words, images, and text. In coming pages, I devote a considerable amount of more detailed analysis to how words, shapes, and images are being integrated in visual language (for syntax →Ch. 3; for semantics →Ch. 4).

We can imagine a kind of continuum of coupling in visual language that ranges from no connection at all among the elements, through very loose coupling, to moderate and very tight coupling of words, images, and shapes. Such a continuum probably represents the reality of communication more exactly than does an either/or characterization of no coupling or complete coupling.

Words and images are visual language

Garbage
Trash

Words, images, and shapes integrated into one single

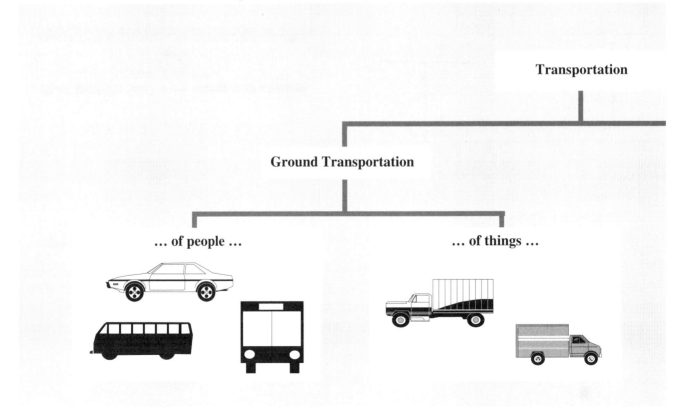

Transportation

Ground Transportation

... of people ...

... of things ...

Words and shapes are visual language

Images and shapes are usually visual language

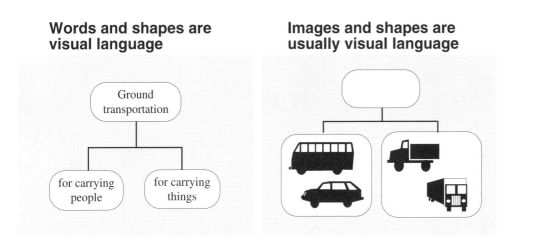

communication unit are always visual language

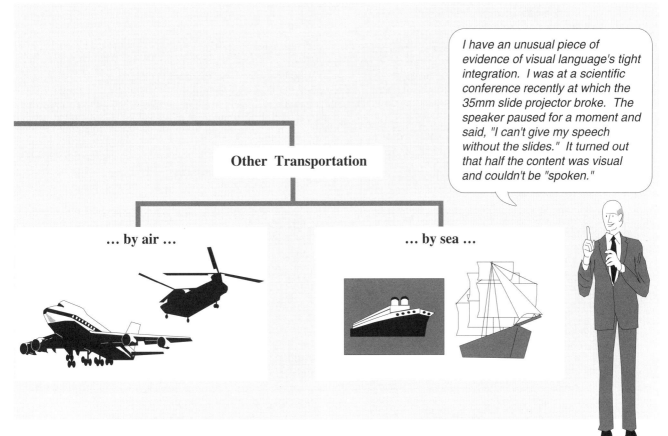

I have an unusual piece of evidence of visual language's tight integration. I was at a scientific conference recently at which the 35mm slide projector broke. The speaker paused for a moment and said, "I can't give my speech without the slides." It turned out that half the content was visual and couldn't be "spoken."

Why Is Visual Language a Language?

My main claim

The main claim of this book is that something new has emerged on the scene of human communication. Based on my research, I am calling it a new language (or something very close to a language). It is here and is continuing to grow and develop.

To substantiate the claim that visual language is in fact a language, I need to determine the criteria to be used to identify a language and then examine visual language against those criteria. What should the criteria be?

Visual language

✓ Can it be analyzed linguistically?

I will have to show that visual language can be analyzed from the standpoint of traditional linguistic categories. That is, I have to show that it shares some rules of syntax with prose and some rules of composition with visual art, while having a distinct syntax and semantics of its own. I take up syntax in chapter 3 and semantics in chapters 4, 5, and 6.

**Syntax
Semantics
Pragmatics**

These borrowed rules are helpful but insufficient to describe the overall integration of visual language and how it works. I point out how and where we need to add other analyses to those borrowed ones, especially when exploring the property of tight integration of visual and verbal components.

Visual language, thus, has distinct properties that make it different from natural languages of words and from purely artistic languages. It has a more complex syntax and requires more diverse and complex analysis. (➔73)

One of the reasons for the emergence of visual language is its ability to express things that are difficult or impossible to say in ordinary spoken or written language. The 2 chapters on functional semantics explore this characteristic in depth. (➔Chs. 4 and 5)

✓ Used by a community?

Ludwig Wittgenstein, the pivotal modern philosopher, and Charles Morris, one of the founding figures of modern semiotics, agree that a language must have enough of a community of use to enable its users to interpret the same signs in the same way. In other words, the meaning of a language cannot be private. A variety of professions already use visual language widely. I am using it in this book. Furthermore, there is evidence that visual language can be taught systematically and used by many people. Nonspeakers can become speakers and thus communicate with other speakers. Communities of users are surveyed in chapter 7.

✓ Sufficiently complete and distinct?

I have to show that the communication units I have identified as visual language are distinguishable from other communication units that either are not visual language or else cannot stand alone as visual language communication units. I do this in chapter 3.

✓ Distinct history?

Like other languages, visual language has a distinct evolutionary history—different time periods during which specific components and communication units were invented. In chapter 2 I take up this history, not to cover the topic exhaustively but to discuss some of the main inventions and their inventors.

✓ Full expression possible?

We would expect a language to be capable of expressing a full range of human interests, needs, thoughts, and emotions. Examples of visual language can be found in many different situations, from explanations and descriptions to emotive and highly symbolic situations. (➔Ch. 7)

☑ Novel units of communication?

Visual language has distinctive communication units that are not found in natural languages. I divide these by size and devote a portion of a chapter to discussing them. (➔55–64)

☑ Systematic explanation of effectiveness?

A language must be "explainable." That is, the reasons it works as a communications tool must be able to be described and enumerated. This aspect of the analysis of visual language still needs much work. However, there are specific components of visual language, such as diagrams, that have received considerable attention in this regard, and it appears that systematic explanations of their effectiveness are available. Furthermore, it is clear that any explanations of the systems by which visual language comes by its effectiveness will have to incorporate the principles of cognitive science. (➔237–238)

☑ Plurality of common signs?

Charles Morris, in defining languages, identifies two basic characteristics. First, "a language is composed of a plurality of signs," and second, "in a language each sign has a signification common to a number of interpreters." Visual language clearly meets the 1st criterion and is in the process of settling upon a large vocabulary of common signs. Much of this book examines just this process.

☑ Combinable signs?

Morris also suggests that "the signs in a language must constitute a system of interconnected signs combinable in some ways and not in others in order to form a variety of complex sign-processes." The possible and impossible combinations of visual language signs are discussed in chapter 3.

☑ Sufficient ambiguity?

Natural languages tend to provide words that have many meanings that are interpreted differently depending upon context. Visual language also has this property. It appears to have both sufficient ambiguity and sufficient congruence of interpretation, making it flexible enough to support many kinds of communication. This quality is demonstrated throughout this book.

☑ Sufficiently arbitrary and conventional?

Ferdinand de Saussure, the great French linguist, made the case that language is primarily composed of the differences between arbitrary symbols that do not necessarily have a connection with the items to which they refer. They are arbitrary and conventional. Visual language contains many arbitrary conventions—for example, in the vocabulary of diagramming. Many other of its expressions, however, have immediate resemblances to natural or human-made objects, as did the language of the ancient Egyptians.

Why Have We Overlooked Visual Language?

How have we missed identifying visual language for so long?

1. We tend to see either/or situations. When we choose one "side"—art or writing—we tend to diminish the "other" to the role of communication supplement, instead of allowing both to serve side by side as the main elements.

2. Visual language is a Creole or pidgin language, composed—in this phase of its development—of bits and pieces. Such languages, by their very nature, grow on the fringes of established languages. We can safely say that visual language is not a fully developed language as yet. How exciting that we get to participate consciously in the development of a new language. We have the opportunity to identify its strengths, as well as investigate its weaknesses and missing areas.

3. The separateness of English and art departments is a deeply entrenched tradition in our

educational institutions. Something that draws from both disciplines will not enjoy immediate popularity.

4. Because at first glance, its visual aspect sometimes overwhelms its communicative purpose, visual language is often classified as art (merely expressive) or, even worse, dismissed as "just cartooning." But it is a mistake to not take seriously one of the most powerful communications languages available today.

What Is Driving the Emergence of Visual Language?

The modern world of high technology, global business, and telecommunications has brought together a group of influences that is driving the increased use of visual language. This page illustrates just one way to map these influences. The arrows can be read as "drive(s)." Only the major driving forces and connections are shown.

As the world increases in complexity, as the speed at which we need to solve business and social problems increases, as it becomes increasingly critical to have the "big picture" as well as multiple levels of detail immediately accessible, visual language will become more and more prevalent in our lives.

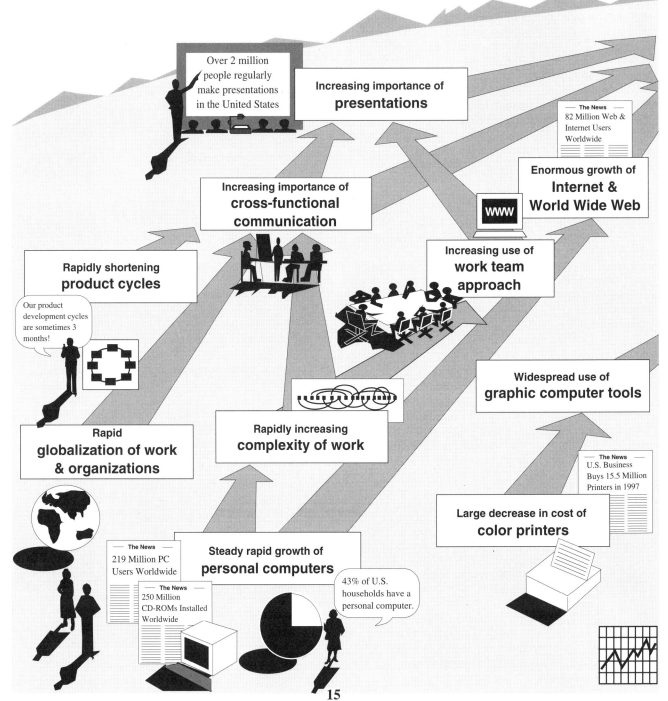

15

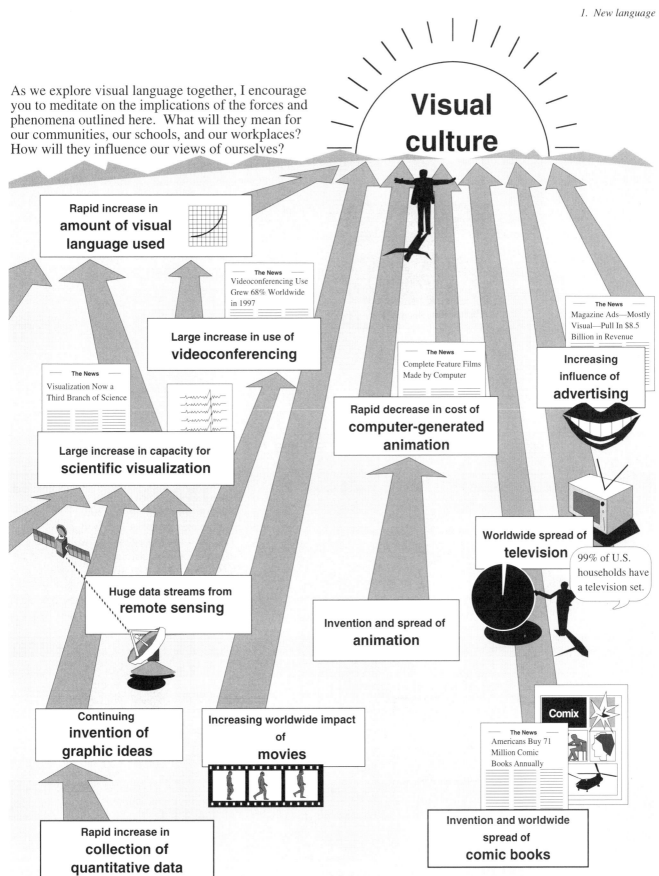

As we explore visual language together, I encourage you to meditate on the implications of the forces and phenomena outlined here. What will they mean for our communities, our schools, and our workplaces? How will they influence our views of ourselves?

Visual culture

Rapid increase in amount of visual language used

The News
Videoconferencing Use Grew 68% Worldwide in 1997

Large increase in use of videoconferencing

The News
Magazine Ads—Mostly Visual—Pull In $8.5 Billion in Revenue

Increasing influence of advertising

The News
Complete Feature Films Made by Computer

The News
Visualization Now a Third Branch of Science

Large increase in capacity for scientific visualization

Rapid decrease in cost of computer-generated animation

Worldwide spread of television

99% of U.S. households have a television set.

Huge data streams from remote sensing

Invention and spread of animation

Continuing invention of graphic ideas

Increasing worldwide impact of movies

Comix

The News
Americans Buy 71 Million Comic Books Annually

Invention and worldwide spread of comic books

Rapid increase in collection of quantitative data

16

Why Is the Graphic Computer So Important?

Because of the development of graphic computer tools, we don't have to be skilled artists to use visual language. With these tools and a few hours of training, visual language can be "spoken" by anybody.

What tools do we have?

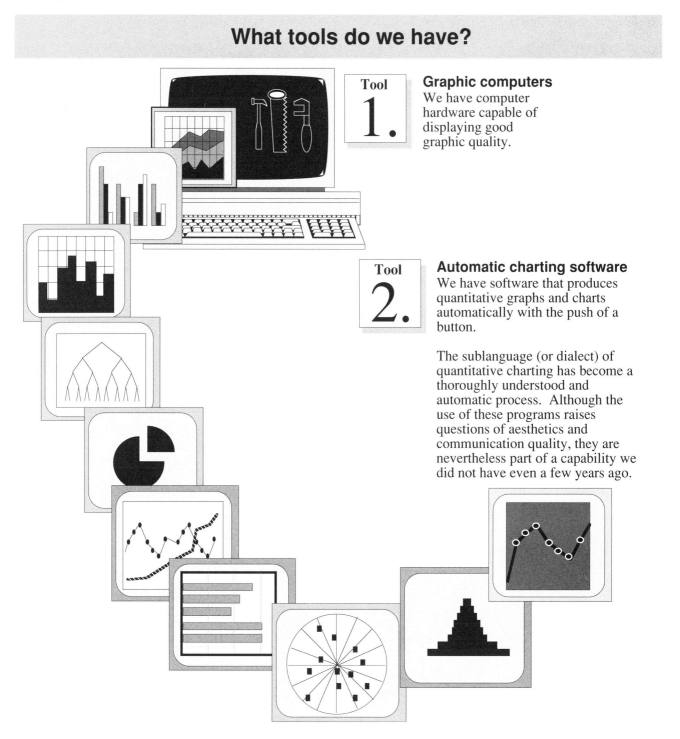

Tool 1.

Graphic computers
We have computer hardware capable of displaying good graphic quality.

Tool 2.

Automatic charting software
We have software that produces quantitative graphs and charts automatically with the push of a button.

The sublanguage (or dialect) of quantitative charting has become a thoroughly understood and automatic process. Although the use of these programs raises questions of aesthetics and communication quality, they are nevertheless part of a capability we did not have even a few years ago.

Tool 3.

Drawing and page-composition software

We have a great variety of easy-to-learn drawing and page composition software, including programs that manipulate photographs, draw in 3 dimensions, and do animation.

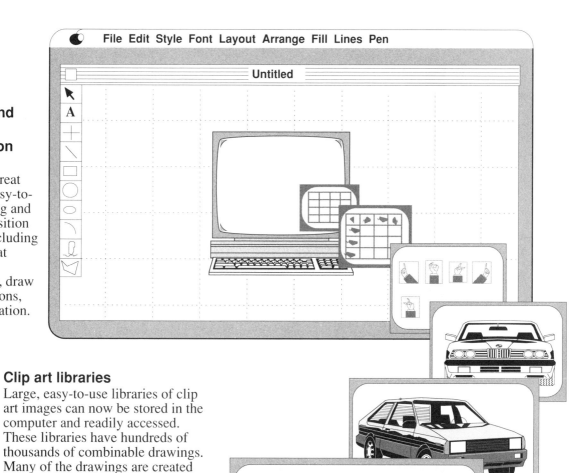

Tool 4.

Clip art libraries

Large, easy-to-use libraries of clip art images can now be stored in the computer and readily accessed. These libraries have hundreds of thousands of combinable drawings. Many of the drawings are created so that you can take them apart and use the parts in a new drawing, even stretching them to a new scale as necessary.

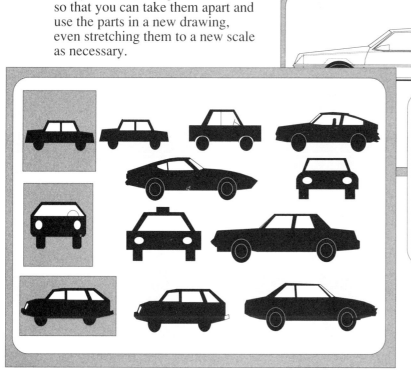

I have emphasized tools for the layperson on these 2 pages. Of course, multimedia authoring tools and graphic tools for manipulating visual compositions, for editing, and for page makeup have flourished in the past few years—revolutionizing how professionals in those fields work.

This Book Will Change Your Idea of Visual Language

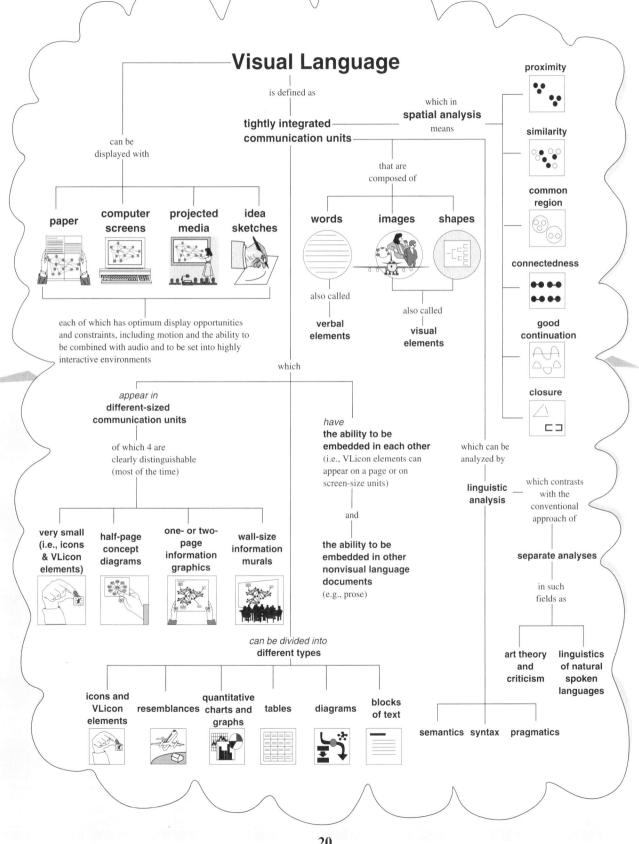

Visual Language

is defined as

tightly integrated communication units

can be displayed with

paper   computer screens   projected media   idea sketches

each of which has optimum display opportunities and constraints, including motion and the ability to be combined with audio and to be set into highly interactive environments

which in **spatial analysis** means

that are composed of

words   images   shapes

also called **verbal elements**

also called **visual elements**

which can be analyzed by

linguistic analysis

which contrasts with the conventional approach of

separate analyses

in such fields as

art theory and criticism   linguistics of natural spoken languages

semantics   syntax   pragmatics

proximity

similarity

common region

connectedness

good continuation

closure

which

appear in **different-sized communication units**

of which 4 are clearly distinguishable (most of the time)

very small (i.e., icons & VLicon elements)   **half-page concept diagrams**   **one- or two-page information graphics**   **wall-size information murals**

have **the ability to be embedded in each other** (i.e., VLicon elements can appear on a page or on screen-size units)

and

the ability to be embedded in other nonvisual language documents (e.g., prose)

can be divided into **different types**

icons and VLicon elements   resemblances   quantitative charts and graphs   tables   diagrams   blocks of text

Do You See What I Mean?

Members of the National Science Foundation committee on scientific visualization asked in 1987: What if we each had a display screen built into our foreheads and connected to our brains? They asked the question rhetorically, to focus attention on the fact that the "output" devices with which we humans come equipped do not include visualization.

The committee members answered their own question by speculating that such a screen, connected to our brains, would allow us all to see what was on each others' minds. I could see what you think and you could see what I think. Communication might be vastly improved.

If we had such capabilities, how much better would communication be? Perhaps it would be a great deal better. After all, some neuroscientists estimate that we get up to 80 percent of our information by visual means. A visual display of the insides of our minds would certainly amplify our display output.

Then again, perhaps communication would only be somewhat better because we'd have to hide a lot of our thoughts. But at least we would have the output capability.

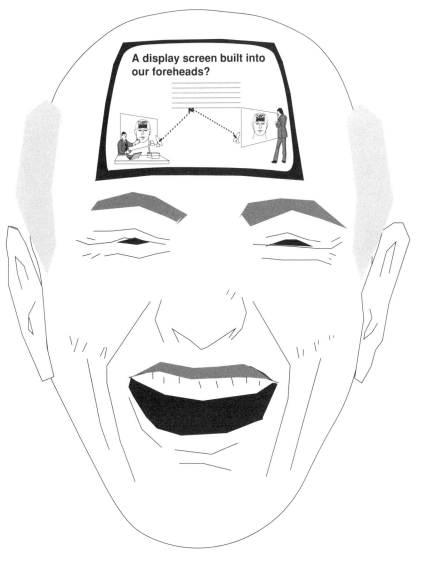

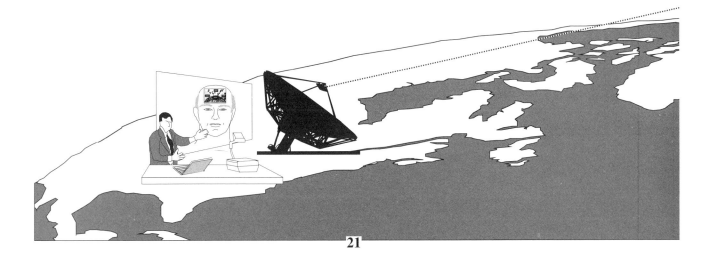

We do already have portable and adequate output devices. With laptop graphic computers we can already conveniently communicate with visual language.

With larger display devices and projectors we can show large groups how we see the world. Even more amazing than using forehead-mounted devices, we can communicate with visual language in real time over long distances, literally around the globe. In many ways, the capacity to show people what is on our minds is already here.

The era of the wearable computer has also arrived. Thin screens that can be worn as breastplates are an idea already on the drawing board.

Not far behind are ultrathin screens (so-called electronic paper) that could be comfortably pasted on our foreheads in the morning. Suppose they could be connected to gigantic wafer-thin memory boards with tremendous storage capacity, controllable through a pocket or belt-mounted keyboard. You begin to see that the NSF scientists were not dealing in science fiction.

Whatever the output devices, the critical question is, what language would we use to display our ideas? *I think the best choice—for clarity, efficiency, ease, and creativity—would be the precise combination of words, images, and shapes that I am calling visual language. If I am right, then we need to learn the vocabulary, grammar, and semantics of this new language. Join me as we explore all of the possibilities that visual languages offers for better communication.*

Chapter 2
A Brief History of Innovations

Time line: From prehistoric through classical age

Earliest data recording. At least 30,000 years before any written language was developed, animal bones were etched with what appears to be the lunar calendar. Early humans used conceptual thought and valued orderly presentation of information. **Dordogne, France, c. 38,000 BCE**

Earliest lists and tables. Extensive lists and tables of marks representing inventory and trade existed prior to pictographic writing. **Mesopotamia, c. 6000 BCE**

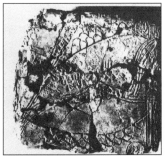

Oldest-known map. Shows early development of concepts of spatial relations. Uses a one-to-one correspondence and symbols to represent features of territory. Clay tablet with Akkadian map shows all of northern Mesopotamia. **Nuzi, c. 2300 BCE**

Most languages have developed over time, and their origins are obscured by the lack of a written record. Fortunately, we can reconstruct a relatively good history of many of the major inventions and inventors of visual language. This chapter outlines the history of visual language's development in a time-line format. The time line especially focuses on significant innovations in the structure or templates of information (such as lists and branching) as well as some of the more important foundational innovations (such as the invention of paper), without which visual language would not be possible. The time-line is interspersed with more detailed summaries of some of the more interesting central figures and inventions.

5000 BCE   4000   3000

Early artwork. Paintings on walls of caves show advanced representational capability very early in human history. **Lascaux, France, c. 20,000 BCE**

First pictographic writing. Early Sumerians used about 2,000 signs, which also contained phonograms and determinatives. **Mesopotamia, c. 3200 BCE**

Early coordinate system. Surveyors located specific points in space in a manner similar to the Cartesian system. **Egypt, c. 3200 BCE**

23

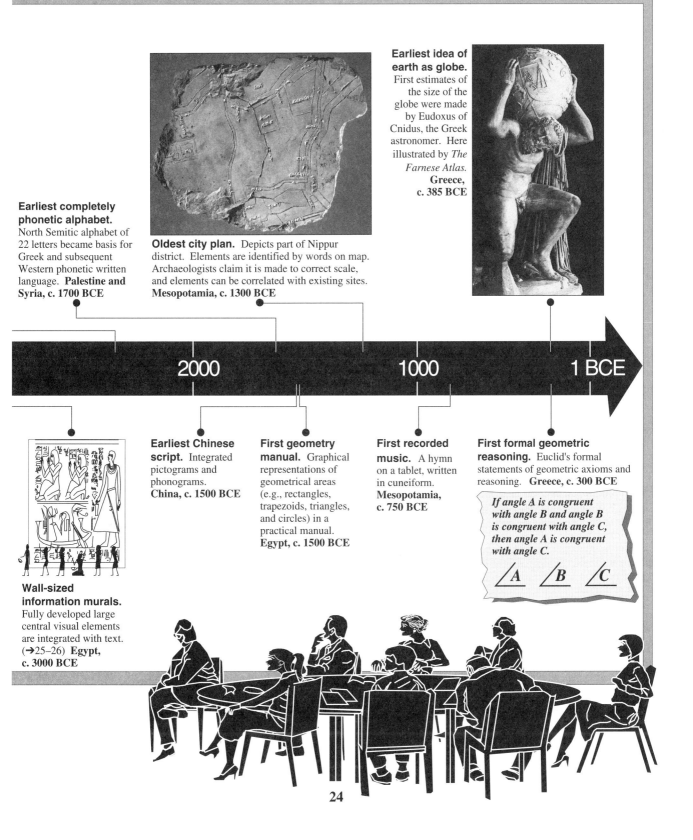

Earliest idea of earth as globe. First estimates of the size of the globe were made by Eudoxus of Cnidus, the Greek astronomer. Here illustrated by *The Farnese Atlas.* **Greece, c. 385 BCE**

Oldest city plan. Depicts part of Nippur district. Elements are identified by words on map. Archaeologists claim it is made to correct scale, and elements can be correlated with existing sites. **Mesopotamia, c. 1300 BCE**

Earliest completely phonetic alphabet. North Semitic alphabet of 22 letters became basis for Greek and subsequent Western phonetic written language. **Palestine and Syria, c. 1700 BCE**

2000   1000   1 BCE

Earliest Chinese script. Integrated pictograms and phonograms. **China, c. 1500 BCE**

First geometry manual. Graphical representations of geometrical areas (e.g., rectangles, trapezoids, triangles, and circles) in a practical manual. **Egypt, c. 1500 BCE**

First recorded music. A hymn on a tablet, written in cuneiform. **Mesopotamia, c. 750 BCE**

First formal geometric reasoning. Euclid's formal statements of geometric axioms and reasoning. **Greece, c. 300 BCE**

If angle A is congruent with angle B and angle B is congruent with angle C, then angle A is congruent with angle C.

Wall-sized information murals. Fully developed large central visual elements are integrated with text. (➔25–26) **Egypt, c. 3000 BCE**

24

Ancient Egyptian Language

The ancient Egyptian hieroglyphic system seems to have had many components similar to today's visual language and to have integrated them in somewhat similar ways. We can say it was the first fully developed visual language in the West.

There were 5 major components of Egyptian language. Jan Assmann suggests that the different language elements enable 3 functions in writing. "The first is to explain the picture ... the second is to identify the persons (therein) ... the third is to supplement the rendering of speeches, that is, to record sound, in multiple media." These 3 functions also appear routinely in modern visual language.

1. Pictographs

We usually think of Egyptian as a language in which each little picture (called a pictogram) meant what it resembled: the familiar idea of one picture is one word, such as these equivalents.

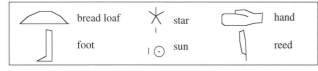

In the visual language that we see today, resemblances such as these are used, but they are not usually used as substitutes for words in sentences, except occasionally in advertising. (→197) Resemblances are primarily used as illustrations, perhaps to show location or appearance. (→163–166)

2. Ideographs

Pictographs were relatively rare. Egyptian also had hieroglyphics in which an action was represented by some characteristic element.

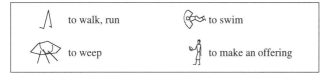

In fact, Egyptian was a hybrid language of what would today be called "words" and "images," although this distinction is perhaps too neat, given that words are themselves often images.

3. Phonograms

Egyptian also contained phonograms, in which graphic symbols, some resembling real objects, stood for sounds, just as the 26 letters of the current English alphabet stand for sounds. Words were spelled out in sounds as well as depicted by pictures. That was Thomas Young and Jean-Francois Champollion's great discovery.

Young in 1819 discovered that hieroglyphics like these:

were actually phonetical spellings of the name Ptolemaios, or Ptolemy.

We can look at the list of sound equivalents that Young and Champollion developed for Egyptian. The writing of the sound by showing a picture of something whose name contains the sound is called a rebus, and is a little-used element of visual language today. The use of shapes for syntactic and semantic purposes was not as extensive in Egyptian as in contemporary visual language; see, for example, visual language's extensive use of diagrammatic shapes to organize information. The oval shape around the words, known as a cartouche, is found around all royal names in hieroglyphic script.

Areas of text in hieroglyphic form appear in various convenient or useful clusters, particularly in the large, wall-sized murals.

There are other kinds of phonograms in Egyptian, around 80 signs that indicate double sounds, usually a consonant. Here are just a few:

The 24 single consonant signs are:

	a		p		ḥ		k
	i		f		ḫ		ḳ
	y		m		ẖ		g
	'		n		s		t
	w		r		š		ṯ
	b		h		s		d, ḏ

4. Determinatives

To handle homonyms (words that sound alike but have different meanings, such as *sun* and *son* in English) and other such ambiguities, Egyptian employed a group of signs that were added to words in order to designate the domain to which the word belonged. For example, the sign

would be added to a word to indicate the general domain of books, writing, or abstract ideas, and a seated man or seated woman would indicate male or female domains:

man, person

woman

Also, some Egyptian icons were to be interpreted as the thing represented, rather than as a sound. These determinatives were indicated by a convention of a single stroke to the side or below the icon. In this example,

the picture of the cobra by itself stands for the consonant "d,"

whereas the cobra with a vertical stroke stands for "cobra."

The determinative indicates that the picture is intended to represent the object (i.e., the cobra) it resembles.

5. Information murals

Assmann describes the uses of different scales of hieroglyphics in Egyptian. "Protodynastic pictorial narrative uses picture-signs on two distinctly different physical scales. The large pictures portray a 'scene,' and the small pictures identify actors and places by including names. The small pictures therefore refer to language (names), the large pictures refer to the world (acts). It would be a mistake, however, to categorize only the small pictures as 'writing.' The large pictures also act as writing ... This type of recording is successful only when both types of signs, the small ones with language reference and the large ones with world reference, work together. Neither of the two 'media' is self-sufficient in recording the intended or any other meaning."

Later in this book I suggest that many visual language communication units beyond the size of the icon (➔55–56) usually have dominant central visual elements around which the rest of the communication unit revolves. It appears that Egyptian scribes and artists confronted similar requirements of communication and similarly arranged the components in an integrated fashion.

Egyptian information mural

Visual language shares qualities with Egyptian

Regarding ancient Egyptian, Tom Hare concludes that the interaction "of picture and writing creates an integral whole which can scarcely be attained in writing systems like the Greek or Roman alphabets, relying as they do on conventional and arbitrary relations between sound and the written word, and insensible, as they are, to the iconic dimension of writing which was so important and so engaging to the Egyptians."

Tight integration of words and images, the use of one or more central visual elements, and wall-sized units of communication are 3 key qualities that visual language shares with ancient Egyptian. Our media—computer screens and large electronic whiteboards, for example—differ from the stone temple walls of the Egyptians. Nonetheless, it is clear that we face some of the same communication challenges—including the expression of large-scale, complex messages that can be viewed by large groups of people simultaneously—that the Egyptian scribes and artists faced 5,000 years ago.

26

Time Line: From Hellenistic Period through Middle Ages

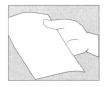

Conventional date for invention of paper. Prior to the making of paper from tree bark and rags, writing had been done on bamboo or silk in China and on papyrus made out of reeds and animal skins in the Middle East. **Ts'ai Lun, China, 105 CE**

Leaving spaces between words. Reinvented during Charlemagne's reform of writing, the leaving of spaces between words enabled many readers to switch from reading aloud (which was the common way to read in the Middle Ages) to reading silently. **France, c. 800 CE**

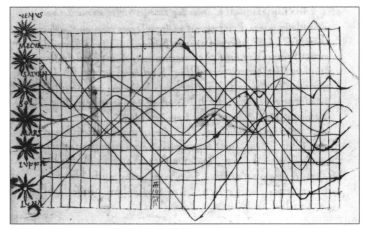

First curves plotted on a time grid. Found in transcription of Commentary of Macrobius on Cicero's *In Somnium Scipionis,* the chart shows planetary orbits. First-known chart that shows motion plotted abstractly through time. **Unknown astronomer, 10th or 11th century**

1 CE   500

Substitution of codex for the roll in creation of books. Previously, books were made from sheets of papyrus approximately 9 inches wide and glued together to make a 20- to 30-foot-long roll. Earliest codex is dated about 100 CE. **1st to 3rd centuries**

Early use of tables. Used to tabulate astronomical information to aid navigation, tables have become standard for organizing data, especially for easy comparison. **Ptolemy, Egypt, 2nd century**

Extensive tabular information. An elaboration of the idea of using tables to compare information, cannon tables were widely used in the medieval period. **Henry II's gospels, England, c. 1020**

First-known graphic branching structures. The genealogical tree appeared in the Middle Ages, and seems to be the 1st conception of a branching configuration. This visual rendering of multiple paths leading from one root led to the development of a large class of diagrams. The initial form was the "crane's foot" used in genealogical charts and shown in this detail of the genealogy of King Edward I (1296). An 11-foot roll, all done with branching technique, it is one of the most extensive structured information designs to that date. **Early Middle Ages**

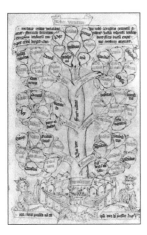

Common use of branching structures in diagrams. Use in lists of virtues and vices, structures of knowledge, genealogical pedigrees. Branching lines give structure to a subject matter and guide the eye in seeing the organization. **Throughout Middle Ages**

Schematic diagrams. In medieval manuscripts, various diagrams, often grouped around illustrations, provided early prototypes for what in this book are called infographics. **Throughout Middle Ages**

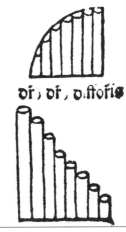

First-known bar graph. Sometimes called a proto–bar graph because no quantities are present. Illustrates a theoretical function. Shows that spatial analogs of quantities had begun to be conceptualized. **Nicole Oresme, French mathematician, c. 1350**

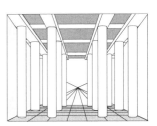

Invention of perspective rendering. Perspective method enabled artists to create geometrically controlled space on a two-dimensional surface, providing illusion of three-dimensional space. **Leon Battista Alberti and Filippo Brunelleschi, Italian architects, 1435**

1000

1500

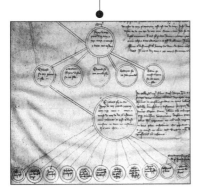

Books printed from movable type. The Gutenberg Bible, which began widespread changes in the dissemination of knowledge, is regarded as one of the fundamental turning points of Western culture. **Johannes Gutenberg, German printer, c. 1455**

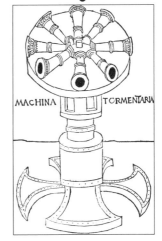

First technical book with illustrations. The book, *De re militari*, contains woodcuts of engines of war. **Roberto Vaturio, author, Joannes Nicodai de Verona, printer, Italy, 1472**

Routine use of page numbers for books. As books began to be much more widely available, the reader's ability to access the information quickly became more important. Aldine Press pioneered this search tool. **Aldus Manutius, Venice, 1499**

Time Line: 16th through 18th Centuries

Rectilinear tree structures introduced. The structure of the ubiquitous modern organization chart first appears during this period, in genealogical charts. **16th century**

Tables of empirical data. Extensive data collection accompanied the rapid development of science in the 16th and 17th centuries, which eventually led to the elaboration of tabular display of numbers. **Die Tabbellen-Statistik, Germany, early 17th century**

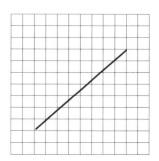

Coordinate system relates graphed line and equation. Used in ancient surveying, but not developed mathematically until this time, the coordinate system provided the groundwork for a whole new field of mathematics and, in applied work, the ability to do precise mechanical drawing. **René Descartes, French mathematician,** *La Geometrié,* **1637**

1500   1600

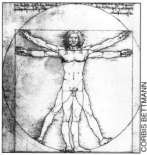

Extensive use of visualization in science and engineering. Used in detailed plans for fortifications, vehicles, aids to human flight, bridges, and in elaborations of theories of mechanical motion, etc.; the idea sketch became a hallmark of creative problem solving. **Leonardo da Vinci, Florence, c. 1500**

Extensive use of woodblock carving and printing. The development of science and technology were facilitated by the sudden extensive use of woodblock carving, which permitted the distribution of repeatable illustrations so important in biology (for the recognition of plants), anatomy, and many other disciplines. **16th century**

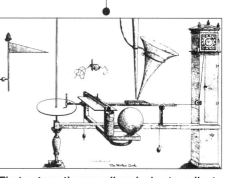

First automatic recording device to collect data. The invention of a weather clock, based on the use of a recording needle on a moving drum to graph changes in temperature, was the initial and crucial idea for automatic data recording. **Christopher Wren, English architect and scientist, 1664**

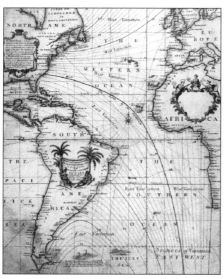

Data mapping. Isobar map showing lines of magnetic declination for the world launched the field of thematic mapping—the plotting of data on geographical maps. **Edmond Halley, English scientist, 1700**

First printed coordinate paper. A time saver for scientists and engineers plotting data, the invention indicates how rapidly the plotting of data was spreading. **Dr. Buxton, England, 1794**

1700 1800

Biographical time line invented. The now widely used technique of plotting data on time lines was initiated in this period. (➔31) Priestley acknowledged the existence of prior time lines that plotted data other than people's lifespans. **Joseph Priestley, English chemist and high-school teacher, 1765**

Bar chart invented. The ubiquitous bar chart, perhaps 1 of the 2 or 3 most useful quantitative data presentation devices, was invented and 1st printed in a book of statistics of political and economic affairs. (➔33) **William Playfair, British social scientist, 1786**

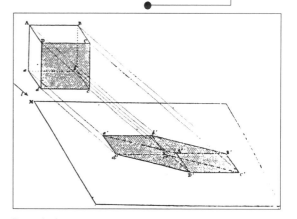

Descriptive geometry. The 1st book on descriptive geometry served as the foundation for the development of engineering drawing, which was essential for the Industrial Revolution. **Gaspard Monge, French mathematician, 1795**

Priestley: Inventor of Biographical Time Lines

Joseph Priestley, known best for his work in experimental chemistry, is a fundamental figure in visual language. He invented the time line chart in 1765. His first chart contained 2,000 of the names "most distinguished in the annals of fame." It showed the length of these people's lives as lines on a grid that was marked off in years. The chart measured 2 feet by 3 feet and stretched from 1200 BCE to 1800 CE. Unknown birth or death dates were shown as dotted lines. Priestley spent much of his life teaching and used these historical charts in his classes. They were very successful and went through many editions.

Priestley's rationale

Priestley wrote a small book about his experience of designing the chart, called *A Description of a Chart of Biography*. In this book, he describes some of the key advantages of visual representations of information over purely textual ones, especially for abstract or complex concepts. "As no image can be formed of abstract ideas, they are, of necessity, represented in our minds by particular, but variable ideas; ... that is, if ... the idea be nothing that is the object of our senses, it is nevertheless universally represented in our minds by the idea of some sensible thing."

A chart of biography

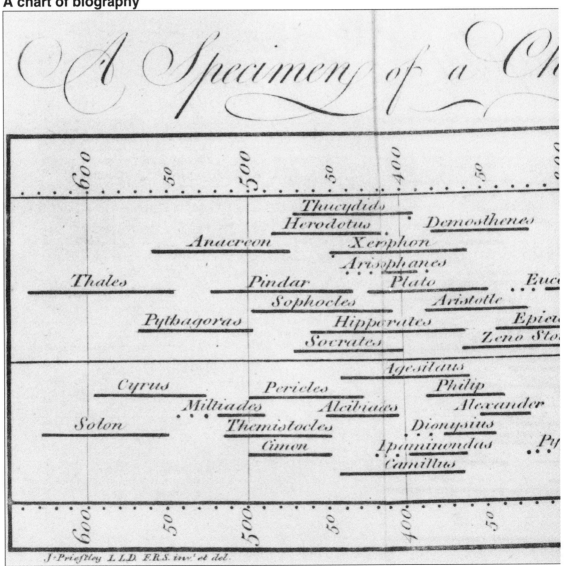

"Thus the abstract idea of time, though it be not the object of any of our senses, and no image can properly be made of it, yet because it has real quantity, and we can say a greater or less space of time, it admits of a natural and easy representation in our minds by the idea of a measurable space, and particularly that of a line; which, like time, may be extended in length, without giving any idea of breadth or thickness."

Priestley's inspiration

Apparently Priestley was inspired by a time line of empires (which I have been unable to locate). He writes, "Who hath not seen this exemplified in the chart of history imported from France and published with improvement in England? It is past all dispute that a few minutes' inspection of that chart will give a person a clearer idea of the rise, progress, extent, revolutions and durations of empires than he could possibly acquire by reading: and it is almost certain that when a person hath once impressed his imagination with the figure which any particular country makes in that chart he can never wholly lose the idea of it."

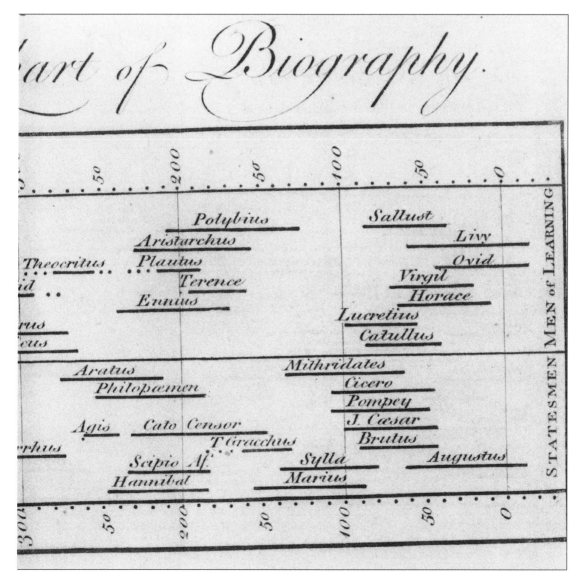

Playfair: Innovator in Visualizing Statistics

The English political economist William Playfair (l759–1823) is credited with developing or improving many of the major numerical charts. For example, the first known time series using economic data was published in Playfair's remarkable book, *The Commercial and Political Atlas*. Playfair did his work in the context of an enormous increase in the collection of statistics and in the use of such statistics to solve social problems.

Playfair wrote about his work, "Information, that is imperfectly acquired, is generally as imperfectly retrained; and a man who has carefully investigated a printed table, finds, when done, that he has only a very faint and partial idea of what he has read; and that like a figure imprinted on sand, is soon totally erased and defaced. The amount of mercantile transactions in money, and of profit or loss, are capable of being as easily represented in drawing ... though, till now, it has not been attempted. Upon that principle these Charts were made."

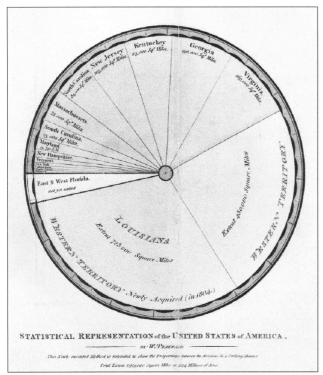

First pie chart

Playfair called it a divided circle and emphasized its value in showing proportions. This chart shows the relative size of different states and territories of the United States shortly after the purchase of Louisiana Territory from France by President Jefferson. This chart appeared in *Statistical Account of the United States of America* in 1805.

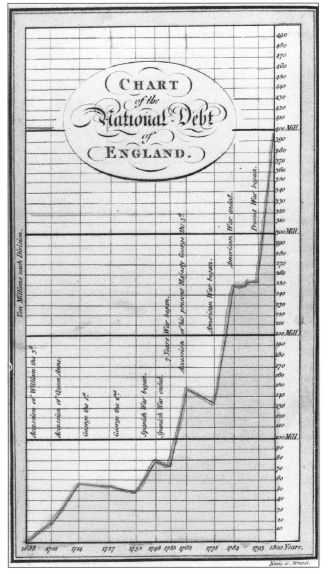

First extensive modern use of time series

Playfair probably didn't invent the time series per se, but he developed the methodology and presentation to a level that is entirely equivalent with modern usage. This chart is one of many that appeared in Playfair's *Commercial and Political Atlas* in 1786.

33

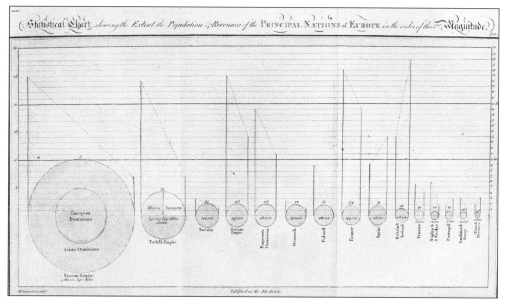

First circle graph

Playfair invented this form of chart to compare relative sizes. The circles are proportionate to the number of the inhabitants. This form of charting is little used today because it has been shown that it is difficult to compare areas accurately. This chart appeared in the *Statistical Breviary* in 1801.

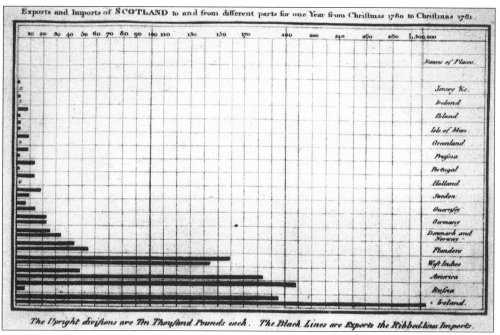

First modern bar chart

Some observers say that Playfair invented the bar chart but there are a few other examples that go back as far as 1350. Playfair certainly developed the precise technique to a level of completeness and precision that had not been used before. This chart appeared in the 2nd edition of the *Commercial and Political Atlas* in 1787.

Time Line: 19th and Early 20th Centuries

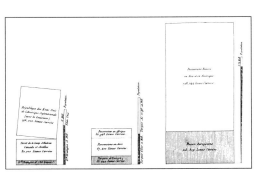

Subdivided bar graph invented. With this chart began the detailed comparative analysis of data. **Alexander von Humboldt, German scientist, 1812**

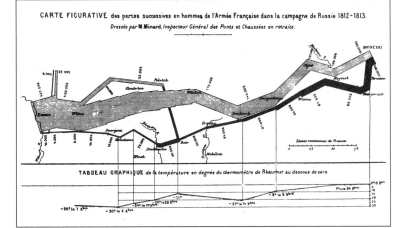

Map incorporating statistical diagrams. The brilliant integration of several types of graphic presentation and multiple variables on the same chart was developed and, many say, perfected by Minard. **Charles Joseph Minard, French engineer, 1851**

Cumulative frequency graph invented. This chart enabled statisticians to examine the rate of growth of a variable. **J. B. J. Fourier, French mathematician, 1821**

Curve-fitting to scatterplot invented. This invention launched a whole new branch of statistics, difficult to do without visualization. **J. F. W. Herschel, England, 1832**

Three-dimensional population surface (or "stereogram"). Importance is plotting of 3 variables on a three-dimensional surface. **Gustav Zeuner, Germany, 1869**

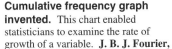

1800　　　　　　　　　　　1850

Circle graph invented. (→33) **William Playfair, England, 1801**

Pie chart invented. Showing proportions provided a means for comparing percentages. (→33) **William Playfair, England, 1805**

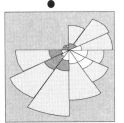

Invention of the polar area diagram. Besides inventing the polar area diagram, Nightingale inaugurated the extensive use of graphs and charts for systematic analysis of data, with an 800-page report on British hospital administration. (→38) **Florence Nightingale, English nurse, 1858**

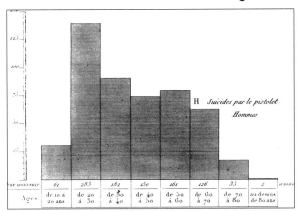

Histogram invented. The grouping of data extends the ability to summarize and see patterns. This histogram shows rates of suicide by different methods among different age groups of Frenchmen. **A. M. Guerry, French statistician, 1833**

Development of visual storytelling techniques. Töpffer's stories synthesized extensive storytelling in frames with dialogue. (→37) **Rudolphe Töpffer, Swiss professor and artist, 1845**

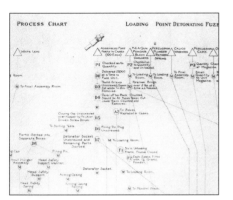

Work flow charts invented. Gilbreth's work marked the beginning of wide use of diagramming to solve business efficiency problems. **Frank Gilbreth, American engineer and consultant, 1919**

ISOTYPE: International System of Typographic Picture Education. The invention of a comprehensive approach to presentation of statistical data for rapid learning and wide use in public education began with the Museum of Social Statistical Graphics, Social and Economic Museum, Vienna. (→40) **Otto Neurath, Austrian sociologist, 1924**

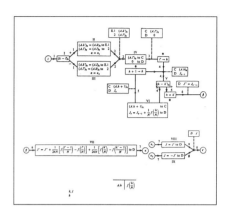

Computer flow charts invented. The flow chart enabled the computer programmer to analyze complex problems. (→43) **John von Neumann, Hungarian-American mathematician, 1945**

1900

1950

Pictogram for pictorial statistics invented. Began the modern use of icons especially for statistics. (→39) **Michael Mulhall, England, 1884**

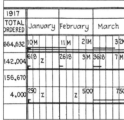

Gantt and progress charts invented. Systematic industrial planning depends on precise and measurable standards, which are displayed with these charts. (→41–42) **Henry L. Gantt, American engineer and consultant, 1900–1911**

First college course in graphical statistics. Began the systematic dissemination of this branch of visual language. **M. F. P. Costelloe, professor at Iowa State College, 1913**

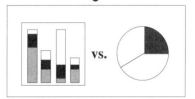

First comparative study of pie and subdivided bar charts. These studies launched the empirical investigation of communication effectiveness of visual language techniques. **Walter C. Eells, United States, 1926**

Töpffer: Inventor of Visual Storytelling and the Comics

Rudolphe Töpffer (1799–1846), storyteller and artist, is credited with inventing the thorough combination of illustrations and words to tell a story. As such, he is the father of the modern comic book as well as of the illustrated children's story and of the visual novel. E. H. Gombrich gives Töpffer additional credit for the realization that viewers can be relied upon to fill in what is absent in the drawings—the space between the frames—from their own experience.

Although stories had been told with words and images before Töpffer, he thought through a number of the most important components of visual storytelling, including:

- multiple panels on a single page
- the ability to show movement from one panel to the next
- the use of multiple figures to show motion

A series of frames from *Monsieur Crepin, Monsieur Pencil*

Töpffer's forecast

In discussing the "great appeal" of the picture story compared to prose literature, Töpffer enumerates many of the advantages of contemporary visual language, which are outlined in chapter 7. "With its dual advantages of greater conciseness and greater relative clarity, the picture story, all things being equal, should squeeze out the other [i.e., prose story telling] because it would address itself with greater liveliness to a greater number of minds, and also because in any contest he who uses such a direct method will have the advantage over those who talk in chapters."

Nightingale: Pioneer in Social Statistics and Inventor of the Polar Area Diagram

Florence Nightingale, an almost mythical figure in the founding of nursing, was also a major reformer of the British hospital system. She is also a significant figure in visual language due to her invention of the polar area diagram and to her work in pioneering "the revolutionary notion that social phenomena could be objectively measured and subjected to mathematical analyses."

The polar area diagram represents each statistic as proportional to a wedge in a circular diagram. Nightingale called these diagrams "coxcombs" because each wedge was colored in soft pastels.

Florence Nightingale was an extraordinary hospital administrator. She was responsible for installing broad improvements in sanitary conditions in British military hospitals, which were showing that, on an annual basis, the entire army would have to be replace 4 times due to deaths from infectious diseases.

After her wartime service, she wrote a long report for a royal commission from which this diagram is taken. It shows the death rate of British soldiers "on an annual basis as a fraction of the patient population." Her major sanitary changes were installed in March. It is clear from the chart what an enormous difference they made.

Nightingale's polar area diagram

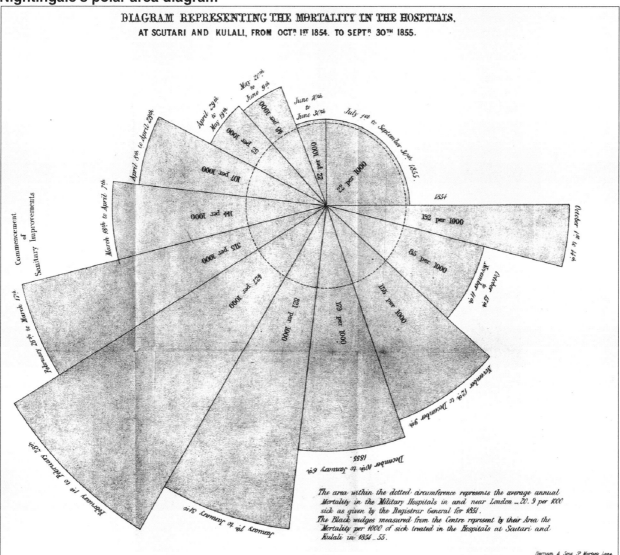

Mulhall: Inventor of Pictorial Statistics

Michael George Mulhall (1836–1900), geographer and statistician, is credited with the invention of pictorial statistics, or the use of pictographs in quantitative displays of information. He authored several geographical works in addition to other collections of data. His innovations in visual language can be seen in *The Dictionary of Statistics* (1892) and *History of Prices Since the Year 1850* (1885), which he both wrote and illustrated.

The reader will note that although these charts show enormous originality and represent a dramatic departure from the way quantities were represented up to that time, they nevertheless leave much to be desired. For example, the relative sizes of areas as represented by the cows or ships are difficult to estimate and compare accurately. Later developments in the use of pictorial statistics, especially those of Neurath, addressed this difficulty.

Mulhall's illustration of yearly meat production in different countries

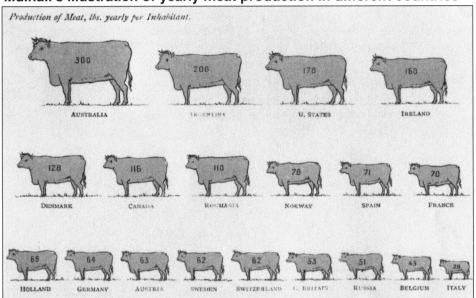

Mulhall's illustration of ocean-going trade volume over 3 decades

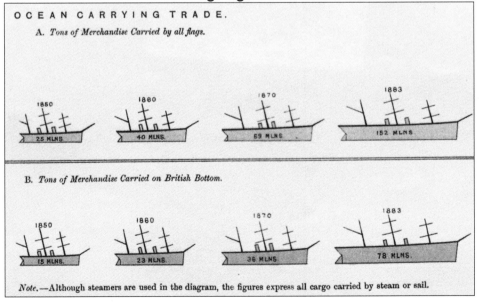

Neurath: Pictorial Statistics to Improve International Understanding

In the early 1930s in Vienna, an Austrian social scientist, Otto Neurath (1882–1945), pioneered an approach to using pictographic visuals for quantitative display of information. As an educator, he thought that "at least in the initial stages of acquiring new knowledge, pictures are a better means of communication than words."

Neurath's approach to visual language was to develop pictures that could be an adjunct to any spoken or written language but that would be understood across borders.

He called his approach ISOTYPE, an acronym for International System of Typographic Picture Education. He led the way in careful consideration of the criteria for pictographs so that they would be understood by the largest number of people. Neurath thus began to systematize Mulhall's pictorial statistics. He also produced many other innovations in pictorial diagrams and charts.

Examples of Neurath's approach to systematizing pictographic charts

If the data is organized by ...	... then use the principle ...	Example
Time and quantity	The eye starts in the upper left corner: organize the graph so that units of measurement can be seen immediately upon 1st glance. Time, Neurath recommends, should flow downward from top to bottom, and quantity from left to right.	
Age and quantity	Ages should flow upward, with lowest ages at bottom.	
Time and multiple sites	Arrange sites across the top and time down along the left axis to take advantage of the eye's tendency to start in the upper left corner.	
More than one quantity at multiple sites	Show different measurements with different pictographs to aid quick perception and comprehension.	

Gantt: Gantt and Progress Charts

The Gantt chart has become one of the visual staples of modern management. Invented and perfected in the period 1900–1911, the chart is a symbol of the scientific management movement in the early part of the 20th century. Henry L. Gantt (1861–1919) was a consulting management engineer who developed a variety of methods for cost record keeping, production recording, planning, and giving bonuses. As part of this work he developed the Gantt chart and the progress chart to focus management attention on the future,—that is, on the difference between what has been done and what needs to be done.

Key to Gantt charts
The key to Gantt charts is that they show both the work completed and the work planned in the same limited area, in proportional relations to each other and to time. The charts not only provide a schedule for project completion, but allow continuous comparison between that schedule and the actual work done.

Gantt chart
Width of daily space represents working hours of the plant.

Each worker's effort is represented on a separate line.

Each person has 2 totals, 1 for the day and 1 for the week.

Advantages of Gantt charts
Easy to draw: *There are now a variety of computer programs that draw them.*
Easy to read: *The relative thickness of lines enables readers to easily eyeball proportions and make comparisons.*
Visualization of the passage of time: *One of the most important components of the Gantt chart is the representation of where production is in relation to time.*
Fixes responsibility for success or failure: *When the output of many workers and machines is brought together on one chart, it is possible to identify problem areas quickly.*

Progress chart
This progress chart records deliveries. The time frame during which articles are to be delivered is marked with angles (⌐ ¬). The amount to be delivered during the time frame is at the left edge of each time frame; the total amount delivered to date is at the right edge of each time frame.

The length of the lines running across the calendar represent the amount of actual deliveries. For example, on October 22, only about half of Article C was delivered. The thick black line shows the cumulative amount of goods delivered to date.

Gantt chart

| Man | RECORD CHART FOR | DEPT. | DATE Week Ending March 8th 15th 1919 |

NAME	NO	Mon. 3	Tues. 4	Wed. 5	Thurs. 6	Frid. 7	Sat 8	Mon. 10	Tues. 11	Wed. 12	Thur. 13	Frid. 14	Sat.15
PALEN		64%			5%A	28%				72%		28%	
Griffen	501	T	I		I	T	I	T	T	T	T	T	
Palen	503	GR	G	G	G	G	G	RG	T	I	G	T	
Millspaugh	507												
Owens	514	T		A	A	A				R			
Rogee	517			R						I			
Williams	519	T	I	T			T						
Martell	527				I	I	I						
Stewart	535	6	GR	G	G	G	G	G	G	GR	TR		
REYNOLDS		46%		24%A		30%		54%		12% A		34%	
Marchand	508				T	I	A	A	T		T		
Bradford	518	T	T	T		T	T	T	T	AT	T		
Rusk	525			R					T				
Gerhardt	526	A		A	A								
Forbes	529	T	T	T	T		G						
Lewis	530			T	T		T	T					
Groth	531	R	T	T	X	A	A	LEFT					
Plepzig	532	A	A	A	A	A	A	T	R	T	T		
Swartz	533	A	A	A	A	A	T	T	LEFT				
Shorter	534	T	T	T	T	G	T	T	T				
Healey	537	R	B	R	W	W			T				

Progress chart

ARTICLES	1917 TOTAL ORDERED	January	February	March	April	May	June	July	August	September	October	November	December
A	664,632	10M	11M 21M	32M	43M 16M	59M 37M	96M 22M	118M 20M z 138M 152M	190M 157M	347M 257M	604M 439M	643M	
B	142,004	618 z	2618	3M 3618	7M 3M	10M 4M	14M 4M 18M 11M	29M 11M	40M 21M	61M 22M	83M 26M	109M 23M	132M
C	156,670			18 z	z	16	2M z 2M 2M	4M 7M	11M 22M	33M 34M z	67M	101M	
D	4,000	250 z	z 500	750	1000 252 1252 0	z 1252 0	z 1252 0	z 1252 673 z 2125 2625	2750	3375	4000		

Fig. 6 Progress Chart

von Neumann: Computer Flow Charts

John von Neumann (1903–1957) is acknowledged as the inventor of the modern computer. He first suggested the idea of a stored memory and worked out the architectural details of the process, including the idea of a computer program (or software) that could be changed depending upon the problem to be solved. Early computers were thus called stored-program computers. The modern personal computers that sit on our desks are referred to as embodying "von Neumann architecture."

One problem that arises in the development of complex computer programs is how best to represent the computer instructions to human beings. Von Neumann is generally credited with inventing the now ubiquitous flow chart as he was working out his ideas for how to store programs of instructions for the computer. The flow chart was the earliest version of an information structure that has proliferated into many different kinds of analysis systems. (→127–132)

An early flow chart

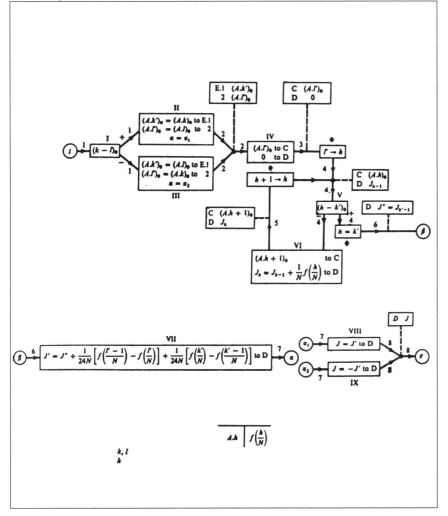

The different components of a flow chart have a semantics, the details of which are discussed in chapter 4.

Kavanagh: Decision Logic Tables

Although tables were invented very early in human history (→23), the arrival of the computer, which could compute logical statements, produced a new variation of the table. Decision logic tables (also called decision structure tables or simply decision tables) were developed by T. F. Kavanagh and a group of programmers at General Electric for the purpose of analyzing complex computer programs.

Example: A decision logic table
Several early authors of articles on decision logic tables used an example table that instructs its readers on how to identify an elephant or giraffe, as shown below.

animal	legs	nose length	neck length	name
yes	4	not less than 3'	less than 3'	elephant
yes	4	less than 3'	not less than 3'	giraffe
yes	-	not less than 3'	not less than 3'	freak

As you can see, the decision logic table is composed of as many columns and rows as are necessary to specify all of the possible logical alternatives in the situation or problem. The reader reads across each row, skipping to the next row as soon as one condition is not met. Schmidt and Kavanagh wrote, "Each row is evaluated in sequence from top to bottom. If all the conditions in a row are satisfied then the corresponding actions are executed and the table is considered solved."

Major advantages of decision logic tables
Burton Grad has summarized the major benefits of decision logic tables.
Clarity and conciseness. They are easy to prepare, read, and teach to others. They take perhaps 25 to 50 percent less writing than flow charts to create, and they often reduce programming time.
Completeness. You can see whether a cell in a table is blank and make corrections. Fewer errors are made and debugging is simplified.

Display of meaningful relationships. Tables sharpen cause-and-effect understanding. Relationships are seen quickly and easily. As Kavanagh wrote in one of his early articles, "Logic tables are a way of thinking as well as an organized way of expressing those thoughts. ... The logic of a problem can always be written out in words and sentences, but this necessitates a sequential consideration of alternative paths rather than the more desirable simultaneous consideration. The written definition of the logic may be exact, but it is prone to misinterpretation and hence erroneous conclusions."

Example: A decision logic table in business

HOW TO APPROVE OR DISAPPROVE AN ORDER

IF credit limit is . . .	and IF pay experience is . . .	and IF special clearance has been obtained . . .	THEN . . .
o. k.			approve order
questionable	favorable		approve order
not favorable	not favorable	yes	approve order
not favorable	not favorable	no	return order to sales dept.

Proliferation of Diagrams: PERT and CPM Charts

History

During the mid-1950s, it became apparent in several industries—defense, aerospace, construction, and petrochemicals—that projects were becoming so large and complex as to exceed management capabilities to plan, schedule, track, and evaluate. This led to a major period of invention of diagrams to represent systems of immense complexity. Once again the demands of comprehending and managing huge amounts of detail challenged the human imagination, and once again the response was a visual language invention.

Many types of diagrams were invented during this period. These 2 pages summarize the conceptual development and first application of a network arrow diagram, along with idea of a "critical path," which was pioneered as a joint venture of E. I. du Pont de Nemours and Company and the Sperry-Rand Corporation. In September 1957, the first computerized Critical Path Method (CPM) system, using a UNIVAC I computer, was launched. At approximately the same time the U. S. Navy Special Projects Office hired Booze, Allen, and Hamilton and the Lockheed Missiles and Space Company to develop a similar Program Evaluation and Review Technique (PERT) for the Navy's Polaris submarine project.

Structure and purpose of the charts

Both PERT and CPM charts present a project as a network of tasks (represented by rectangles), all of which are related to one another and connected by arrows representing "must be completed before." The arrows also represent time and are quantified—that is, different length arrows represent different amounts of time. A computer program then calculates each path through the network to determine which one(s)—if not completed on time—could delay the rest of the project.

Without aid, our minds are quite unable to cope with the sheer size, interrelatedness, and complexity of projects with thousands of tasks. Such planning charts permit management to plan and schedule component parts of a project without losing coordination and control of the whole.

Key ideas

Time estimates. Three time estimates are normally assigned to each activity to allow for uncertainty in planning:
- optimistic (minimum amount of time the activity will take)
- most likely (normal time an activity will take)
- pessimistic (maximum time an activity will take under adverse conditions)

The critical path. The critical path is often represented by a heavier line on the chart. Its connections, plus the time estimates, give managers a chance to decide whether it is worth allocating more resources to a project that is behind schedule in order to get it back on track.

Two types of activities. Real activities describe the tasks that must be accomplished in order to move from one event to another. Real activities expend money, time, human resources, and equipment. (Note: Arrows do not indicate amount of resource expended.)

Dummy activities represent the dependency of one event upon another. Dummy activities may have zero time associated with them. Examples of situations that might require the presence of dummy activities include inactivity, redundant activities, and schedule-convenience delay times.

PERT chart

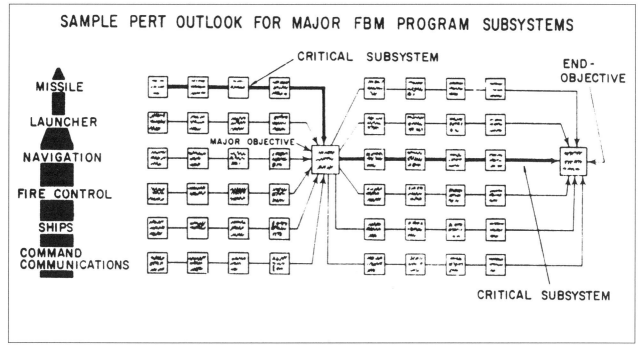

PERT chart (critical path marked with darker line)

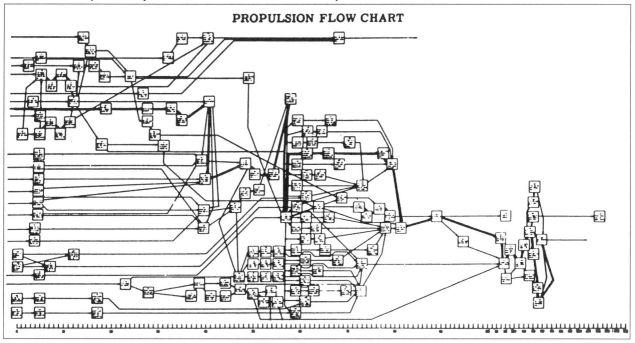

Time Line: Late 20th Century

Proliferation of new diagrams. Driven by the software programming revolution and by the growth in size and complexity of industrial organizations, this period has produced a tremendous variety of diagramming. In one sense it can be called the golden age of diagrams, because so many new varieties appeared. This section of the time line highlights a few of these new diagrams. (➔45) **1950s through 1980s**

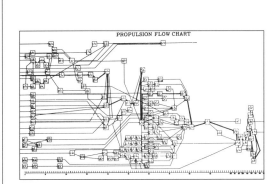

PROPULSION FLOW CHART

PERT/CPM charts invented. Permitted the planning and management of extremely complex projects with tens of thousands of events and activities. (➔45) **du Pont; Sperry Rand; Booze, Allen, and Hamilton; Lockheed Martin, 1957**

Computer software for drawing invented. The graphical computer has played a fundamental role in the increasingly widespread use of visual language for communication. Sutherland invented much of the functionality of drawing programs that permits this tool to be used by so many. **Ivan Sutherland, American computer engineer, 1963**

1950

1960

IF

THEN

Decision logic tables invented. Enables analysis of logic in computer programs, complicated regulations, and instructions. (➔44) **T. F. Kavanagh, American engineer, and General Electric Group, 1958–1960**

Theory of verbal/visual rhetoric. First attempt to analyze the deep integration of words and images. (➔105–106) **Gui Bonsiepe, Swiss designer, 1966**

Surface rendering invented. Renders the three-dimensional surface of an object on a two-dimensional computer screen, while hiding from view the underlying geometric shapes of which the object is constructed. **John Warnok, G. W. Romney, and Gary Watkins, American software engineers, 1960s through 1970s**

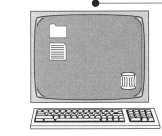

Graphical user interface and desktop metaphor. Development of the modern computer interface took more than a decade. The release of the Xerox Star computer triggered worldwide recognition of importance of icons and metaphor in interface design. **Alan Kay and Xerox PARC Team, American software engineers, 1970–1983**

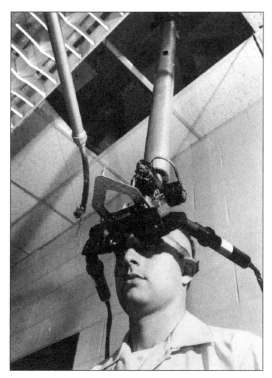

Virtual reality invented. Importance: The ability to create three-dimensional worlds that viewers feel they are inside of rather than just viewing and in which they can move about. **Ivan Sutherland, American computer engineer, 1968**

Theory of linear and nonlinear reading. Calls attention to the varieties of reading required in visual language. (→229–230) **Michael Twyman, British art historian, 1979**

Theory of externalization of ideas in problem solving. Crystallization of thinking about creative problem solving and visual thinking. (→213) **Robert McKim, American designer, 1980**

World Wide Web invented. Rapid increase in use of visual language is concomitant with the growth of the Web and the browser software that makes creation and use easy and colorful. **Tim Berners-Lee, British physicist, 1991**

1970

1980

Present

Systematics of making group process visible. Widespread application in organizational meeting rooms of value of visual recording and facilitation. (→215–216) **David Sibbet, American organizational consultant and information designer, 1979**

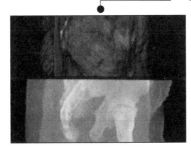

Volume rendering. The rendering of three-dimensional volumes of data, not just surfaces but contents, on the computer screen. **Loren Carpenter, Pat Hanrahan, and Bob Drebin, American software engineers, Pixar, 1980s**

Theory of semiotics of graphics. First definitive, semiotic analysis of quantitative charts and graphs. Still a classic. (→227–228) **Jacques Bertin, French semiotician, 1981–1983**

Excellence in quantitative presentation. Focused worldwide attention on quality and accuracy in quantitative graphical presentation with such concepts as avoiding chartjunk and the data-ink ratio. Spearheaded the professionalization of information design. (→236) **Edward Tufte, American political scientist and statistician, 1982**

Technology and Complexity Drive Periods of Growth

As we look back on this abbreviated history, we see that the challenges of coping with complex data and information have been among the most important drivers of the development of visual language. One driver, for example, was the huge volumes of statistics that were collected, often about social issues, in the 17th century. Another driver is the "firehoses of data" that scientists are facing at the end of the 20th century. Each of these periods has triggered visual language innovations.

Furthermore, 3 major technological inventions—photography, improvements in the printing press, and the graphic computer—have catalyzed innovations in visual language.

Late 19th Century

Late 18th Century

Photography and printing

In the late 19th and early 20th centuries technological innovations in the printing industry and in photography gave the book, magazine, and newspaper industries a gigantic boost in capability. This spectacular increase in the use of visuals worldwide meant that much more of humanity was able to see the world without leaving home.

Quantitative data

During the scientific revolution of the 17th century, scientists began to accumulate a huge variety of data, both physical (e.g., temperature) and social (e.g., numbers of deaths and births). Previously, the major way to convey such data had been the table of numbers. But in the latter part of the 18th century a number of key inventions made the visual language of quantitative data available. While literacy, even today, is not universal for such graphs and charts, there is no question that they now have a standard role in science and technology.

Just Yesterday

Early 1980s

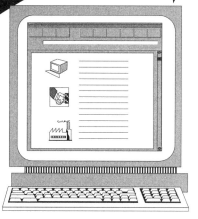

World Wide Web

Another revolution began in 1991
with the introduction of the
World Wide Web. Suddenly, not
only are millions of computers
connected to the Internet, but the
capability of publishing visual-
language pages has reached
millions more. This has produced
an outpouring of creativity and
communication. Together with
virtual reality, these capabilities
will again revolutionize human
communication.

Graphic computer

In 1983, with the introduction of the
Macintosh computer, the capability to produce
integrated word–image communication units
again increased dramatically. Today well over
50 million computers worldwide are capable
of producing visual language. The widespread
availability of drawing software, clip art,
CD-ROMs for storage, and multimedia
projection devices, and the realization that
visual language is vital to modern
organizational communication has produced
another dramatic increase in use. The graphic
computer has also resulted in a gigantic
increase in the use of visualization in scientific
computing.

*Currently, visual language is in a period of tremendous
growth all over the world and in all arenas of human
communication. Such global developments make it
difficult to get an accurate perspective on very recent
developments. To some degree, that makes it difficult
to see how current innovations will fit with the rest of
the historical patterns of visual language's
development. One thing is certain: When a complete
history of the language is written, our times are sure to
be remembered as a flourishing of creativity in the use
of visual language.*

50

Chapter 3
Communication Units, Morphology, and Syntax

Analysis of visual language as a language, as opposed to as a dialect or a design methodology, must begin within the framework of natural language linguistics. This is the 1st of 3 chapters that undertake such a linguistic study; the other 2 cover semantics (the study of meaning) and pragmatics (the study of use), respectively.

This chapter investigates visual language morphology—the basic building blocks of any language—and syntax. It will quickly become clear that, while such a study can begin within the constraints of natural language linguistics, the special characteristics of visual language—especially the tight integration of verbal and visual elements, and the requirement that they be considered in parallel—requires old concepts to be extended and new concepts to be developed. When applicable, I borrow distinctions and frameworks from art theory, art criticism, and cognitive science.

The questions I address are: What are the basic units, the building blocks, of visual language? What should rules for combining those basic elements into meaningful units of communication be based on? And, what do meaningful units of communication look like in visual language? In answering these questions, more questions are raised—which I take as a sign that visual language linguistics is a topic of study worthy of further attention from researchers. Syntax, in particular, is abundant with opportunities for further research, study, and theory.

Finally, let me note that the uneasy relationship between shape and function, between syntax and semantics, raises its head in a linguistic analysis of visual language, just as it torments all other studies of language. The questions are fascinating: How does shape create function or meaning? How does meaning rely on form? My preliminary survey of visual language syntax tackles some, but by no means all, of these thorny issues.

mor • phol • o • gy /n/
1. in linguistics, the study of words, independent of their relationships in sentences. Words are analyzed into their smallest meaningful components and into all of the variations that may be associated with them (e.g., the word *misunderstanding* can be divided into three components: *mis-*, *understand*, and *-ing*). Sometimes, rules for the formation of gender and number and for declension and conjugation are identified. **2.** in visual language, the study of the primitive components (verbal and visual).

syn • tax /n/
1. in linguistics, the way in which basic components—words—are put together in phrases, clauses, and sentences. [fr. GK *syntaxis* arrangement] **2.** in visual language, the study of the combinations and relationships of verbal and visual elements, specifically the identification of the permissible combinations of components.

Contents of Chapter 3

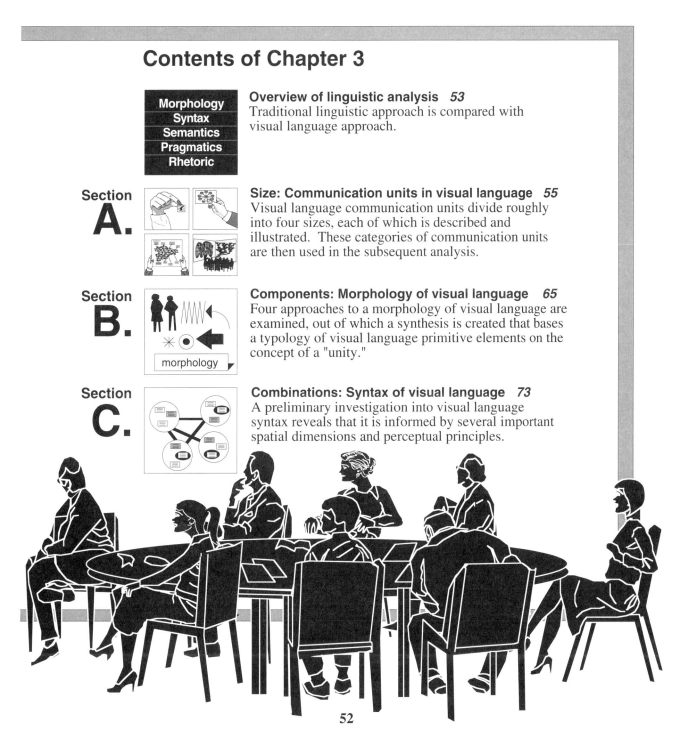

Overview of Linguistic Analysis

This overview compares traditional linguistics analysis with my approach to visual language analysis. Several of the traditional linguistic categories must be revised, because the components of visual language by definition include images and shapes in addition to words. For example, the study of morphology of visual language will incorporate words, but will require identification of visual primitives as well. (→65–72)

It is important to note that, in general, visual language incorporates what is known about the patterns of purely verbal communication. That is, it uses words, sentences, and paragraphs. But it integrates them with visual elements in new ways that create visual language syntax. Something as simple as the variety of ways in which elements can be arranged on the page (→77–80) provides an example of the flexibility and richness of visual language syntax.

This chapter focuses principally on the linguistic analysis of this new syntax. It would be interesting to do a comprehensive syntactical analysis of the verbal part of visual language to discover the ways in which it might be different from that of natural language.

At this stage in the development of visual language, I examine the large organizing principles. Undoubtedly, as time goes on, there will be those who will bring to visual language analysis the kind of axiomatic, rule-based analysis that is currently used in some branches of natural language linguistics.

Components of language

Morphemes
The components of a word. For example, *mis*, *understand*, and *ing* are 3 morphemes.

Phonemes
The permissible sounds in a language, that is, the vowels and consonants and their components. English has about 40 phonemes, Hawaiian has 15. No human language contains more than 50 or so phonemes.

are used to build

Words
The combination of morphemes into unique units of meaning. English has about 450,000 words, of which the average high-school graduate recognizes perhaps 80,000 and uses, according to various estimates, from 10,000 to 20,000.

are used to build

Phrases and clauses
The subunits of sentences. Phrases and clauses are the components of a language that are used to "build up" meanings in syntactically permissible ways.

are used to build

Sentences
Usually regarded as the minimal unit of communication of "complete" thoughts. Sentences are also subject to syntactic constraints.

are used to build

Paragraphs
Usually defined as groups of sentences about a single topic. The definition of both "group" and "topic" varies widely, and paragraphs range in length from one sentence to many pages.

are used to build

Documents
Written with a particular readership in mind. As the connection between writer, intended message, reader, and reader interpretation, it provides the context for the more elementary parts of communication.

The organization of traditional versus visual language linguistics

Morphology

In language, the study of the basic individual elements—morphemes and words. Morphology is the foundational study upon which syntax and semantics are built. Morphology of visual language requires identification of its basic elements.

Syntax

The study of how the basic elements can be identified and combined into units. In many linguistic studies, syntax describes the permissible combinations of classes of basic elements and the permissible transformations of basic elements. Some studies of syntax form categories of basic elements based on semantics or meaning. Other studies of formal languages specify syntax independent of meaning. The syntax of visual language requires the identification of how visual and verbal elements can fit together and in what ways they are combinable.

Semantics

The study of how language conveys meaning, how words can refer to referents, and how language enables communication. Studying the semantics of visual language is a major undertaking that involves examining how specific combinations of words and visual elements together convey meaning. The semantics of visual language is one of my particular interests and one of the focal points of this book. Chapter 4 provides perspective on visual language semantics, and chapters 5 and 6 treat functional semantics in depth by asking, what do words do best and what do visual elements do best when they are working together?

Pragmatics

The study of how language is used in the wider social contexts of communication, including the various social functions it performs. It includes the study of social conventions that we follow about what to say and not to say in particular occasions, which are informed by the influences of social class, status, role, and ethnic diversity. The study of visual language pragmatics includes an exploration of the ways that reading a visual language page or computer screen is considerably different from reading a page of linear prose text. The pragmatics of visual language also necessarily involves the study of the application of visual language to specific human problem-solving and similar activities, as well as to information design, or the attempt to make communication units effective and efficient.

Rhetoric and Composition

The study of how sentences can be combined to form larger units of communication. As with natural languages, the rhetoric of visual language addresses the practical, "how-to" issues of composing for specific purposes and in particular contexts. Investigations into the rhetoric of visual language will be easier once the syntax and semantics are more fully worked out.

54

Visual Language Communication Units

The first step in understanding the components of visual language is to find the coherent units of meaning. I propose we use 4 basic types of communication units, divided roughly on the basis of size. The characteristics and properties of each major size of visual language communication units are the subjects of the following pages.

Of course, the 4 basic types cannot be sharply delineated. They are not discrete, and one can find examples that fall in the boundary region between the communication units. But generally, visual language communication units can be sorted into 4 sizes. These categories are therefore an accurate representation of the territory.

Name	Description	Size
Icon/VLicon elements (➜57–58)	Smallest unit of meaning in visual language. Usually a simple graphic. One type of icon, called a VLicon element, contains 1 or 2 words, or a phrase, to clarify the visual elements.	Generally small (less than one-inch square)
Concept diagram (➜59–60)	A simple to moderately complicated graphic (often a diagram) accompanied by one or a few sentences. Usually cannot stand alone as an autonomous communication chunk, but appears in the context of a sequence or grouping.	Roughly a quarter to a half page
Information graphic, or "infographic" (➜61–62)	Larger spreads usually containing a large and often complex central visual element or group of visual elements. Frequently contains several blocks of text. Can stand alone as an autonomous communication chunk.	Half-, 1-, or 2-page spread
Information mural, or "infomural" (➜63–64)	Includes one or more infographics. Types usually recognizable by format: landscapes, mandalas, matrices, process diagrams, time lines, and so forth.	Usually the size of a wall or part of a wall

Purpose and significance

• Focuses attention
• Identifies function or content
• Discriminates among similar items
• Adds or maintains visual interest
• Provides commentary
• Sets a mood

• Represents a characteristic thought size
• Organizes moderate amounts of information into optimum thought chunks
• Provides an example for a generalization
• Disambiguates complex information
• Reinforces a particular point
• Represents passage of time, multiple points of view

• Large enough to represent all but the most complex subjects
• Identifiable by the presence of one or more central visual elements
• Communicates at an overview level while preserving access to detail
• Self-contained, within the limits of context

• Illuminates subjects with deeper levels of complexity
• Frequently used in group problem analysis, decision making, or data collection
• Facilitates creative problem solving, cross-cultural communication, exploration of deeper connections

I would like to comment on the origin of names I've selected.

Icons *are common enough these days.* ***VLicon*** *is a term I invented to distinguish between icons that do not incorporate words and those that do.*

Concept diagram *is a compromise. Architects frequently use the term to describe this form of communication (which they use often).*

Information graphic *(or* ***infographic****) is the term that newspaper and magazine graphics illustrators use for their products, which are often of the size I've indicated.*

The term ***information mural*** *(or* ***infomural****) really captures the idea of the larger size.*

Icons and VLicon Elements

i • con */n/*
1. any relatively small picture or symbol used to identify a thing or idea. **2.** a small picture or symbol used to identify a tool, document, command, etc., on a computer interface. *Syn.* logograph, glyph, (sometimes) pictograph.

Icons are usually thought of as pictures that do not have words associated with them. Icons are what many people think of initially as visual language. Some even think that visual language consists only of icons, citing traffic signs and computer interfaces as examples.

Research on icons

A fair amount of research has been conducted on the degree to which an icon can be recognized either by itself or in the context of a collection of icons. The results generally indicate that icons by themselves fail to communicate adequately. The exceptions—like the stop sign, P for parking, and a circle with a slash through the center—enjoy recognizability based on their frequent, long-term, and universal usage. We continue to use them because they take up less "real estate" and are readily discriminable from one another, even when their individual meanings are obscure.

Use words

But the use of icons for effective, efficient communication continues to be compromised so long as users fail to remember or guess their meanings. One popular solution is to always include a word of phrase of text with an icon to disambiguate its meaning, or to only use text if the meaning of the icon is likely to be ambiguous.

Why icons without words are inadequate ...

1 | Meaning frequently not unique

Images, like words, are ambiguous. For example, here are 2 different iconic uses of a heart symbol:

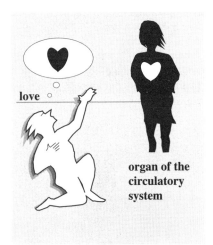

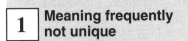

organ of the circulatory system

Examples such as this one abound. Only context, usually in the form of some accompanying text, can disambiguate such symbols.

2 | Change over time

The common shape of an object can change considerably over time. It is sometimes difficult to tell simply from an illustration that it is the same object, even though it may have exactly the same function and use the same design principles. For example, the telephone has metamorphosed greatly in 75 years. No single one of these telephone icons could be used outside the era in which it was dominant to unambiguously symbolize the idea "telephone."

3 | Meaning not always clear

In one international study of 108 symbols—32 of which are in wide use—86 were clearly understood by less than 50 percent of the respondents. Only 3 of the symbols were understood by more than two-thirds of the sample. Other studies have produced similar results.

... and why VLicon elements work.

Consider the one-way sign.

What would happen if we used just the words by themselves?

ONE WAY

Or just the arrow?

Standing alone, neither the words nor the sign adequately convey the intended message. Without the words, the meaning of the arrow is unclear. Without the arrow, the question becomes, which way? The one-way sign neatly illustrates the importance of words and images working together at the iconic scale.

The example of the one-way sign, along with the research into the ineffectiveness of stand-alone visual icons and the regularity with which visual icons are misunderstood, suggests the need for a different approach to iconic communication—namely, the VLicon element.

> **VLi • con™ element** /n/
> **1.** any relatively small picture or symbol combined with a textual label and used to identify a thing or idea in visual language; an icon used with words. [fr. visual language + icon] **2.** a trademark used by Robert E. Horn.

Either/or fails

Such solutions, however, are predicated on an either/or belief about the use of visuals and text, an underlying theme of this book. Here, as in other parts of our discussion, I recommend a both/and position. Research clearly demonstrates that words and visual elements not only can but need to work together to produce more effective communication.

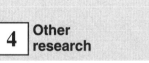

4 | Other research

The findings of several other studies of the use of icons (or sets of icons) are relatively consistent and can be summarized as follows:

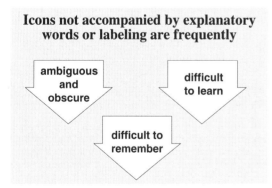

Such research findings should be familiar to users of graphical computer interfaces in which 2 dozen or more icons appear without labels, often creating frustration or slowing the learning process. Many software producers have adopted the "balloon help" convention, in which a small cartoon speech balloon appears to explain the function when the cursor rolls over the icon. Is there any way to make icons clear, distinct, learnable, and memorable? No one has presented convincing evidence that such a goal can be accomplished.

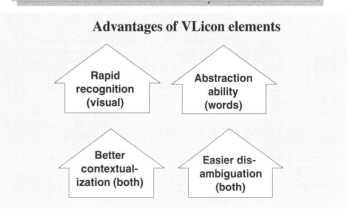

Concept Diagrams

con • cept   di • a • gram /n/
Diagrams that express a single concept. Usually a simple to moderately complicated graphic accompanied by one or a few sentences. Usually cannot stand alone as an autonomous communication chunk, but appears in sequence with other concept diagrams. Roughly a quarter- to a half-page in size.

This category may be the most pervasive category of visual language components. Concept diagrams most often comprise 1 or 2 sentences and a central visual component. They are about the size of the usual slide in a presentation and contain about the same amount of information. In print, they usually appear as a set of panels to be read sequentially. On computer screens, they are often the size of a single screen.

The concept diagram seems to represent some characteristic thought size. I speculate that they may be a kind of optimum thought chunk, probably based on the amount of visual language our working memories can hold easily. (→237)

Like other visual language units, concept diagrams are tightly integrated. The words support the visual elements and vice versa. Just about any kind of visual element can form the central visual component of this size of communication unit. Concept diagrams are extremely flexible; almost any sentence or 2 can provide the verbal element, and virtually any form of visual can provide the central focus.

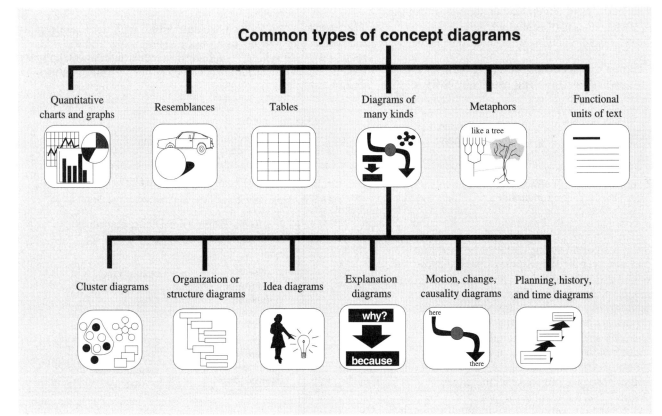

Example of concept diagrams from Total Quality Management

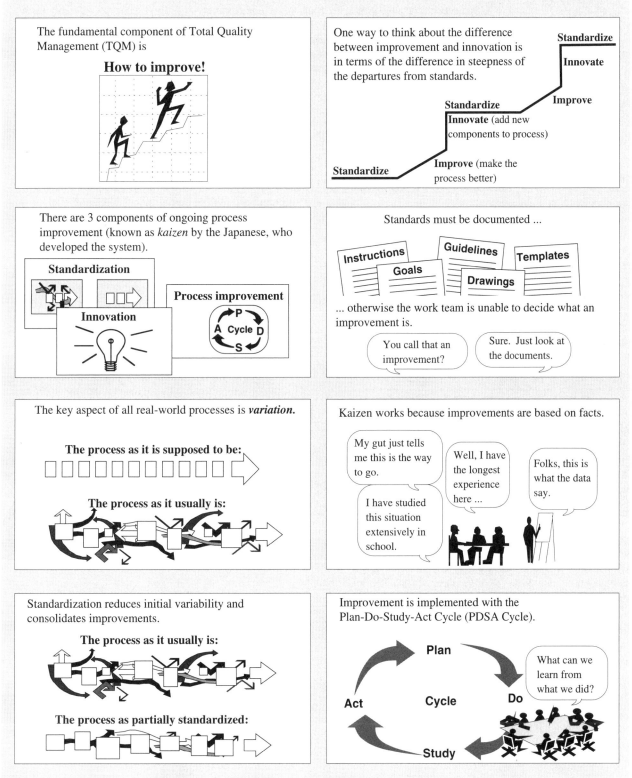

The fundamental component of Total Quality Management (TQM) is

How to improve!

One way to think about the difference between improvement and innovation is in terms of the difference in steepness of the departures from standards.

Standardize
Innovate
Improve
Standardize
Innovate (add new components to process)
Improve (make the process better)
Standardize

There are 3 components of ongoing process improvement (known as *kaizen* by the Japanese, who developed the system).

Standardization
Innovation
Process improvement
P
A Cycle D
S

Standards must be documented ...

Instructions
Guidelines
Templates
Goals
Drawings

... otherwise the work team is unable to decide what an improvement is.

You call that an improvement?

Sure. Just look at the documents.

The key aspect of all real-world processes is *variation*.

The process as it is supposed to be:

The process as it usually is:

Kaizen works because improvements are based on facts.

My gut just tells me this is the way to go.

Well, I have the longest experience here ...

Folks, this is what the data say.

I have studied this situation extensively in school.

Standardization reduces initial variability and consolidates improvements.

The process as it usually is:

The process as partially standardized:

Improvement is implemented with the Plan-Do-Study-Act Cycle (PDSA Cycle).

Plan
Cycle
Act
Do
Study

What can we learn from what we did?

60

Information Graphics

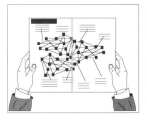

in • for • ma • tion   graph • ic /n/
Moderately sized, meaningful combinations of words, images, and shapes that together constitute a complete communication unit. Visual and verbal elements are tightly integrated. Is as self-contained as possible on 1 or 2 pages or on a large screen. Usually contains considerably more information than a concept diagram, although an information graphic may use any of the types of concept diagrams as its central visual element. Usually contains several blocks of text. **Abbr.** infographic. **Syn.** MacroVU® communication unit.

The information graphic, or infographic, is the basic communication unit that integrates many visual language elements into wholes. The roots of the form are traceable at least as far back as medieval documents (➔28), which displayed tight integration of a large number of smaller units of both text and images.

Central visual element
Infographics are notable for the frequent use of one or more central visual elements. The text is frequently arranged around the visual element and/or linked to it with lines that guide the eye and thus increase reading efficiency. In the example on the facing page, the most central visual element is the structural diagram of the eyeball. Note, however, another central visual element: a compressed two-column table with one column listing and describing structures of the eye and the other column describing their functions.

Example of nonintegrated text and diagram

Parts of the eye and their functions
The eyeball has three main groupings: (1) the outer layer, (2) the middle layer, and (3) the inner layer. In the outer layer are the cornea and extrinsic muscles. The transparent cornea allows passage of light rays though the eye. The extrinsic muscles permit and limit movements of the eyeball within the orbit of the eye. Next comes the middle layer. There is a circular opening in front, the pupil, which allows light to enter. There is a colored muscular ring surrounding the pupil called the iris. It controls the size of the pupil and the amount of light entering the eye. Next to the pupil is the ciliary muscle, which contracts and moves the lens. Aqueous humor, which fills the area between the cornea and the lens, is produced by the ciliary body. The suspensory ligament suspends the lens and relaxes to allow curvature of the inner lens. Finally, the crystalline lens brings light rays to focus on the light-sensitive area. The innermost layer contains the lining at the back of the eye, which is called the retina. It is highly specialized to convert light energy into nerve impulses. The optic nerve conveys impulses to visual centers in the occipital (posterior) part of the brain.

Anterior chamber (Aqueous humor)
Suspensory ligament
Extrinsic muscles
Ciliary body
Ciliary muscle
Retina
Cornea
Lens
Iris
Inner lens
Optic nerve

Figure 1. The Eye

Creating a coherent visual whole
The infographic is particularly qualified to bring together disparate chunks of information into a coherent visual whole while preserving access to detail. So far as possible, an infographic is self-contained. That is, within the limits of context, it should permit the reader to understand a single portion of the subject matter. Perhaps we can refer to infographics as "what diagrams become when they grow up."

Nonintegrated vs. integrated
Readers are urged to compare the traditional approach with the visual language approach. Contrast the example of nonintegrated text and diagram (at left) with the infographic on the facing page. Note that the infographic undertakes to guide the reader's eye as to the sequence and importance of elements. In the nonintegrated text and diagram, the reader is forced to try to understand the text and diagram separately, which burdens short-term memory with the load of carrying information from the text to the diagram and vice versa. An important line of research has shown that placing such a burden upon short-term memory produces significantly greater error when learners attempt to solve problems. Learners have fewer such problems with the infographic communication unit.

compare

You will gather how important I believe the infographic is by observing how many of them I use in this book.

61

Example of an infographic communication unit

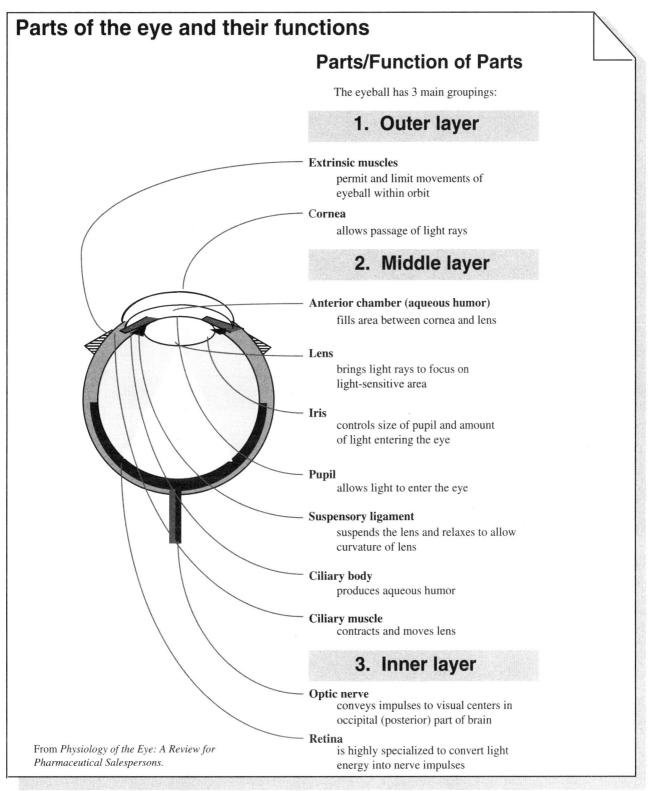

Parts of the eye and their functions

Parts/Function of Parts

The eyeball has 3 main groupings:

1. Outer layer

Extrinsic muscles
permit and limit movements of
eyeball within orbit

Cornea
allows passage of light rays

2. Middle layer

Anterior chamber (aqueous humor)
fills area between cornea and lens

Lens
brings light rays to focus on
light-sensitive area

Iris
controls size of pupil and amount
of light entering the eye

Pupil
allows light to enter the eye

Suspensory ligament
suspends the lens and relaxes to allow
curvature of lens

Ciliary body
produces aqueous humor

Ciliary muscle
contracts and moves lens

3. Inner layer

Optic nerve
conveys impulses to visual centers in
occipital (posterior) part of brain

Retina
is highly specialized to convert light
energy into nerve impulses

From *Physiology of the Eye: A Review for
Pharmaceutical Salespersons.*

Information Murals

in • for • ma • tion   mu • ral /n/

Large, highly integrated displays—usually the size of a wall or part of a wall—that include one or more infographics. Often highly interlinked with a variety of displays (or windows) representing multiple levels of detail and perspective. May be created in real time on paper or as interactive display units. Frequently used in conference rooms for situation reporting and decision making.

The special utility of the information mural comes from its great size, which allows it to hold large amounts of information. Unlike a prose document, the information in a mural is all visible at a glance. This type of communication unit lends itself well to broad, systems-level overviews of complex situations or ideas. Access to detail, however, can be preserved via linkages to other visual language documents. Of the 4 communication units, information murals have the greatest potential to positively affect how we communicate about "big ideas."

The increased complexity of the world often requires hundreds of factors to be considered in a single decision. Mural-based thinking enables decision makers to bring more expertise to bear on contemporary problems, and aids group discussions and decision making by representing nearly infinite numbers of interrelationships and viewpoints in one composition. Information murals are increasingly being used in the conference rooms of business, industry, and government for brainstorming, planning, and decision making.

The Bradford Project

Overview
The Bradford Project is the flagship project of our next 5-year company plan. This infoscape shows the major project stages (as floating platforms) and their interconnections.

Status
Presently we are in the crucial phase of building the initial prototype. We expect that the prototype will be completed within two quarters.

Initial Beta Test
Marketing has already completed contacts with key customers to perform initial beta tests.

Patent Application Process

Patent Search

Legal Dept. Involved

Special Safety Simulations

Initial Prototype Built

Revised Pilot Project Approved

Offsite Critique Session

Pilot Project Approved

Morphology—The Study of Visual Primitives

> **mor • phol • o • gy** */n/*
> **1.** in linguistics, the study of words, independent of their relationships in sentences. Words are analyzed into their smallest meaningful components and into all of the variations that may be associated with them (e.g., the word *misunderstanding* can be divided into three components: *mis-*, *understand*, and *-ing*). Sometimes, rules for the formation of gender and number and for declension and conjugation are identified. **2.** in visual language, the study of the primitive components (verbal and visual).

Many approaches to understanding a subject matter begin by analyzing it down to its most primitive components and then building up from there. Morphological studies, apart from being intrinsically interesting, provide the basic elements for syntactical and semantic studies. The primitive elements identified in a morphology are used for further analyses and explanations. Thus the level at which one identifies primitive elements must be chosen to serve syntactical purposes.

A review of morphological analyses

Many people have examined graphic illustrations and diagrams in attempts to identify visual primitives. This section examines 2 robust, formalist morphological approaches for their usefulness for a morphology of visual language.

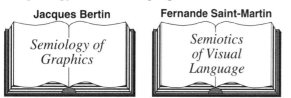

Although they are important, the formalist approaches do not serve the needs of the syntactic analysis I undertake in the next section. After analyzing the formalist approaches, I briefly consider the relevance of Irving Biederman's theory of three-dimensional perception to a morphology of visual language. Finally I agree with Evelyn Goldsmith that formalist approaches do not give us the right set of primitives for visual language. I will propose a classification of major morphological elements of visual language that is based on the distinctions between words, images, and shapes.

Jacques Bertin

An important delineation of visual morphological variables was developed by Jacques Bertin in his study of two-dimensional maps, diagrams, and network charts. He identifies one morphological primitive, the "mark" (any ink on a page), which can have these variables.

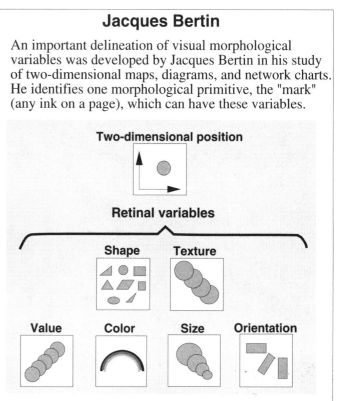

With the application of combinations of these 7 variables (8 if you count the 2 dimensions of the plane) to the "mark," anything can be visually represented. "They form the world of images. With them the designer suggests perspective, the painter reality, the graphic draftsman ordered relationships, and the cartographer space," Bertin says.

Bertin is thorough in his identification of these variables, and his book on the semiology of diagrams and maps is an unsurpassed classic. But his analysis fails us in that it neglects illustrations and is less than satisfactory in its treatment of the integration of words and images.

Fernande Saint-Martin

Fernande Saint-Martin, in *Semiotics of Visual Language*, provides a detailed and elaborate outline of visual primitive elements in terms of lines, shapes, and forms. Her detailed taxonomic distinctions (as between curves and angles, symmetrical and asymmetrical, and single and compound) provide an excellent vocabulary for any morphological analysis that encompasses only formal relationships. However, the distance between her primitives and any kind of meaningful syntax is too wide to help us develop a morphology for visual language.

Here are some examples—but by far not a complete list—of Saint Martin's taxonomy.

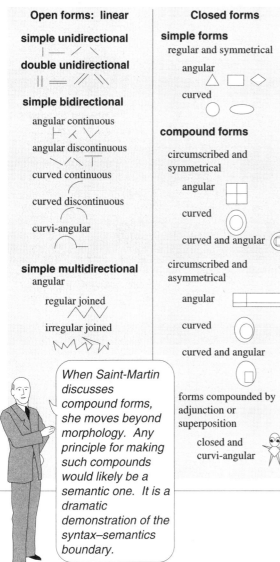

When Saint-Martin discusses compound forms, she moves beyond morphology. Any principle for making such compounds would likely be a semantic one. It is a dramatic demonstration of the syntax–semantics boundary.

Formalist approaches inadequate

Formal morphological analyses such as those reviewed here focus on the identification of parts. It is easy to decompose visual components into these morphologies of shapes and lines. But, though it is easy to decompose, it is difficult to build meaningful units from such simple primitives. The rules and guidelines for combination are not easy to write and their number would be enormous if one were to undertake to specify them—which would be, I believe, a futile exercise.

Suppose we describe the tree below using the visual morphological terms supplied by the formalists. We might try to describe in some way the trunk lines and the texture of the leafy portion.

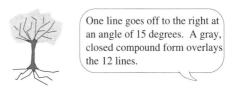

One line goes off to the right at an angle of 15 degrees. A gray, closed compound form overlays the 12 lines.

Would such an analysis ever get us close to the idea of "tree"? No. No matter how detailed the description is, no matter how many of the primitives are combined in the description, it would not mean "tree" to a reader or listener. Thus, we find the outer limits of a purely formal morphological analysis's ability to serve syntactical purposes, that is, to give us clues about how visual language communicates meaningful information.

Neither Bertin's nor Saint-Martin's morphology solves the problem of moving from formal analysis to a utilitarian morphology in which a tree can be identified as a tree—as a coherent unit of meaning. There are no sufficient principles for combining these elements into larger compositions without some way of considering the whole tree as a form, as a unit. This is exactly where we meet the limits of morphological analysis based on forms. One limited exception to that conclusion is this book's analysis of the semantic ability of certain kinds of lines to convey feeling or mood. (→147–148)

Three-Dimensional Components as Morphological Primitives of Perception

We live in a three-dimensional world. Many of the visual elements of visual language are perceived to exist in that world. Thus, a theory that accounts for our perception of three-dimensional objects will help us understand the cognitive processes that enable us to think of a tree (or, in the example below, an elephant)—as opposed to a line, as St. Martin would have us do—as a morphological primitive in visual language. Irving Biederman, a perceptual psychologist, has a promising theory that goes a long way toward identifying the stages of the object perception process.

"Geons" as morphological primitives

Just as we apprehend spoken language through the repetitive combination of a few phonemes, Biederman says we recognize three-dimensional objects by segmenting them into simple, regular, geometrical elements (e.g., blocks, wedges, cylinders, etc.).

Each of these elements is easily identified and distinguished from one another when viewed from any position. Below are some primitives of object recognition, according to Biederman.

Biederman identifies 36 primitive components (called "geons" for "geometrical icons"), which the theory identifies as generalized cones. A cone is a volume created by projecting a shape along a straight or curved axis. Cones are usually symmetrical and have the gestalt property of good continuation. (➜75–76) Different combinations of the same geons enable us to recognize different objects:

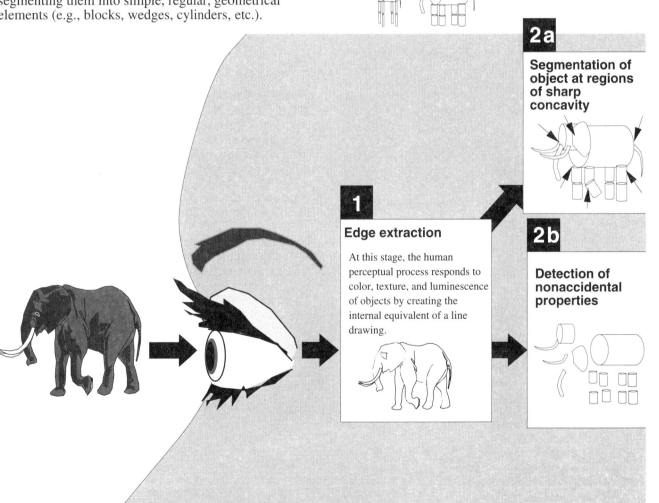

2a

Segmentation of object at regions of sharp concavity

1

Edge extraction

At this stage, the human perceptual process responds to color, texture, and luminescence of objects by creating the internal equivalent of a line drawing.

2b

Detection of nonaccidental properties

Biederman's theory aids our analysis

In Saint Martin's morphological analysis, Biederman's geons would have to be built out of primitive lines and shapes before they could be built up further into an elephant; whereas Biederman identifies the geon as the basic building block of perception and recognition. Biederman's perceptual primitives—the geons—focus on the right level of morphological analysis of visual primitives, that is, on a level from which the jump to syntax is conceivable.

For that reason, if Biederman's theory accurately describes how our perceptual processes work, then it should be studied more extensively for its application to the development of visual language. However, his theory obviously does not account for the principles and processes of tight integration of visual and verbal elements, which is critical in a morphology of visual language.

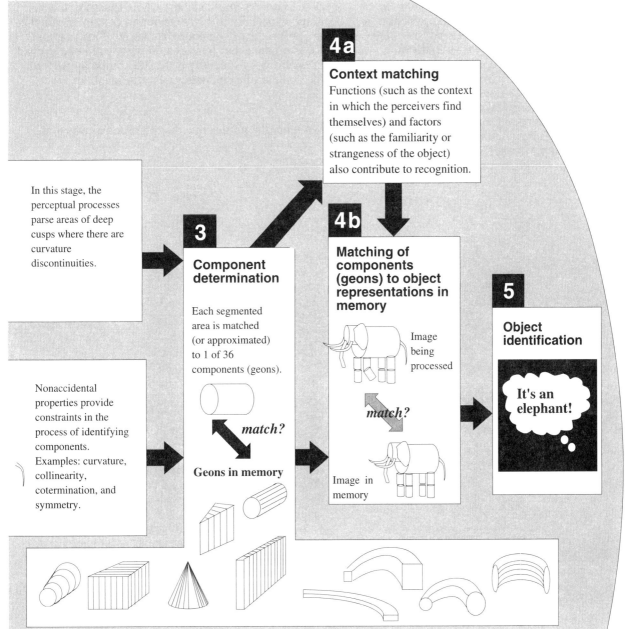

4a

Context matching
Functions (such as the context in which the perceivers find themselves) and factors (such as the familiarity or strangeness of the object) also contribute to recognition.

In this stage, the perceptual processes parse areas of deep cusps where there are curvature discontinuities.

3

Component determination

Each segmented area is matched (or approximated) to 1 of 36 components (geons).

match?

Geons in memory

Nonaccidental properties provide constraints in the process of identifying components. Examples: curvature, collinearity, cotermination, and symmetry.

4b

Matching of components (geons) to object representations in memory

Image being processed

match?

Image in memory

5

Object identification

It's an elephant!

Morphological Units in Visual Language

Evelyn Goldsmith makes a convincing argument against formal approaches to morphological analysis. She suggests that analysis of visuals must begin with what she calls a "unity," referring to "any area in a picture which might be recognized as having a separate identity, even if the identity is not known." She argues that the approach of analysts who start with points and lines—like Bertin and Saint-Martin—cannot get us anywhere in the analysis of a picture.

Humans see unities

In looking at the picture below, viewers will notice themselves using Goldsmith's unities approach—which is supported by Biederman's analysis of how our perceptual processes function—to perform a morphological analysis of the picture. In other words, when asked to select unities from the landscape, viewers will list items like mountains or mountain range or mountain, village, lake, cow, bushes, and so forth. Viewers will tend not to select as unities curved lines, angular lines, or asymmetrical curved closed compounds. Even the curved lines in the sky will usually be seen as clouds, not as curved lines.

When another unity is added to the drawing to communicate an additional idea, the new unity also changes how we look at the background, which becomes context. Even the cow, which is ostensibly in the foreground of the picture, becomes background.

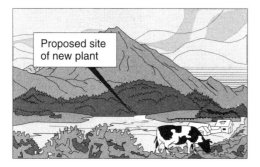

Unities are context dependent

The formalists' analyses of morphological primitives could not allow context to play a role in the identification of morphological primitives, which is where their analyses fail visual language. The following illustration of part of a face provides an example of how identification of unities depends on the context in which the viewer places the portrait.

Some viewers might say the whole illustration is a unity, especially if they're trying to determine whether the portrait is of someone they know. Others might focus on the eyes alone as a unity, or even one eyeball or eyebrow—especially if the illustration appears in the context of a cosmetics advertisement.

What are the unities in a diagram such as this one?

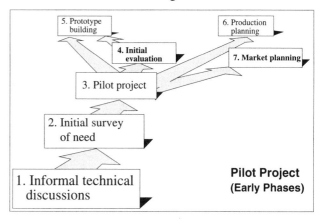

I understand the unities to be these objects:

because they can each be recognized as having a separate identity. The shadows on the panels give them a separate identity, and because we live in a three-dimensional world with a sun, the panels become tangible objects. The arrow is a conventional symbol with a collection of "family resemblance" meanings such as "leads to" or "comes next," which are called into play when they are placed between other objects or separate identities. This discussion indicates the way that semantics and syntax enter into the definition of morphological primitive elements.

Introduction to a typology of morphological units

Goldsmith's and Biederman's insightful analyses will help us as we begin to construct a typology of morphological primitives for visual language. The construction process is somewhat messy, and there are porous boundaries between some of the concepts, but we have established a sufficiently robust approach to enable us to create a typology of the most important units, which can be used in the analysis of syntax and semantics.

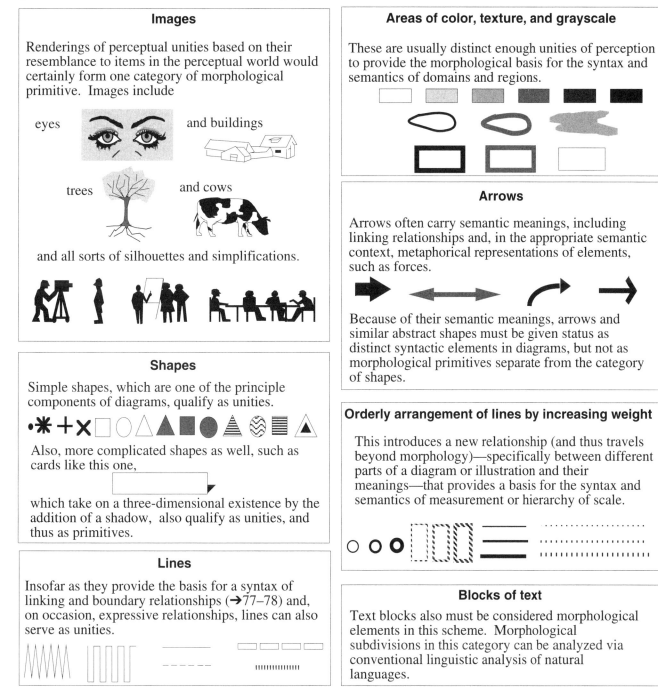

Images

Renderings of perceptual unities based on their resemblance to items in the perceptual world would certainly form one category of morphological primitive. Images include

eyes

and buildings

trees

and cows

and all sorts of silhouettes and simplifications.

Shapes

Simple shapes, which are one of the principle components of diagrams, qualify as unities.

Also, more complicated shapes as well, such as cards like this one,

which take on a three-dimensional existence by the addition of a shadow, also qualify as unities, and thus as primitives.

Lines

Insofar as they provide the basis for a syntax of linking and boundary relationships (➔77–78) and, on occasion, expressive relationships, lines can also serve as unities.

Areas of color, texture, and grayscale

These are usually distinct enough unities of perception to provide the morphological basis for the syntax and semantics of domains and regions.

Arrows

Arrows often carry semantic meanings, including linking relationships and, in the appropriate semantic context, metaphorical representations of elements, such as forces.

Because of their semantic meanings, arrows and similar abstract shapes must be given status as distinct syntactic elements in diagrams, but not as morphological primitives separate from the category of shapes.

Orderly arrangement of lines by increasing weight

This introduces a new relationship (and thus travels beyond morphology)—specifically between different parts of a diagram or illustration and their meanings—that provides a basis for the syntax and semantics of measurement or hierarchy of scale.

Blocks of text

Text blocks also must be considered morphological elements in this scheme. Morphological subdivisions in this category can be analyzed via conventional linguistic analysis of natural languages.

Summary of Morphology

The previous pages examined a number of approaches to morphological analysis of visual primitive elements. Based on that examination and aided by the preliminary discussion of visual language unities begun on the previous page, I now present a typology of visual language primitives that will well serve our further investigations into the structure and meaning of visual language.

Sources for this typology

This typology uses categories from traditional fields where helpful. The best example here is natural language linguistics, which is difficult to improve upon in a morphological analysis of the verbal component of visual language. I have also concentrated on finding the right level of analysis and have discarded the formalist approach in favor of a functional approach informed by the work of Evelyn Goldsmith and Irving Biederman.

Two levels: Primitives and properties

The typology has 2 levels. The 1st level is the primitives themselves: words, images, and shapes. The 2nd level consists of properties: visible characteristics that can be imposed in nearly limitless combinations onto each of the primitive elements. The combinations of primitive elements with properties is the beginning of a syntax of visual language, itself the subject of the next section.

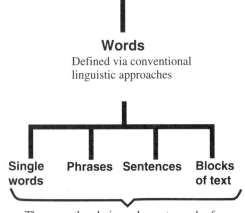

Words
Defined via conventional linguistic approaches

| Single words | Phrases | Sentences | Blocks of text |

These are the obvious elements, each of which functions syntactically and semantically in different ways. Morphological analysis required at a finer-grained level relies upon the studies made in traditional linguistics of natural languages and the analysis of pictures and illustrations.

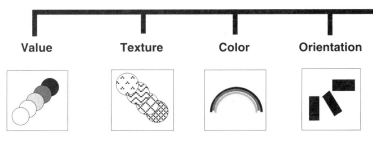

Value   Texture   Color   Orientation

The major morphological elements of visual language

Shapes

Defined as abstract gestalts that stand out from the background as unities but that do not resemble objects in the natural world

Images

Defined as visible shapes that resemble objects in the perceivable world

Point

Defined as something that cannot have anything in front of it without being covered or obliterated or otherwise made unidentifiable. Thus, small shapes such as ✱ ✛ ✖ ⊙ ● can also qualify as points (particularly in diagrams).

Line

Defined as an extended shape, but so thin a shape that nothing can be put in front of it without obliterating it and making it unidentifiable.
Example:
~~Some words in front~~

Abstract shape

Defined as a gestalt form that stands out from the background as a unity and does not resemble objects in the perceivable world.

Space between shapes

Defined as a kind of shape that is usually perceived as background, but that in certain circumstances becomes foreground.
Example:

eyes and buildings

trees  and cows

and all sorts of silhouettes and simplifications.

Properties of primitives

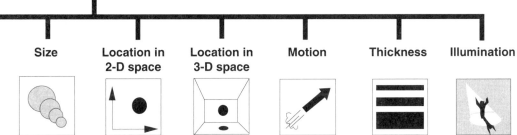

Size   Location in 2-D space   Location in 3-D space   Motion   Thickness   Illumination

Introduction to Visual Syntax

syn • tax /n/

1. in linguistics, the way in which basic components—words—are put together in phrases, clauses, and sentences. [fr. GK *syntaxis* arrangement] **2.** in visual language, the study of the combinations and relationships of verbal and visual elements, specifically the identification of the permissible combinations of components.

The study of syntax in linear prose sentences consists of identifying how different kinds of elements arrange themselves within that sequence. Similarly, visual language syntax studies the patterns of arrangement of elements in two-dimensional space on pages or screens or in three-dimensional space in virtual reality.

The simplest approach to syntax in visual language begins with combinations of discrete unities, the elements we identified in the previous section as the basic morphological units, and analyzes the various dimensions of the combinations and spatial arrangements of those unities.

Analytic strategy: Arrange words in space

We can start with a simple collection of words, or functional units of text. The different meanings communicated by various ways of organizing the same collection of words in combination with visual elements provides us with intuitions about what a syntactical analysis of visual language should entail. We need to look at spatial arrangement and pay particular attention to the relationships among the visual elements and between the visual elements and the text.

Example one: Facilitate reading

If we use the example of automobile repair, we could itemize some of the important parts of a car, such as the engine, electrical system, transmission, brakes, and tires.

What do we learn about visual language syntax when we convert that textual paragraph into a list?

> engine
> electrical system
> transmission
> bakes
> tires

The list lines up the words such that each item is an isolated component, yet all of them are clustered together in a meaningful way.

How does a list change how we read?

**Obviously,
we can
read down
a list rather
than
across
the page**

**and that changes how quickly
we absorb the information.**

Example two: Facilitate action

Or we could indicate to ourselves that we have to get the mechanic to fix the window-washer motor, adjust the brakes, change the oil, check the clutch, and listen to that bumping noise in the back. The verbal syntax is different as well the semantics: It is task oriented and imperative.

What happens when we make another list?

> fix window-washer motor
> adjust brakes
> change oil
> check clutch
> listen to bumping noise

The 1st impact is a semantic one: The words are even more directive. Lists, as all know from our own "to do" lists, facilitate action. Items arranged in a vertical syntax on a list can also be counted or checked off more easily than if they are lined up in continuous lines, as in a paragraph.

>   fix window-washer motor
> √adjust brakes
>   change oil
> √check clutch
>   listen to bumping noise

Example three: Add visual elements

The next level of complexity in visual language syntactic integration involves adding simple visual elements called focusers (➔185–186) to lists. What happens? Look at these lists:

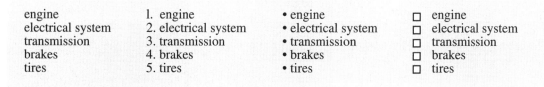

How does the impact of the list change? Do the individual items stand out more? Is one list better than another? Do the different lists have different purposes? Among the comments I receive when I ask panels of readers those questions are:

Example four: Add larger shapes

Shapes, including straight lines, guide the eyes and mind in distinct ways. What happens when different shapes are added to the basic list? Are there differences in impact?

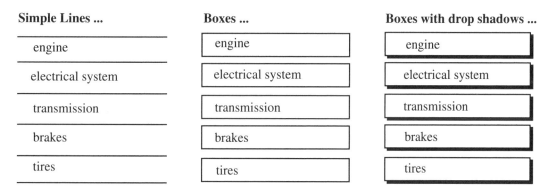

What do panels of readers say about these integrations of text and visual elements?

Conclusion

An important part of the analysis of syntactic relationships in visual language will involve successive elaborations on the arrangements presented on these pages. Lists and other spatial arrangements comprise a large part of visual language syntax, which owes a great debt to Gestalt principles of perception.

Syntax and Gestalt Theory

In visual language, syntax depends upon the arrangement of the elements spatially on a page. And our ideas about proper arrangement depend upon particular ways that our perceptual systems function. Early in the 20th century, a group of psychologists known collectively as the Gestalt psychologists (after the German word for "form") discovered a set of perceptual principles upon which much of the spatial syntax of visual language depends.

Figure/ground

The foundational discovery of the gestaltists was that we tend to split our perception between foreground and background. Ralph Haber and Maurice Hershenson explain, "This phenomenal appearance occurs regardless of the complexity or simplicity of the stimulation in the retinal projection. It is considered so basic that this segregation has usually been taken as the starting point of organized perception. Thus, any inhomogeneity in the retinal projection leads to a perceptual segregation of the field into one part called a figure and another part called a ground. These parts are usually separated by a contour which may be said to divide figure from ground, although the contour seems to belong to the figure. Generally only one of two homogeneous parts of a field may be seen as the figure and the other as the ground ... Thus figure-ground segregation may be said to be immediate and self-evident."

Face or vase?

The familiar "face or vase" optical illusion is often used to demonstrate the strength of the perceptual forces within us that separate foreground and background. We have great difficulty not flipping one or the other—the face or the vase—into the foreground.

Six principles

The Gestalt psychologists described 6 general ways in which we group things spatially. These empirical principles have been established by a good deal of research into perception. The principles help us organize the world around us into meaningful units and directly affect how we find meaning in clusters—or assemblages—of text, images, and shapes in a visual language composition. Because Gestalt principles are so critical to our perception of meaning, they must necessarily form the foundation of visual language syntax.

Complex syntax: Combining Gestalt principles

Some clusters simply exhibit one Gestalt principle: for example, proximity.

Other clusters use several of these principles simultaneously, allowing us to discriminate several levels of commonality or connection.

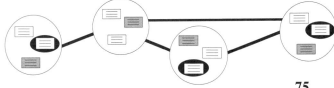

Gestalt principle

Principle of proximity

Principle of similarity

Principle of common region (or closed forms)

Principle of connectedness

Principle of good continuation

Closure principle

Definition of principle   Use of principle

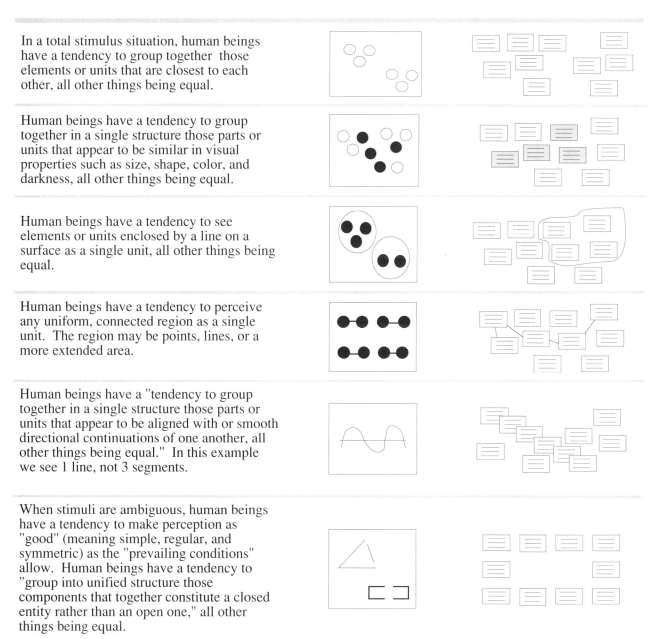

In a total stimulus situation, human beings have a tendency to group together those elements or units that are closest to each other, all other things being equal.

Human beings have a tendency to group together in a single structure those parts or units that appear to be similar in visual properties such as size, shape, color, and darkness, all other things being equal.

Human beings have a tendency to see elements or units enclosed by a line on a surface as a single unit, all other things being equal.

Human beings have a tendency to perceive any uniform, connected region as a single unit. The region may be points, lines, or a more extended area.

Human beings have a "tendency to group together in a single structure those parts or units that appear to be aligned with or smooth directional continuations of one another, all other things being equal." In this example we see 1 line, not 3 segments.

When stimuli are ambiguous, human beings have a tendency to make perception as "good" (meaning simple, regular, and symmetric) as the "prevailing conditions" allow. Human beings have a tendency to "group into unified structure those components that together constitute a closed entity rather than an open one," all other things being equal.

76

Possible Arrangement of Elements

In the introduction to this section (➜73–74) we saw what happens to a simple list of words when we changed the arrangement, added various kinds of focusers, and placed various shapes between the words. We have also seen how Gestalt principles help us organize our visual perception.

Visual language has a huge potential vocabulary based on possible syntactical combinations. The table on these 4 pages charts many, but by no means all, of the basic syntactical arrangements available in visual language. The examples here use words as the arranged elements, but similar arrangements can be created with any of the visual language primitives.

	Elements alone	Elements and focusers	Elements surrounded by shapes
Horizontal list	word word word word word	(1) word, (2) word, (3) word, (4) word, (5) word	word word word / word word
Vertical list	word word word word word	(1) word (2) word (3) word (4) word	word word word
Upper left to lower right	word word word word word	(1) word (2) word (3) word (4) word	word word word
Group proximity	word word word word word	(1) word (5) word (2) word (4) word (3) word	word word word word word
Notes	Follows the Gestalt principle of good continuation	Options for focusers: • bullets A. letters * asterisks icons ☐ checklists ➜ arrows	A variety of shapes and arrangements can be used

77

Elements connected by lines	Elements and boundaries	Elements surrounded by shapes and shading	Elements surrounded by shapes connected by lines
word—word—word	word word word / word word	word word word / word word	word—word—word / word—word
word ▮ word ▮ word	word / word word / word word	word / word / word	word / word / word
word word word word	word word word word word	word word word	word word word
word word word word—word	word word word word word	word word word word	word word word word word
Width and length of lines can vary, as can the topology of the arrangement. Lines can be arrows.	Follows the Gestalt principle of common region	Follows the Gestalt principle of similarity	Follows the Gestalt principle of connectedness

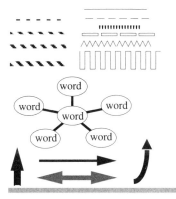

Possible Arrangement of Elements (continued)

Continuing our elaboration of the possible arrangement of elements in visual language syntax from the previous page, we see here how the various properties of visual morphological units can be combined with the unities to develop a syntax.

	Elements oriented differently	Elements with texture	Elements of different size
Horizontal list	word *word* word / word word *word*	word word word / word word	word word word / word word
Vertical list	word / word / word / word	word / word / word	word / word / word / word
Upper left to lower right	word / word / word / word / word	word / word / word	word / word / word / word / word
Group proximity	word / word word / word word	word / word word / word word	word / word word / word word
Notes	Follows the Gestalt principle of similarity	Follows the Gestalt principle of similarity. The texture can be in the background of the text, as above, or in the typeface itself. word	Follows the Gestalt principle of similarity

Elements separated by space	Elements with different position in 2-D space	Elements with different illuminations
word word word	word word word word word	word word word word word
word word word	word word word word word	word word word word word
word word word	word word word word word	word word word word word
word word word word word	word word word word word	word word word word word
Follows the Gestalt principle of proximity	Follows the Gestalt principle of proximity and good continuation	Many visual devices are available to highlight and focus attention.

Visual Topologies

The syntactical arrangement of elements presented on the previous pages can be further organized into a relatively small number of specific topological patterns—that is, different kinds of visible shapes or patterns of shapes. Topologies are also syntactical structures—they effectively communicate meaning because they are based on the Gestalt principles of human perception. When visual language syntax violates those principles, meaning is lost or distorted. The notion of topologies is important to visual language, especially in the understanding of a large class of diagrams, often called cluster diagrams. The tree diagram at right identifies the major topologies.

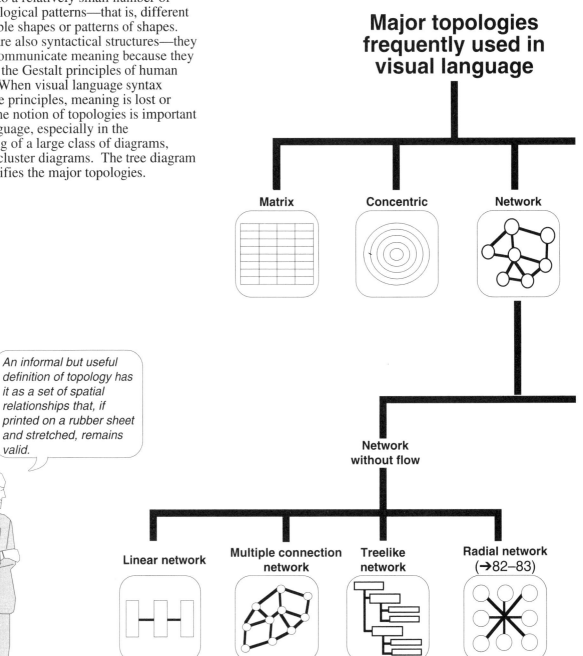

Major topologies frequently used in visual language

Matrix

Concentric

Network

An informal but useful definition of topology has it as a set of spatial relationships that, if printed on a rubber sheet and stretched, remains valid.

Network without flow

Linear network

Multiple connection network

Treelike network

Radial network (➔82–83)

Arranging other elements on topologies

After identifying the topologies, we then need to look at the major ways that words (and other shapes) can be arranged onto them.

An example: We have the following text. "There are 4 levels of functionality in computers: (1) hardware, (2) operating system, (3) application software, and (4) user's document."

To map this text onto a topology, we choose the shape with the most relevance or analogical support. For our example, we choose the "level" topology:

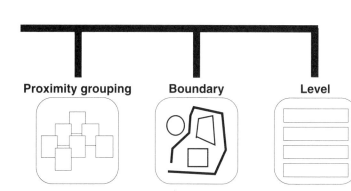

Proximity grouping   **Boundary**   **Level**

Level

The resulting visual language communication unit might look like this:

Four levels of function in computers

User's document
Application software
Operating system
Hardware

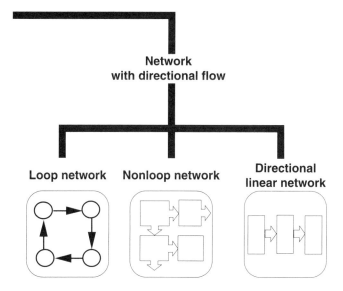

**Network
with directional flow**

Loop network   **Nonloop network**   **Directional linear network**

Each of these topologies has its own set of subtypes. As an example, I have diagrammed the subtypes of one of the topologies—networks—and on the next 2 pages I give examples of sub-subtypes—kinds of radial networks—to explore their syntactical possibilites.

82

Example: Radial Network Topologies

Let's take our exploration of topologies one level deeper by examining one topology—radial networks—in greater detail. We're looking for syntactical possibilities, or how the topology can be used to create meaning out of arrangements of visual language primitives.

Emergent semantic properties

The diagram on the facing page illustrates how different kinds of radial networks have different expressive qualities. Because, as we have seen, lines and shapes and their arrangements in relation to each other have emergent semantic properties, we begin to imbue the topologies on the facing page with meaning even though they contain no content or context. (My investigation into the properties of meaning that a contentless topology can have is continued on the next 2 pages.)

Form and meaning are interconnected

My goal here is not to present every possible type of arrangement of the radial network topology. Rather, I introduce on the facing page just enough of one major type of topology to demonstrate my point: Further semantic meanings emerge from formal differences (e.g., whether the center is explicit or implicit). The need to make meaning interacts deeply with pure form. On one level, we can step back and detach ourselves from the topologies on the facing page. We can describe them as purely geometric connections of lines at such and such an angle. But we react to the topologies in more complex ways as well. We project meaning onto them, yet often feel that the meaning comes from them.

Pure forms thus have levels of meaning for us, sometimes complicated levels. Perception is not a simple interaction: Meanings grow; they interact; they have histories that change over time; they are modified by our experience, for example, as pure forms come into use as symbols. The anecdotal evidence (➔85–86) illustrates how easy it is to change the current state of emergent meanings.

Example of a network topology

How do we apply the radial network topologies to actual usage situations? Illustrated below is an example of a cluster diagram (➔127–128, 187–188) based on one of the network topologies.

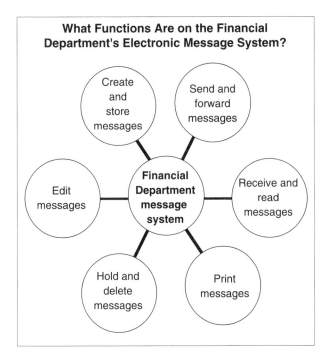

What Functions Are on the Financial Department's Electronic Message System?

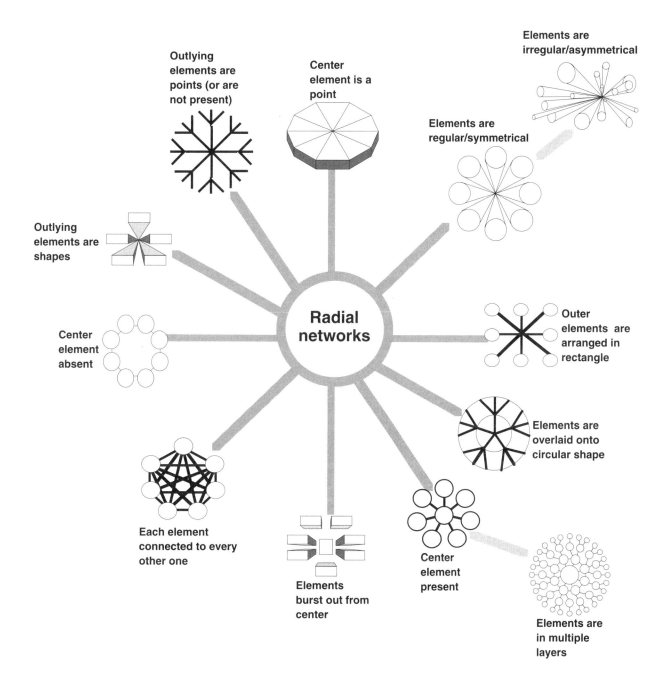

Outlying elements are points (or are not present)

Center element is a point

Elements are irregular/asymmetrical

Elements are regular/symmetrical

Outlying elements are shapes

Center element absent

Radial networks

Outer elements are arranged in rectangle

Elements are overlaid onto circular shape

Each element connected to every other one

Elements burst out from center

Center element present

Elements are in multiple layers

Multiple Associations of Topologies

My realization that people have more than formal reactions to topologies of visual elements prompted me to ask seminar discussion groups to share the associations they had with purely visual elements. I found that individuals nearly always find meanings in form—frequently many meanings. The topologies mean something to people independent of any context that might be suggested by accompanying images or words.

Context tends to override associations

Does the ambiguity presented by the fact that topologies initially suggest different meanings present a guaranteed problem? No. It appears that the word and other elements interacting with the visual meanings of the topologies provide sufficient context (→126, 191–192) to ensure accurate interpretation.

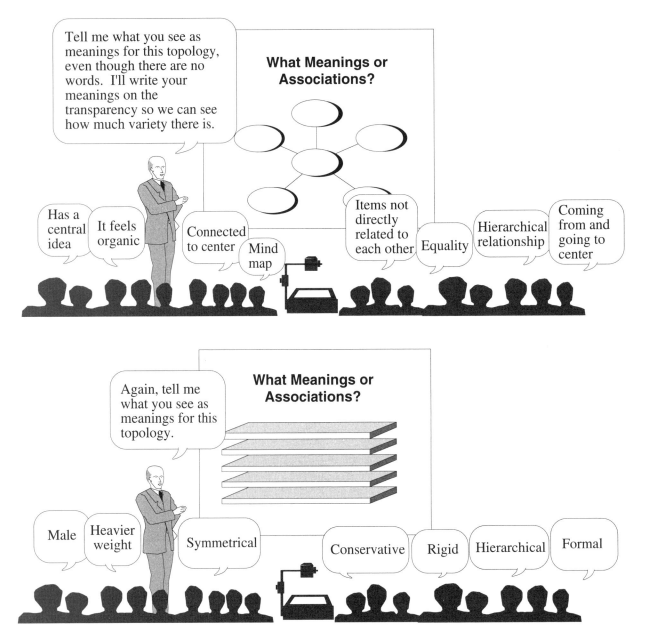

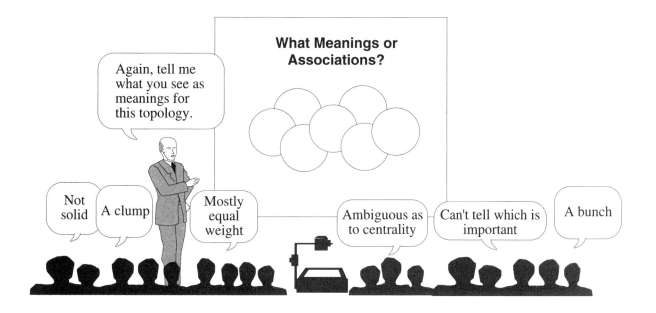

The fact of multiple associations suggests the location in visual language of the blurred boundary between syntax and semantics. Although it may be awkward from the standpoint of linguistic analysis to ask a semantic question ("What meanings or associations?") about purely syntactical objects (the contentless topologies), it is not surprising that people attach meaning to syntactic form.

Very little rigorous research has been done in this area. Much more will be required before truly reliable generalizations can be made. But in the meantime, powerful contextual effects enable us to use topologies confidently.

Same Text, Different Syntactical Topologies

Traditionally, syntax explores purely formal, rulelike relationships. These examples present the same set of words (the components of an aircraft) displayed in a variety of topologies. The formal relationships (i.e., which element is connected to another) is the same for all the topologies, but notice how some of the display arrangements "work" better than others.

Syntax is context dependent

These diagrams exemplify the vast syntactical possiblities that visual language holds, the complexity of its syntactical rules, and the amorphous nature of the boundary between visual language syntax and semantics, which is partly based on the fact of multiple associations. Visual language syntax, like visual language morphology, is somewhat context dependent. From the examples to the right, it becomes apparent that a particular syntactical topology is sometimes better suited to communicate a specific kind of content.

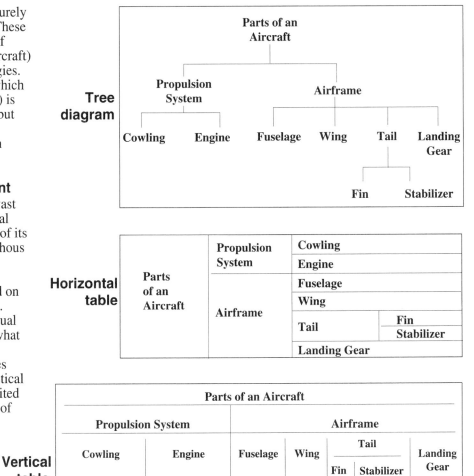

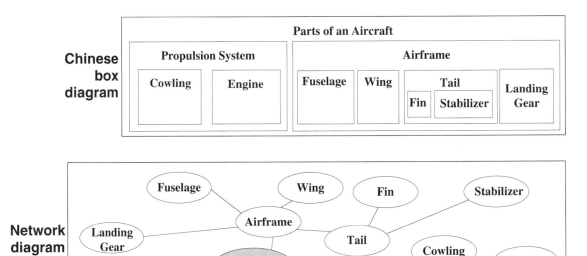

Mandala diagram

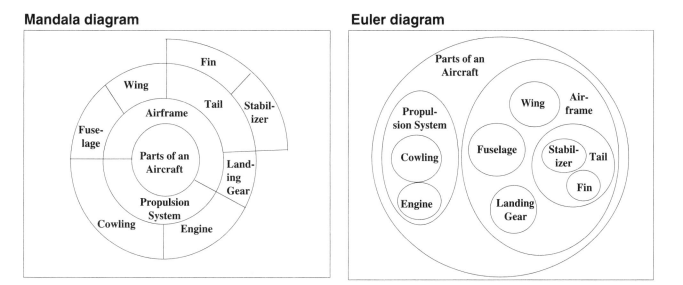

Euler diagram

Visual outlines

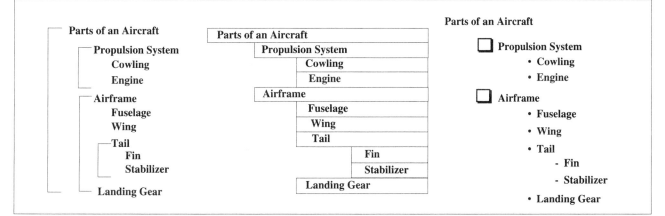

Shaded table

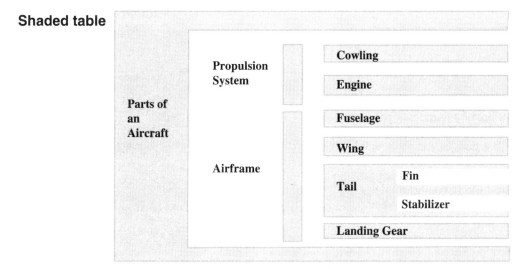

Visual Levels of Topologies

Dimensionality is another, more complex, aspect of visual language syntax. The dimensionality, or visual level, of topologies can be varied as shown in the table at right.

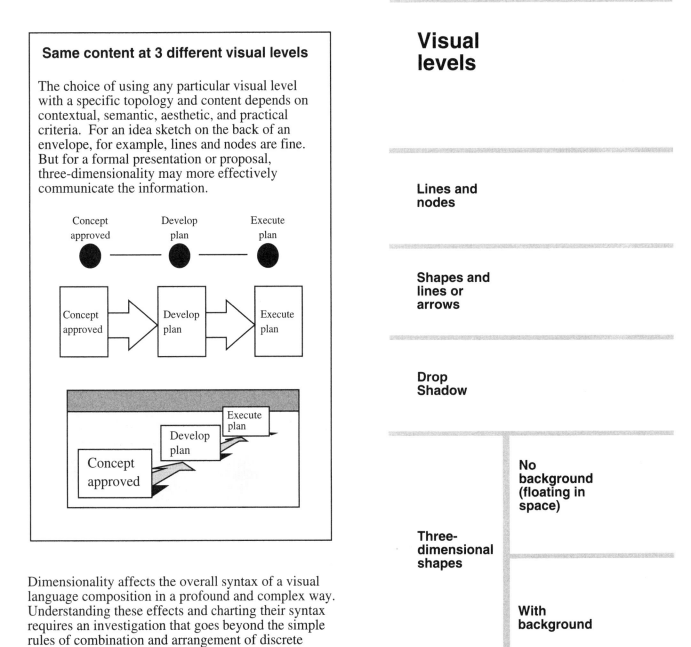

Same content at 3 different visual levels

The choice of using any particular visual level with a specific topology and content depends on contextual, semantic, aesthetic, and practical criteria. For an idea sketch on the back of an envelope, for example, lines and nodes are fine. But for a formal presentation or proposal, three-dimensionality may more effectively communicate the information.

Concept approved — Develop plan — Execute plan

Concept approved → Develop plan → Execute plan

Concept approved / Develop plan / Execute plan

Visual levels

Lines and nodes

Shapes and lines or arrows

Drop Shadow

Three-dimensional shapes

No background (floating in space)

With background

Dimensionality affects the overall syntax of a visual language composition in a profound and complex way. Understanding these effects and charting their syntax requires an investigation that goes beyond the simple rules of combination and arrangement of discrete primitive elements that are the topic of this chapter. For now, I simply flag foreground–background syntax as a separate region of study for visual language.

Topologies

Linear network	Matrix of elements	Simple network

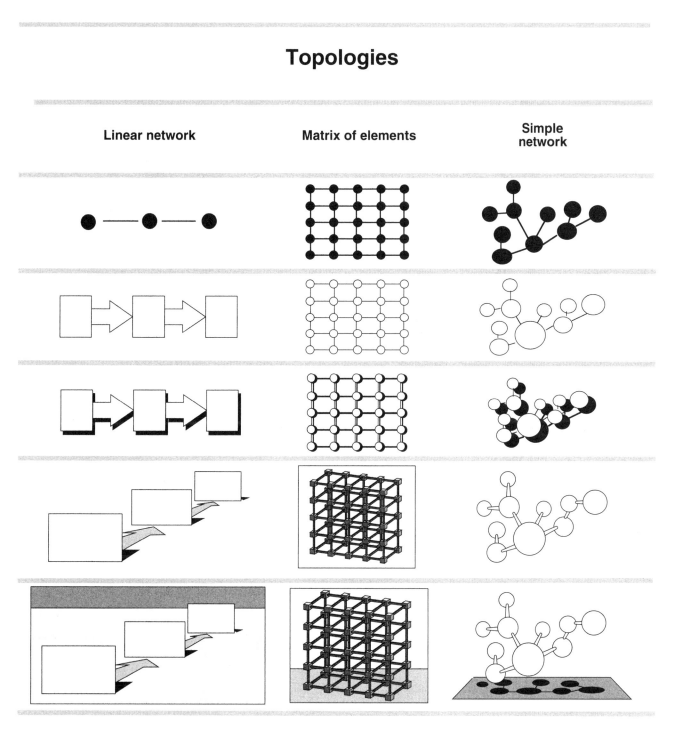

Chapter Summary

Discrete element syntax is based on a morphology of unities and includes complex combinations and arrangements of morphological unities.

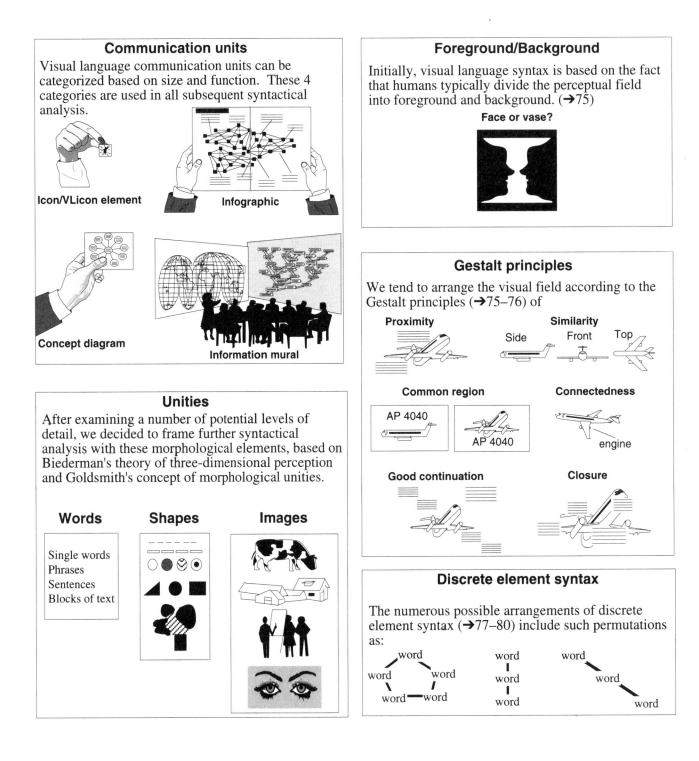

Communication units

Visual language communication units can be categorized based on size and function. These 4 categories are used in all subsequent syntactical analysis.

Icon/VLicon element

Infographic

Concept diagram

Information mural

Unities

After examining a number of potential levels of detail, we decided to frame further syntactical analysis with these morphological elements, based on Biederman's theory of three-dimensional perception and Goldsmith's concept of morphological unities.

Words

Single words
Phrases
Sentences
Blocks of text

Shapes

Images

Foreground/Background

Initially, visual language syntax is based on the fact that humans typically divide the perceptual field into foreground and background. (→75)

Face or vase?

Gestalt principles

We tend to arrange the visual field according to the Gestalt principles (→75–76) of

Proximity

Similarity

Side   Front   Top

Common region

AP 4040

AP 4040

Connectedness

engine

Good continuation

Closure

Discrete element syntax

The numerous possible arrangements of discrete element syntax (→77–80) include such permutations as:

word
word   word
word — word

word
word
word

word
word
word

Topologies

These discrete element arrangements can be organized into a relatively small number (➜81–82) of visual topologies, including:

Matrix **Network** **Concentric**

Each topology has a variety of conceptual and stylistic manifestations, including these examples of the radial network topology. (➜83–84)

Prior associations

Even in their purely formal, contextless form, these topologies have prior associations (➜85–86) that people bring to the purely visual elements.

Has a central idea

It feels organic

Connected to center

Mind map

Context

But these multiple associations, if competing, are generally overridden by other elements in the context. (➜83) In general, verbal and visual meanings should not compete (i.e., a topology should be chosen because its form is suited to its purpose).

What Functions are on the Financial Department's Electronic Message System?

Create and store messages

Send and forward messages

Edit messages

Financial department message system

Receive and read messages

Hold and delete messages

Print messages

Syntactical topologies

The same textual content may be displayed in different syntactical topologies (➜87–88), as I showed with the formal idea of hierarchy.

Dimensionality

Dimensionality is a separate, complex component of visual language syntax. Each topology can be rendered at different visual levels (➜89–90), including:

Lines and nodes

Shapes and lines or arrows

Three-dimensional shapes with background

Syntactical rules normally include that which is forbidden. That is another topic that awaits future development of the language itself, as people begin to say to themselves and others, "You shouldn't do it that way."

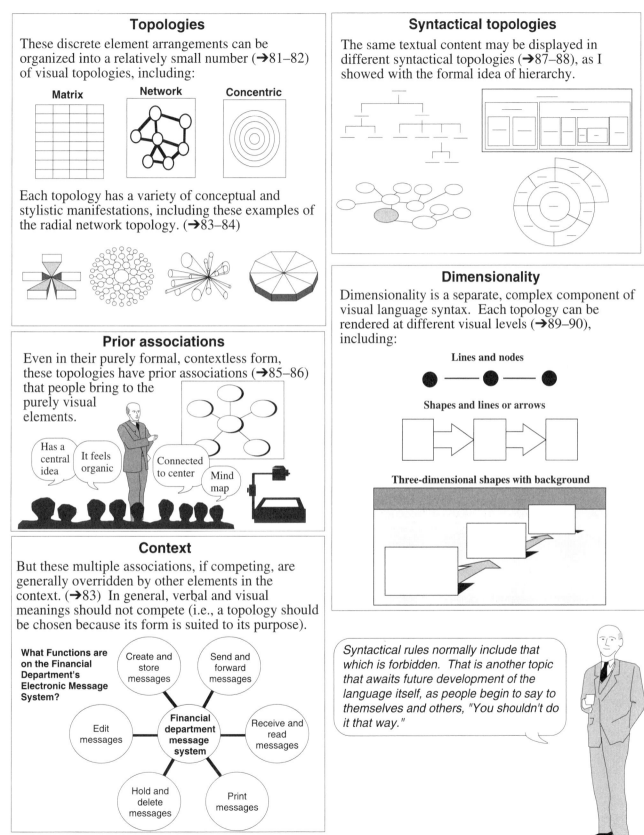

Chapter 4

The Emerging Semantics of Visual Language

se • man • tics /n/
The study of meaning or comprehension in language. In particular, semantics studies the ways in which words and sentences can be mapped onto phenomena.

Semantics is a broad subject to which not only linguists but also philosophers, psychologists, and cognitive scientists have contributed. This chapter explores the diverse sources that are contributing vocabulary and semantic conventions to visual language and examines how these vocabularies and conventions are becoming integrated into units of communication. In many ways, this chapter is the core of the book.

From the principles developed by cognitive scientists and others, we understand that the human brain can receive deep meaning from visual language via processes that include semantic fusion and percept–concept integration. These cognitive processes, among others, allow us to use visual language as an efficient tool for effective communication.

Charles Morris, one of the early figures in the field of semantics, proposed that the outcome of the study of semantics should be a set of rules "which determines under which conditions a sign is applicable to an object or situation; such rules correlate signs and situations denotable by the signs." I would add to his specification that the semanticist must also study and define the conditions under which words, images, and shapes are used, in what combinations, and to what purpose.

Contents of Chapter 4

Section
C.

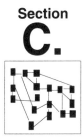

Diagram semantics *123*
Diagramming has proliferated with the increasing complexity of the modern world, and it makes fundamental contributions to the vocabulary and semantics of visual language.

Section
E.

Semantics of space, line, and composition *143*
Notions about the proper arrangement of elements on a page or in 3 dimensions have emerged from the experiments of graphic designers, visual artists, and filmmakers and have become integrated into the expressions of visual language.

Section
D.

Semantics of cartooning *135*
Invented in the last century and early in this century, cartooning has developed a wide variety of semantic conventions that are spreading rapidly around the world and integrating with diagram semantics to provide a rich vocabulary of expression.

Section
F.

Semantics of time *151*
How does visual language represent and signal the phenomena of change and transition? How do we tell when one set of expressions is completed and another begun? How we understand visual representations of time are informed both by theories of perception and by conventions from the world of film and illustration.

Percept–Concept Integration

In traditional communication, concepts have been handled verbally and percepts have been restricted to separate boxes in which illustrations or diagrams appear. Percepts are thought of as impressions of objects received through the senses, and concepts are considered to be mental ideas, possibly connected, but sometimes unconnected, with percepts. Visual language emphasizes the selection, inclusion, and integration of percepts with concepts.

Information Landscapes

The widespread use of information landscapes and other visual language devices has introduced a more direct mode of concept–percept thinking in which representations of objects are mixed with verbal elements. We never see such an information landscape in nature, but the intermingling of percept and concepts seems quite natural, probably because our mental models contain mixtures of these elements. Perhaps what is extraordinary is that this mixture hasn't been used for communication purposes to any great extent until this century.

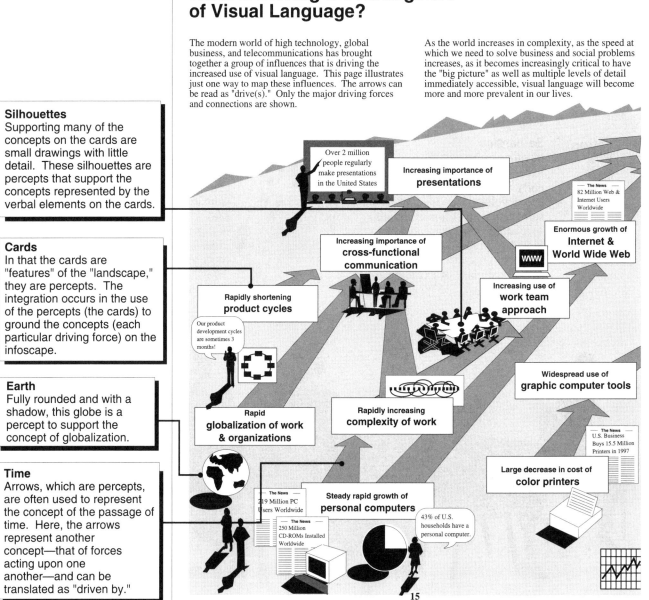

What Is Driving the Emergence of Visual Language?

The modern world of high technology, global business, and telecommunications has brought together a group of influences that is driving the increased use of visual language. This page illustrates just one way to map these influences. The arrows can be read as "drive(s)." Only the major driving forces and connections are shown.

As the world increases in complexity, as the speed at which we need to solve business and social problems increases, as it becomes increasingly critical to have the "big picture" as well as multiple levels of detail immediately accessible, visual language will become more and more prevalent in our lives.

Silhouettes
Supporting many of the concepts on the cards are small drawings with little detail. These silhouettes are percepts that support the concepts represented by the verbal elements on the cards.

Cards
In that the cards are "features" of the "landscape," they are percepts. The integration occurs in the use of the percepts (the cards) to ground the concepts (each particular driving force) on the infoscape.

Earth
Fully rounded and with a shadow, this globe is a percept to support the concept of globalization.

Time
Arrows, which are percepts, are often used to represent the concept of the passage of time. Here, the arrows represent another concept—that of forces acting upon one another—and can be translated as "driven by."

Over 2 million people regularly make presentations in the United States

Increasing importance of **presentations**

The News — 82 Million Web & Internet Users Worldwide

Enormous growth of **Internet & World Wide Web**

Increasing importance of **cross-functional communication**

Increasing use of **work team approach**

Rapidly shortening **product cycles**

Our product development cycles are sometimes 3 months!

Widespread use of **graphic computer tools**

Rapid **globalization of work & organizations**

Rapidly increasing **complexity of work**

The News — U.S. Business Buys 15.5 Million Printers in 1997

Large decrease in cost of **color printers**

The News — 219 Million PC Users Worldwide

Steady rapid growth of **personal computers**

43% of U.S. households have a personal computer.

The News — 250 Million CD-ROMs Installed Worldwide

15

Horizon
The horizon is a percept that is tightly linked in our minds with a number of conceptual ideas. Here, the mountains suggest a vast distance and imply that the infoscape is concerned with big ideas. The arc character of the horizon communicates "there is a global aspect to this" without words. The abstract nature of the landscape tells us that its contents can refer to "anywhere" or "everywhere" in the time frame of an "ongoing now."

Rising Sun
We associate the percept of the rising sun with the concept of future and perhaps speculative thoughts. A percept, the rising sun, is tightly integrated with the concept of visual culture.

Newspapers
The use of the newspapers in this infoscape is an excellent example of the multiple percept–concept associations that individual verbal or visual elements, and their combinations, can have. The newspaper is a percept that is used to convey both the specific concept represented in the headline and the general concept of timeliness. The headline itself is a percept that is being used to convey the general concept of importance and immediacy.

Two-dimensional and three-dimensional objects
Not only does visual language integrate percepts with concepts, it also integrates different kinds of percepts in ways that traditional prose communications avoid. In this infoscape, a mixture of two-dimensional and three-dimensional percepts can be used to reinforce different concepts. They can exist together in the landscape such that the lips float in space, while the TV sits on the ground with a shadow.

Shadows
Shadows are percepts that convey the concept of a real existence in an otherwise abstract landscape.

Transmission signal
The satellite is a percept, connected to the satellite dish by an invisible transmission signal and used to illustrate another percept—huge data streams. The signal is made visible by the gray dotted line: invisible energy made perceptual.

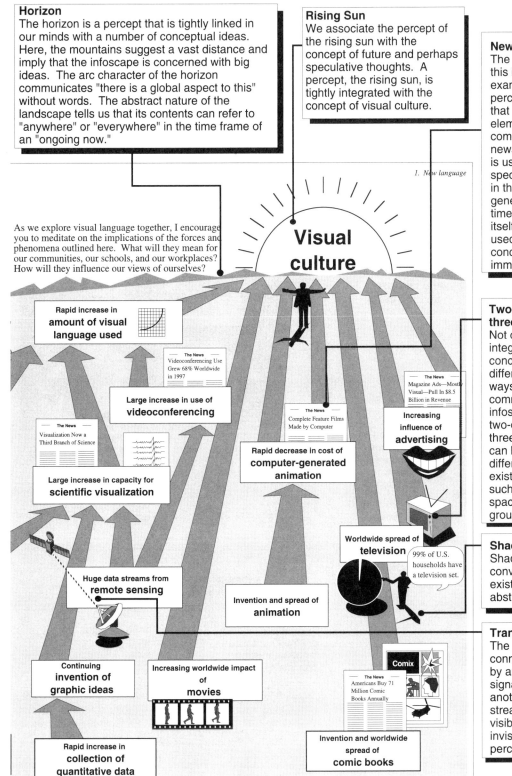

1. New language

As we explore visual language together, I encourage you to meditate on the implications of the forces and phenomena outlined here. What will they mean for our communities, our schools, and our workplaces? How will they influence our views of ourselves?

Visual culture

Rapid increase in **amount of visual language used**

The News — Videoconferencing Use Grew 68% Worldwide in 1997

Large increase in use of **videoconferencing**

The News — Visualization Now a Third Branch of Science

Large increase in capacity for **scientific visualization**

The News — Complete Feature Films Made by Computer

Rapid decrease in cost of **computer-generated animation**

The News — Magazine Ads—Mostly Visual—Pull In $8.5 Billion in Revenue

Increasing influence of **advertising**

Huge data streams from **remote sensing**

Invention and spread of **animation**

Worldwide spread of **television**

99% of U.S. households have a television set.

Continuing **invention of graphic ideas**

Increasing worldwide impact of **movies**

Comix

The News — Americans Buy 71 Million Comic Books Annually

Invention and worldwide spread of **comic books**

Rapid increase in **collection of quantitative data**

16

Semantic Fusion

We know a lot about the cognitive processes involved in making meaning, but we do not understand fully how semantic integration takes place in thought. What happens in the brain when we look at a message like the one in the center of this page ("The Benefits of the New System")? How does the brain combine all the different elements of the message to create an integrated meaning? I call the process of making meaning out of the tight integration of words, images, and shapes "semantic fusion."

Concept maps

The type of diagram on these pages is called a "concept map," and it is a tool that cognitive scientists often use to lay out conceptual schema. This concept map represents the semantic fusion process as applied to the message "The Benefits of the New System." We bring to the message our thoughts and experiences with all of the different elements—arrows, upness, the system, benefits, and boundaries. The particular syntactical arrangement of the elements in the message encourages us to fuse the individual verbal and visual elements together to create a new interpretation and meaning.

A When we look at even a relatively simple concept diagram, a lot of semantic fusion occurs before we create meaning.

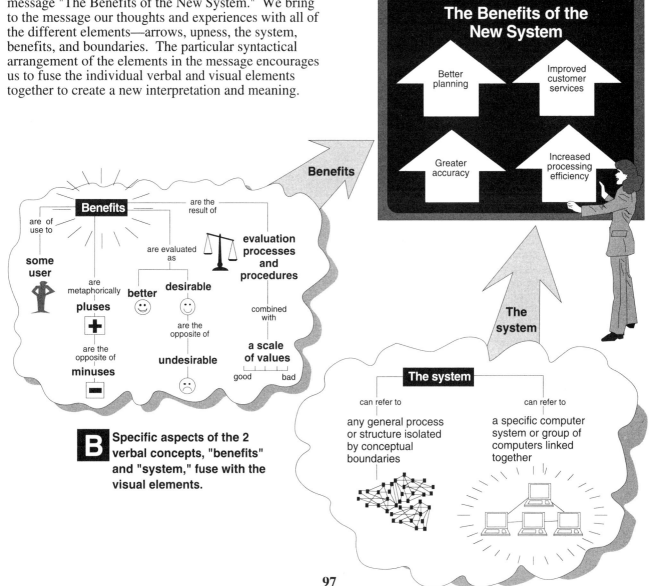

B Specific aspects of the 2 verbal concepts, "benefits" and "system," fuse with the visual elements.

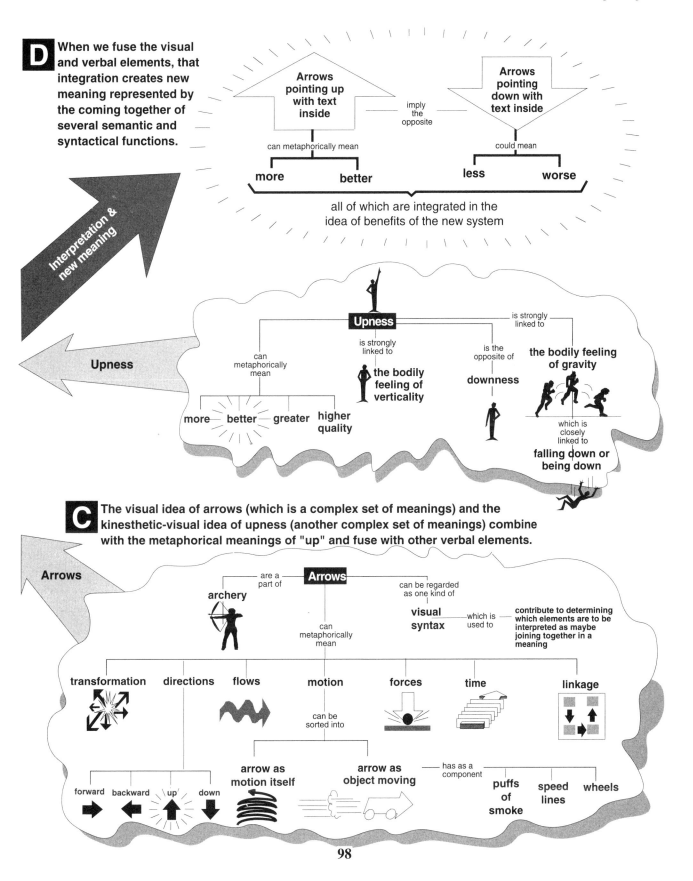

D When we fuse the visual and verbal elements, that integration creates new meaning represented by the coming together of several semantic and syntactical functions.

Interpretation & new meaning

Arrows pointing up with text inside — imply the opposite — Arrows pointing down with text inside

can metaphorically mean

more   better

could mean

less   worse

all of which are integrated in the idea of benefits of the new system

Upness

Upness

can metaphorically mean

is strongly linked to

is the opposite of

is strongly linked to the bodily feeling of gravity

more   better   greater   higher quality

the bodily feeling of verticality

downness

which is closely linked to

falling down or being down

C The visual idea of arrows (which is a complex set of meanings) and the kinesthetic-visual idea of upness (another complex set of meanings) combine with the metaphorical meanings of "up" and fuse with other verbal elements.

Arrows

are a part of — **Arrows** — can be regarded as one kind of

archery

can metaphorically mean

visual syntax — which is used to — contribute to determining which elements are to be interpreted as maybe joining together in a meaning

transformation   directions   flows   motion   forces   time   linkage

can be sorted into

forward   backward   up   down

arrow as motion itself

arrow as object moving — has as a component

puffs of smoke   speed lines   wheels

98

Semantic Investigations

To illuminate the semantics of tight integration from another angle, this table compares a wide variety of visual language communication units with their solely visual and solely verbal counterparts. Along with revealing the communicative power of visual language, the table begins to show some of the subtleties involved in translation between visual language and other languages.

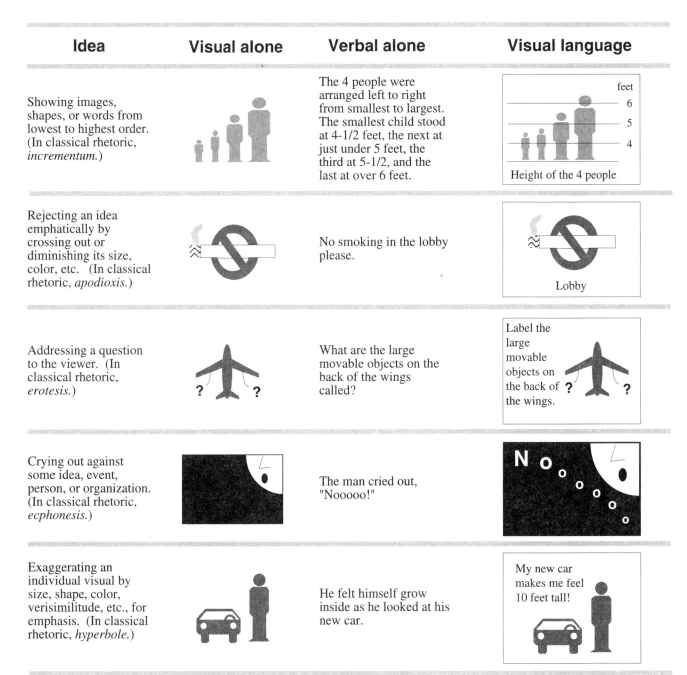

Idea	Visual alone	Verbal alone	Visual language
Showing images, shapes, or words from lowest to highest order. (In classical rhetoric, *incrementum*.)		The 4 people were arranged left to right from smallest to largest. The smallest child stood at 4-1/2 feet, the next at just under 5 feet, the third at 5-1/2, and the last at over 6 feet.	Height of the 4 people
Rejecting an idea emphatically by crossing out or diminishing its size, color, etc. (In classical rhetoric, *apodioxis*.)		No smoking in the lobby please.	Lobby
Addressing a question to the viewer. (In classical rhetoric, *erotesis*.)		What are the large movable objects on the back of the wings called?	Label the large movable objects on the back of the wings.
Crying out against some idea, event, person, or organization. (In classical rhetoric, *ecphonesis*.)		The man cried out, "Nooooo!"	
Exaggerating an individual visual by size, shape, color, verisimilitude, etc., for emphasis. (In classical rhetoric, *hyperbole*.)		He felt himself grow inside as he looked at his new car.	My new car makes me feel 10 feet tall!

Idea	Visual alone	Verbal alone	Visual language
Presenting an inanimate object as a person. (In classical rhetoric, *prosopopoeia.*)		That morning, the sun shone down upon us, like a giant friendly face surrounded by lapping tongues of fire.	In the morning
Achieving a transition by briefly presenting a past image. (In classical rhetoric, *metabasis.*)		Remembering that our definition includes shapes, words, and images ...	**Visual language** Words Images Shapes Integration
Emphasizing a point by reminding the reader of a key event or possible event. (In classical rhetoric, *anamnesis.*)		We must never, of course, forget that we live in the nuclear age when we begin to negotiate about international security.	Context of our negotiations ...
Applying a stereotypical or proverbial image to a new situation. (In classical rhetoric, *paroemia.*)		The heart of the group	The heart of the group
Defining by showing a set of examples or illustrations. (In classical rhetoric, *horismos.*)		Nuts have a great variety of shapes.	**Nuts**
Showing the same thing several ways to refine a meaning. (In classical rhetoric, *exergasia.*)		At least 1 of the 2 engines mounted on the wing can be seen from any point of view.	At least one engine can be seen

100

Types of Semantic Tight Integration

Because tight integration of verbal and visual elements is the unique identifying feature of visual language, a semantic theory of visual language initially needs to identify and classify the different kinds of integration. A useful theory should be able to distinguish between different types of verbal and visual integration.

In principle, a semantic theory should answer the following questions. Why is each element (verbal and visual) present? What function does each serve? What is the relationship between the function of the visual and the verbal elements? These are major tasks for a semantics of visual language. A catalog of the primary kinds of semantic integration is presented here.

Here, the relationship is one of labeling.

The relationship here is one of reinforcement.

Substitution

Definition
Substitution is the relationship between words and visual elements in which each communicates (essentially) the same information. Their effective meanings are so similar as to be interchangeable. When they appear together, their relationship is described as redundant.

Example of substitution

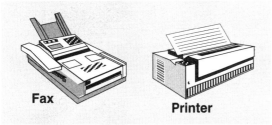

The redundancy relationship, of course, depends on prior knowledge of the meaning of both the verbal and visual elements. Only then can the 2 be regarded as interchangeable.

Software designers rely on users' ability to learn meanings, as well as on the substitution principle, when they design interfaces in which icons appear on-screen without identifying labels. Unfortunately, the proliferation of such icons places learning demands on users that are often burdensome and unwelcome.

Disambiguation

Definition
Disambiguation is the relationship between words and visual elements in which the elements communicate related information and clarify the meaning or interpretation of each other.

Example of disambiguation

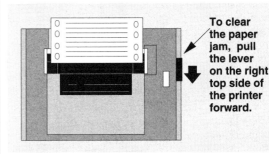

To clear the paper jam, pull the lever on the right top side of the printer forward.

For example, visual elements can verify the location of important pieces of information, thus preventing possible misunderstanding and error. Technically, in the example above, one could clear the jam simply by reading the words. One would have to search for the lever, though, which is designed to blend into the overall look of the printer, and so the task would become more difficult.

Labeling

Definition

Labeling is the relationship in which the words give names to parts or wholes of the visual elements.

Example of labeling

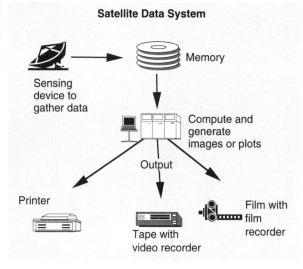

Satellite Data System

In the example above, it could be argued that the pictures could be omitted. But to do so would make more ambiguous at least 2 of the verbal elements:

Sensing
device to   Memory
gather data

Although understandable, those 2 elements are described at a level of abstraction that makes it impossible to know what type of sensing device and what kind of memory might be involved. The addition of the pictures resolves some of that ambiguity.

Removing the words and retaining the pictures puts the reader in the need-for-learning position described under Substitution. (→101) Labeling is one of the most fundamental relationships between words and objects in the sense that much of the edifice of any natural language is based on it.

Example

Definition

Example relationships are those in which the visual and verbal elements are used to relate a class of objects or ideas with its specific instances. Generally, the class of objects or ideas is represented verbally and the instances are represented visually or via a combination of both.

Example of example relationship

A **polygon** is a multisided, closed, straight-lined figure.

Example of example relationship

A great variety of forces, such as personal ethics and organizational goals, are at work on individuals in a group and, when the forces are shared, upon the group as a whole.

Personal
ethics

Organizational
goals

Regulatory
inhibitions

Career goals

Budgetary
reduction

Types of Semantic Tight Integration (continued)

Reinforcement

Definition

Reinforcement is the relationship between words and visual elements in which the visual elements help present a (generally) more abstract idea. They present the idea a second time, even though it may be clearly interpretable from the words alone. Frequently, visual elements add rhetorical qualities such as mood, style, lightness, and so forth.

Example of reinforcement

In the example above, the visual reinforces the ideas presented in words by showing how different certain cognitive models are.

Example of reinforcement

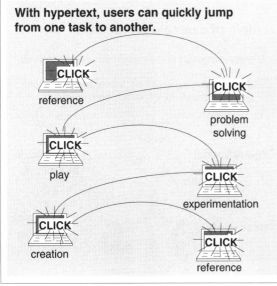

Completion

Definition

Completion is the relationship between words and visual elements in which an idea begun with words is continued and completed visually (or less frequently, vice versa).

Example of completion

Example of completion

103

Chunk, cluster, and frame

Definition

Chunking, clustering, and framing are the relationships between words and visual elements (usually shapes rather than images) in which the shapes provide a visual structure for the ideas communicated by the words, usually via Gestalt perception principles. Most diagrams use this kind of semantic integration.

This type of integration delineates units or chunks of verbal or visual elements and may be used to indicate flow, change of direction, transition, transformation or mutation, passage of time, connection, or different points of view.

Example of framing

The Western African Bioregion Simulation

The International Bioregional Organization

I'm happy to be here via teleconferencing to introduce you to our simulation. Are you there?

Good morning. We're here and ready to go!

Wildlife Management

Tanyaka Wildlife Preserve

You will have primary responsibility for the Tanyaka Wildlife Preserve.

Example of clustering

Example of chunking

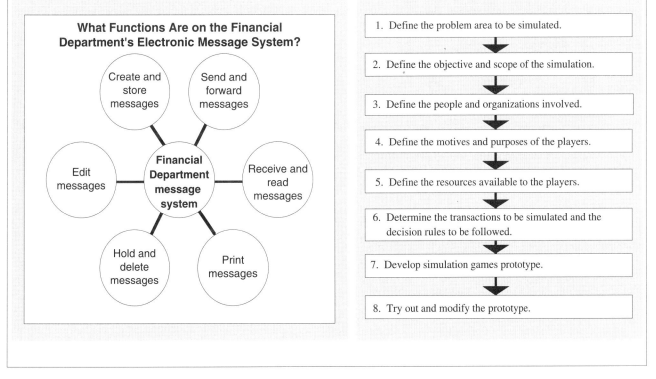

What Functions Are on the Financial Department's Electronic Message System?

Create and store messages

Send and forward messages

Edit messages

Financial Department message system

Receive and read messages

Hold and delete messages

Print messages

1. Define the problem area to be simulated.

2. Define the objective and scope of the simulation.

3. Define the people and organizations involved.

4. Define the motives and purposes of the players.

5. Define the resources available to the players.

6. Determine the transactions to be simulated and the decision rules to be followed.

7. Develop simulation games prototype.

8. Try out and modify the prototype.

Rhetorical Devices and Tight Integration

Semantic relationships between visual and verbal elements are also created via classical rhetorical devices such as metaphor, metonymy, and synecdoche. Close examination of communication units that utilize these rhetorical devices reveals that they exhibit one or more of the types of integration cataloged on the preceding pages in addition to exhibiting a particular rhetorical device. In one sense, then, a kind of multiple integration occurs.

Synecdoche

Definition
In a synecdoche, a part is used to represent a whole, or vice versa.

Example of synecdoche

In the example above, the meal is represented by the plates and silverware. We do not see the food, nor do we see the sequence of the serving of the different courses of food or the people who are eating the meal. Only some elements of the total scene are needed to communicate the idea.

The example also uses both completion and reinforcement forms of integration.

Metonymy

Definition
In metonymy, the name of one thing is used for that of another with which it is associated.

Example of metonymy

Here, the White House stands for the president. The president is not seen and his (or her) name is also not explicitly mentioned. In fact, the "No comment" may not have come from the president but from the White House staff, who "speak" for the president.

Some reinforcement is used, in that both the words White House and the illustration are present.

Metaphor

Definition

In metaphor, one meaning or idea is used to represent a 2nd meaning or idea in order to suggest an analogy or likeness between the 2. Metaphors enable us to think about complex or abstract ideas in terms of more familiar or concrete ideas or experiences.

Visual language metaphor has the capacity to incorporate multiple meanings. The visual elements often provide the impact, emphasis, mood, or tonality that reinforces the main idea but that also triggers supporting or relevant ideas.

In visual language, different mixtures of verbal and visual components make the metaphor a very rich and expressive tool.

At this juncture, we are interested in simply seeing that metaphor functions as a rhetorical device in the tight integration of visual and verbal elements. The next section (➔113–122) contains a deeper analysis of metaphorical integration.

Example of metaphor

Many Possible Intervention Points
In attempting to solve the problem, you should not overlook the possibility of many places for intervention.

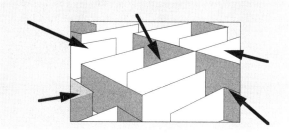

The visual conveys the problem via the spacial metaphor of a labyrinth. The arrows indicate the possible intervention points.

In this example the ideas are probably expressed clearly enough with the text so that the visual cannot be classified as disambiguation. The visual does reinforce the ideas presented by the words.

Example of metaphor

Branch Out in New Ways!

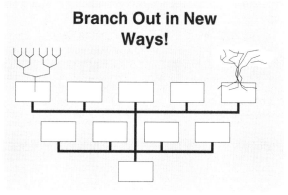

In this example, pictures of a conceptual tree and a natural tree are integrated metaphorically with the idea of "branching out" applied in an advertising firm. It suggests corporate growth or creativity coming out of a traditional organizational chart portrayed upside down.

This metaphor also shows integration with reinforcement.

Temporal Relationships and Tight Integration

Yet other instances of tight integration appear in the context of stories, operations, and other processes that take place through time. A somewhat different set of relationships between verbal and visual elements is seen in such "process" communications than are seen in static displays. More often than not, the verbal and visual elements perform quite different, noninterchangeable tasks.

Division of labor

A kind of division of labor exists in which some tasks (e.g., showing who is talking) are consistently performed by visual elements, whereas other tasks (e.g., quoting the exact speech) are nearly always executed by verbal elements, given that there is no approximately equivalent visual way to present such information. (➔Chs. 5 and 6)

Voice (or sound), source, and situation

Definition
In these situations, voice is usually represented by words (often in speech or thought balloons), and source and situation are shown visually.

Example of voice, source, and situation

Example of voice, source, and situation

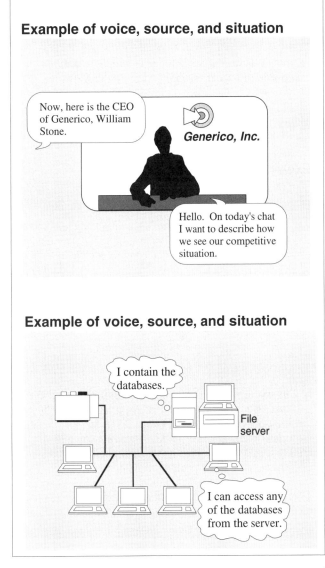

Voice, setting, and mood

Definition
In voice and mood situations the verbal elements often convey some specific information while the visual provides a setting or mood. These functions can be reversed.

Example of voice, setting, and mood

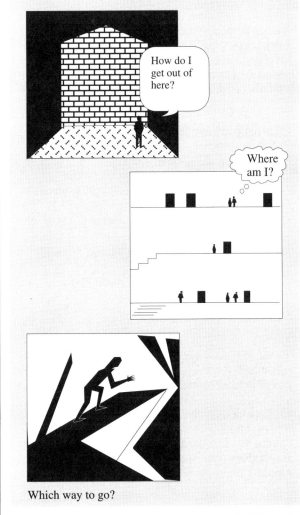

Which way to go?

Description of stasis and change

Definition

Changes or stasis in aspects of a process can be represented in visual language using labels, descriptions, and portrayal of the objects being changed.

Example of description of stasis and change

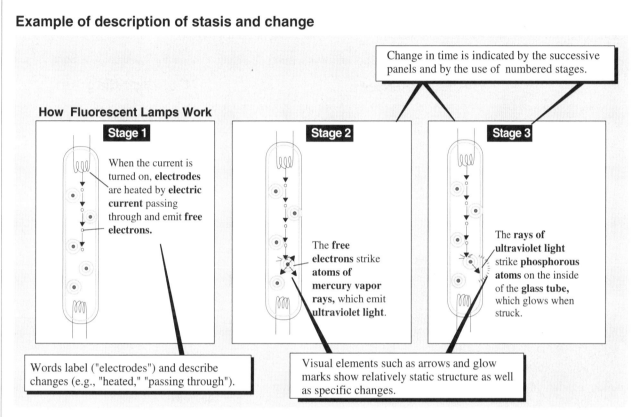

Change in time is indicated by the successive panels and by the use of numbered stages.

How Fluorescent Lamps Work

Stage 1

When the current is turned on, **electrodes** are heated by **electric current** passing through and emit **free electrons.**

Stage 2

The **free electrons** strike **atoms of mercury vapor rays,** which emit **ultraviolet light**.

Stage 3

The **rays of ultraviolet light** strike **phosphorous atoms** on the inside of the **glass tube,** which glows when struck.

Words label ("electrodes") and describe changes (e.g., "heated," "passing through").

Visual elements such as arrows and glow marks show relatively static structure as well as specific changes.

Example of description of stasis and change

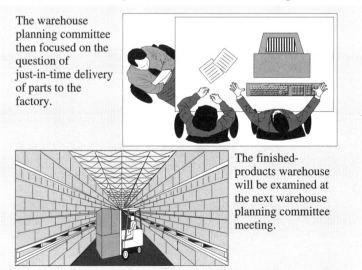

The warehouse planning committee then focused on the question of just-in-time delivery of parts to the factory.

The finished-products warehouse will be examined at the next warehouse planning committee meeting.

This example shows transition from office planning to accomplishment of the plan in the warehouse. Scene-to-scene transitions often also require verbal elements to clarify how the transition should be interpreted. Note that the transitions shown by the verbal and visual elements indicate

- change in time
- change in location
- change in characters
- change in viewpoint.

Size of Communication Unit and Tight Integration

As the size and complexity of a communication unit increase, in general, the size and complexity of the individual elements increase. That is, for example, the amount of text in a single verbal chunk increases, and often the number of verbal chunks increases as well. This greatly expands the ability to convey the whole as well as the parts in the same unit, one of the major advantages of the infographic and infomural.

This table uses the example of 3 differently sized communication units, all dealing with the same subject matter—the eye—to illustrate the different levels of integration that are possible with each type of communication unit. (Information murals, the fourth size of communication unit, have many of the same forms of integration as the information graphic, and are not included here.)

	VLicon element	Concept diagram
Example	Context (not shown): Description of parts of the eye	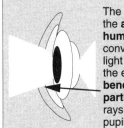 Context (not shown): Series of concept diagrams on the operations of the eye and their malfunctions
Verbal components	Usually consist of a single word or phrase	Contain a single sentence at minimum, but may contain 2 or 3 sentences
Visual components	Usually quite simple, in keeping with the kinds of semantic functions they perform, such as identifying ideas or focusing attention	Range from quite simple to moderately complex
Type of integration	• Labeling	• Labeling • Visual example/verbal description

Information graphic

Parts of the Eye and Their Functions

2. The light waves are initially bent by the **cornea**. The cornea, the outer surface of the eye, acts as an outer lens.

3. The function of the **iris** is to regulate the amount of light entering the pupil. The iris contracts in bright light and opens in dim light.

4. The inner **lens** focuses light on the back of the eye.

5. The **ciliary muscles** flex to alter the shape of the lens, which changes the focus of the lens.

6. Light strikes the **retina**, the area in the back of the eye that registers the photons of light entering the eye. The photons activate the rods and cones, which are specialized cells that act as photoreceptors.

1. Light waves are reflected from the object.

Context (not shown): Series of information graphics on the operations of the eye and their malfunctions

Contain a number of blocks of text. Each block may contain words, phrases, single sentences, or several sentences. The sentences are closely linked to the visual parts (in most cases) by proximity and linear connections, as well as by stylistic devices, such as color.

As complex as the communication situation requires. A major advantage of infographics and information murals is that they can incorporate as much complexity as is necessary and bring together the visual elements with the verbal elements in a communication-enhancing manner.

- Labeling
- Visual example/verbal description

Mere Juxtaposition Is Not Tight Integration

Words and images are usually assumed to be semantically related if they are syntactically linked. But what happens to our thinking process when we place next to one another visual and verbal elements that are not obviously related or are not related at all? Almost all of us will struggle valiantly to create meaning out of nothing, to understand the close juxtaposition of the ideas conveyed by the visuals and the words.

We have an urge, a drive, to fit things into some pattern. We will even seek some obscure, secret, hidden, mysterious meaning because the elements, verbal or visual, are connected in one of the Gestalt ways.

This drive illuminates another feature of semantic tight integration. Mere juxtaposition of verbal and visual elements is not visual language. In fact, arbitrary juxtapositions of elements using any of the Gestalt principles creates semantic obstacles that can, in practical situations, also cause considerable waste of time and human effort. Visual language relies upon semantic fusion and tight integration—not mere juxtaposition—to convey meaning.

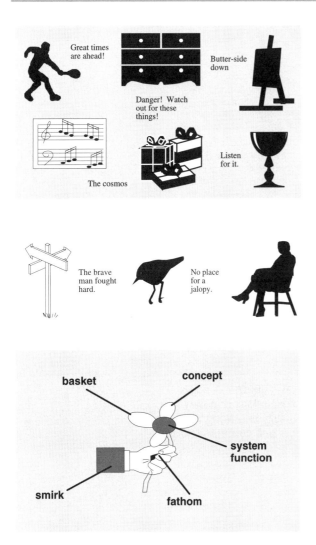

I had no particular reason for selecting this arbitrary collection of things. Yet the Gestalt principle of proximity governing perception makes us want to give meaning to some set of relationships between them. What connects them, however, is only their physical closeness to each other. The lesson is obvious: We must be vigilant in visual language, perhaps more so than in prose, because readers will attempt to make meaning out of elements whose proximity may be accidental.

The Gestalt principle of good continuation suggests subtly that this arbitrary collection of things in a row is somehow connected.

The Gestalt principle of connectedness urges us to make meaning out of connections between objects. In attempting to create meaning out of this illustration, the eye immediately traces the lines connecting the objects and words. We then come to a point of confusion because the words do not connect semantically.

111

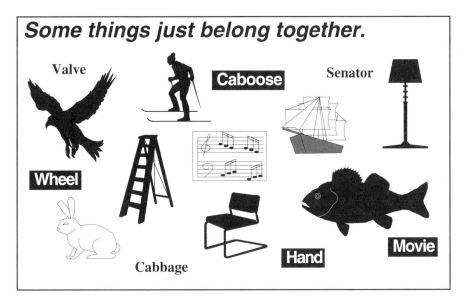

What do you see as belonging together? Here, the individual elements of style (e.g., silhouettes, drawings with more detail, different ways of displaying type) exhibit the Gestalt principle of similarity, which pulls on us to connect these arbitrarily similar items, and our minds attempt to make up some story or pattern that explains the connection.

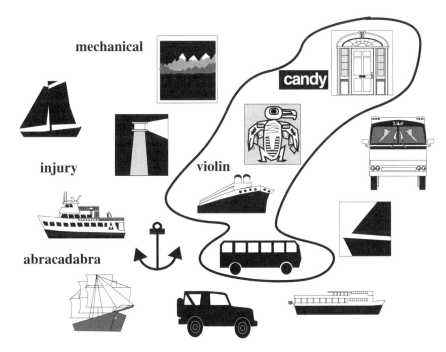

It is difficult not to see the objects that are enclosed within the boundary line as somehow connected. But again, we immediately ask: How? As with the other examples on this page, the objects have been randomly collected, and 4 objects and 2 words were arbitrarily selected to be encircled. There is no meaning or pattern or connection other than the false one created by the Gestalt principle of common region (or closed forms) that guides our perception.

Metaphors in Visual Language

Metaphor, in the classical conception, is a device or ornament added to ordinary meaning. However, theories in modern cognitive science—particularly, those of George Lakoff—indicate that the use of metaphor goes deeper than that. Metaphor, Lakoff suggests, is the fundamental way in which we understand and represent a large number of concepts. Many metaphors are correspondences or mappings that enable us to think about complex or abstract ideas in terms of more familiar or concrete ideas or experiences.

We don't really have a choice about using or not using metaphors. Our cognitive abilities are thoroughly enmeshed in metaphors. If we dig down under just about any communication, we will find that something is very often understood in terms of something else.

Structure of metaphor
Metaphors have a structure in which we use a source domain experience to understand a target domain experience. Some metaphors are relatively simple correspondences.

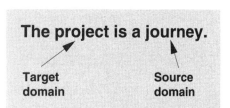

Components of the source experience are used to understand the target experience. Some metaphors are based on complex human experience, which furnishes a multitude of aspects that can support understandings of the target domain.

Entailments
Metaphors have entailments, Lakoff points out. The components of the source domain, in other words, carry over to the target domain. For example, because the structure of a target in an archery contest includes varying degrees of closeness to the bull's-eye, viewers of the slide to the right will understand that their goals for the year have gradations. And because a journey entails a vehicle with a driver, a criticism of a metaphorical journey (a project) will reflect on the metaphorical driver (project leader).

Target: A simple metaphor

Other metaphors for goals
The "goals-are-targets" metaphor entails that a goal can be "shot for," that is, that varying degrees of closeness to the goal can be achieved. Other ways of thinking about a goal are binary—all or nothing. Still other ways of thinking about goals metaphorically are more vague and visionary, such as the sun rising over the distant mountains.

Journey: A more complex metaphor

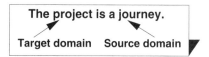

The journey is one of the most powerful metaphors for process. Because most people have taken trips, they share common experiences from which to draw. Many processes are so multifaceted, complex, and unique in their details that they require metaphorical or multimetaphorical expression. Using the idea of a trip as an underlying metaphor enables us to quickly conceptualize and communicate complex ideas about a process using the more familiar experiences in journeys.

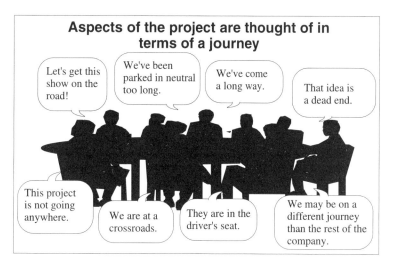

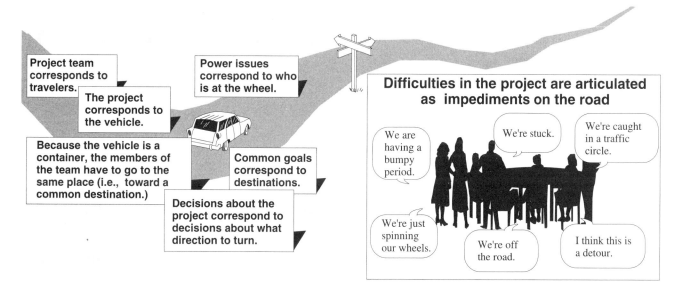

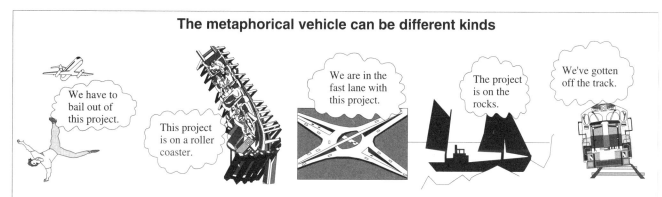

Example: Metaphors for Time

Time is usually understood in terms of metaphors for motion and space. George Lakoff points out that our 5 senses do not include any time detectors. He claims that very early in our lives we notice movement and change and begin to construct an understanding of time metaphorically out of that experience. He concludes, "it makes good biological sense that time should be understood in terms of things and motion." Lakoff's evidence for this claim is primarily linguistic, as we often talk about time as a moving object.

Structure of the metaphor

If time is understood via the metaphor of a moving object, then the structure of our understanding of time is based on the structure of our understanding of motion. Pieces of time are objects that move. We break time into "chunks," which are in motion.

Metaphors have entailments

Lakoff points out that, "since motion is continuous and one-dimensional, the passage of time is continuous and one-dimensional." The metaphor also entails the idea that "time has extension, and can be measured." We use these entailments to understand new things about the target domain.

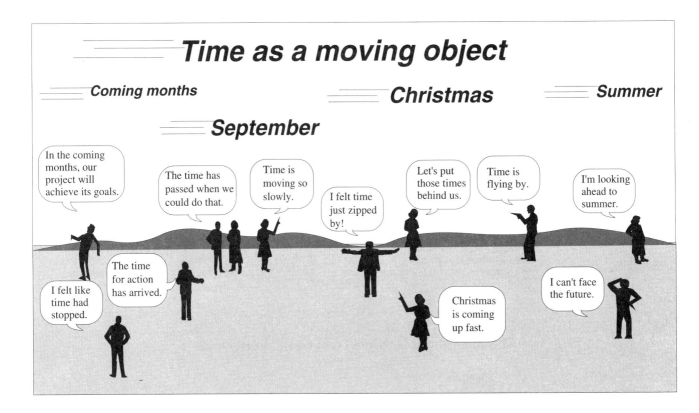

Time as an abstract idea isn't always represented by the same metaphor. In visual terms, it's frequently represented as an arrow, or as divisions in space. These examples of visual metaphors for time illustrate the flexibility of both metaphors and visual language.

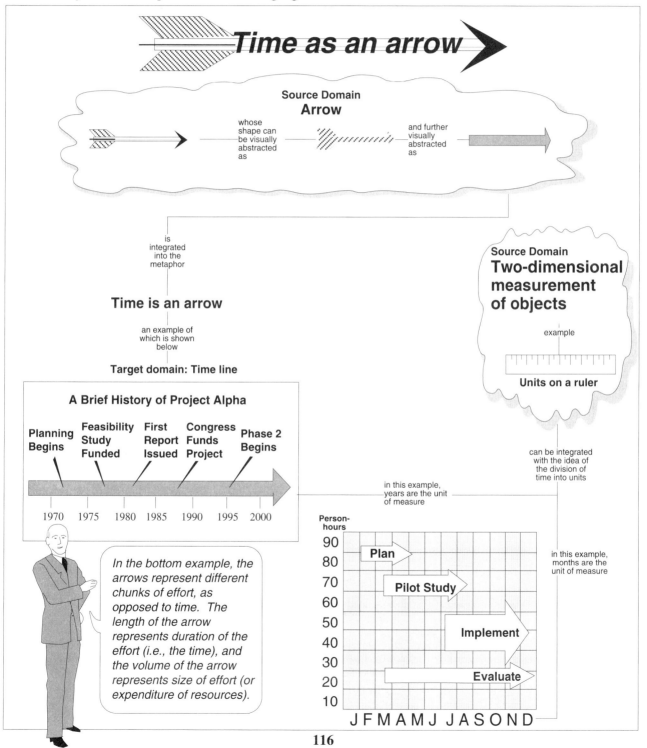

116

The Structure of Visual Metaphors

We create meaning out of metaphors via a semantic fusion process similar to that previously described. (→97) Each visual and verbal source domain of any particular metaphor resonates with several different aspects of meaning. Depending upon the context of the target domain(s), particular aspects are brought to bear on the target domain(s).

The example metaphor on these pages illustrates this process, and also illustrates how important it is that all viewers of a visual metaphor have access to similar ideas about the source domains.

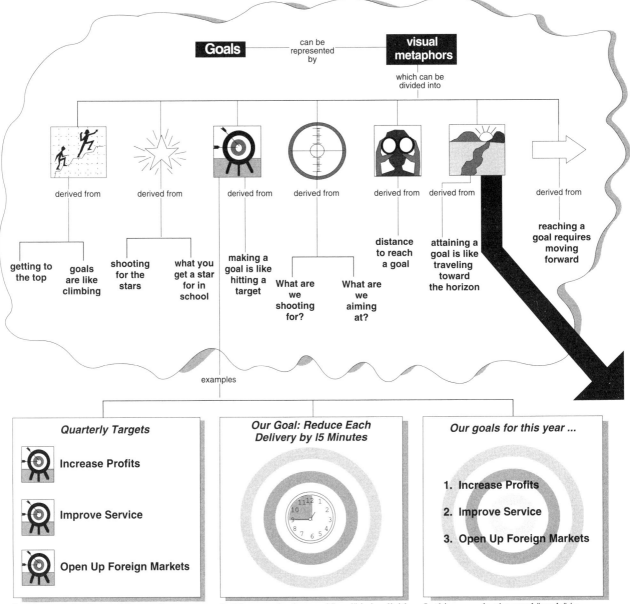

Goals can be represented by **visual metaphors** which can be divided into

derived from — getting to the top / goals are like climbing

derived from — shooting for the stars / what you get a star for in school

derived from — making a goal is like hitting a target

derived from — What are we shooting for? / What are we aiming at?

derived from — distance to reach a goal

derived from — attaining a goal is like traveling toward the horizon

derived from — reaching a goal requires moving forward

examples

Quarterly Targets
- Increase Profits
- Improve Service
- Open Up Foreign Markets

In this example, the word "targets" explicitly links to the visual targets, which also function as *focusers*. (→185)

Our Goal: Reduce Each Delivery by 15 Minutes

In this example, the word "goal" is implicitly linked to the visual target, which serves as a background for the visual representation of the goal itself.

Our goals for this year ...
1. Increase Profits
2. Improve Service
3. Open Up Foreign Markets

In this example, the word "goals" is implicitly linked to the visual target, which serves as a background for the verbal list of goals.

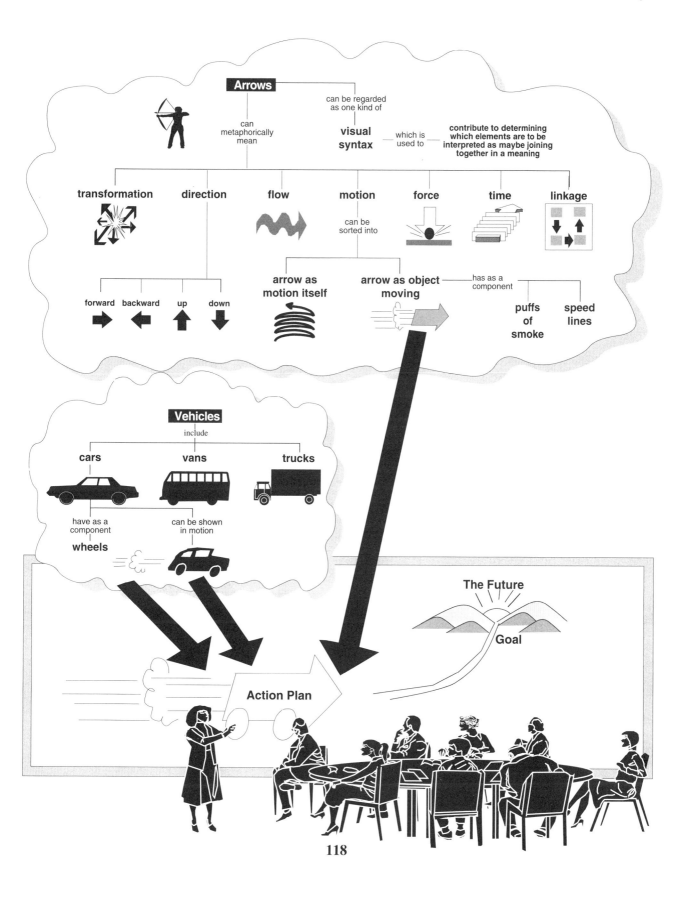

118

Division of Labor in Visual Language Metaphors

Both the visual and the verbal elements of visual language lend themselves well to metaphorical expression. The possible combinations of metaphor and literal statement give visual language users more nuanced ways to communicate meaning.

A visual metaphor can be used to support a literal verbal statement, or vice versa. Both the verbal and visual elements can be metaphorical in nature, or neither may be. The table on these 2 pages sets forth all the possibilities, with notes on relative effectiveness.

Verbal explicit　　　　　　　　　　**Visual explicit**

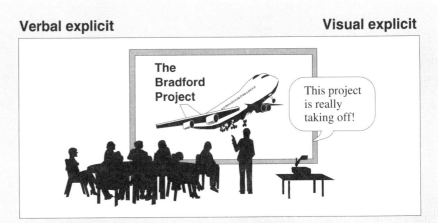

This is an example of congruence, in which the 2 explicit metaphors support each other. In terms of the categories of tight integration discussed in the previous chapter, this example also exhibits mutual reinforcement. (➔103) Note how the use of explicit verbal *and* visual elements strengthens the presentation.

Verbal implicit　　　　　　　　　　**Visual explicit**

Here, the visual shows the metaphor, and although the verbal elements do not mention the "our project is like a journey on an aircraft" metaphor, they are congruent with the visual metaphorical message. Making the visual explicit while keeping the verbal implicit invites reader misunderstanding, however, which may be avoided either by choosing a nonambiguous visual metaphor or by using a verbal metaphor as well.

The comment, "The project is in good shape," actually reveals another implicit metaphor for which the source domain is "good shape" (a Gestalt perception idea; ➔75) and the target domain is "the project." The "good shape" metaphor overlaps with the visual aircraft metaphor.

119

Verbal explicit   **Visual implicit**

This example represents a common situation, in which a communicator uses verbal metaphors that suggest a visual scene but do not support or reinforce the verbal metaphor with any kind of visual element. Situations like these are prime candidates for visual language intervention.

Verbal implicit   **Visual implicit**

If the communication unit contains neither implicit nor explicit reference to a metaphor, there may be no metaphor present. Here, the speaker's rather neutral comment contains no metaphor, and there is no visual to suggest a metaphorical connection to the words.

Using Metaphors in Different Scales of Communication Units

The ways in which visual metaphor can be used to create metaphor depends in part on the size of the communication unit that the metaphor is to be used in.

The table on this page catalogs examples of visual metaphors at different size scales—how they can be used, and for what kinds of purposes.

Icon/VLicon element	Concept diagram

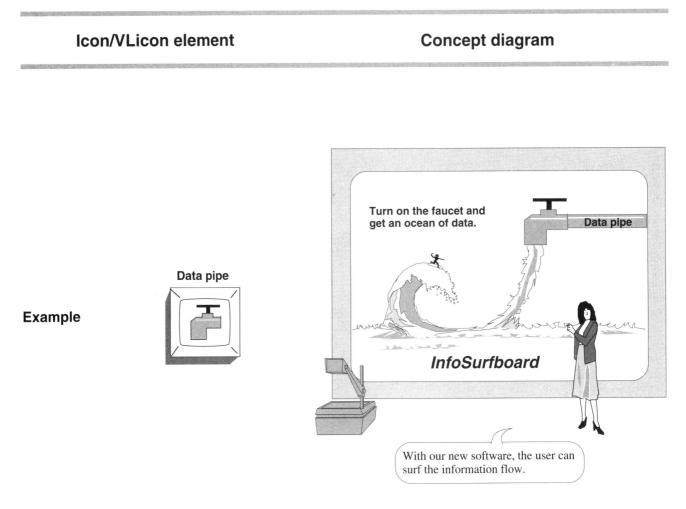

Example	Data pipe	Turn on the faucet and get an ocean of data. — Data pipe — InfoSurfboard — With our new software, the user can surf the information flow.

| **Notes** | At this scale, the source and target domains of a visual metaphor need to be instantly identifiable. Here, a common metaphor in the database profession, the data pipe, is used to identify a function on a software application interface. | Because of limits imposed by size, a concept diagram is rarely able to represent a visual metaphor in its entirety. The important question therefore becomes, what part of the metaphor should each diagram frame? This example illustrates metaphors for data. The idea behind the source domain is that the data flow, if uncontrolled, will overwhelm. The 2nd metaphor—surfing—raises the possibility of skilled data management. Although the data pipe metaphor could be illustrated in more detail, with spigots and pipes and so forth, those components are less central to the message. |

Information graphic or information mural

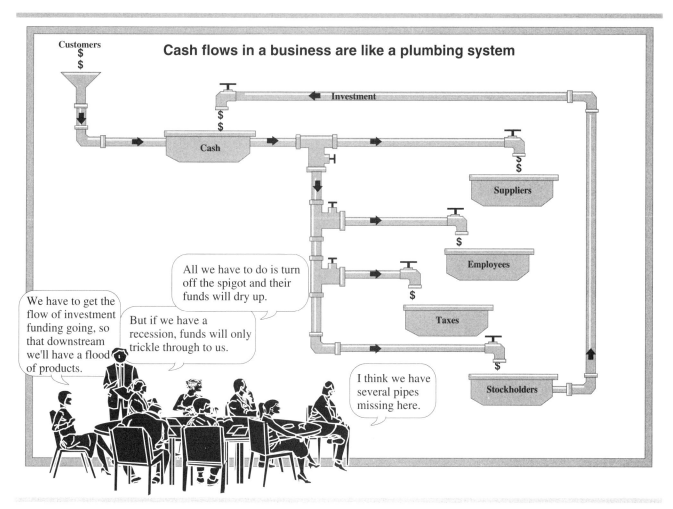

In an information graphic or mural, the metaphor can be more complex and multifaceted, although it is important to remember that a metaphorical representation is still a simplified model.

Diagram Vocabulary

We have noted that a large number of disciplines have contributed to the vocabulary, syntax, and semantics of visual language. Diagramming, one of the foundational disciplines, is the topic of this section. Diagrams qualify as prototypical examples of visual language communication: So tight is the integration in almost any kind of diagram, it is impossible to separate the verbal and visual parts and still retain meaning. One way to highlight the tight verbal-visual integration of a diagram is to observe how meaningless it becomes when separated into its component parts.

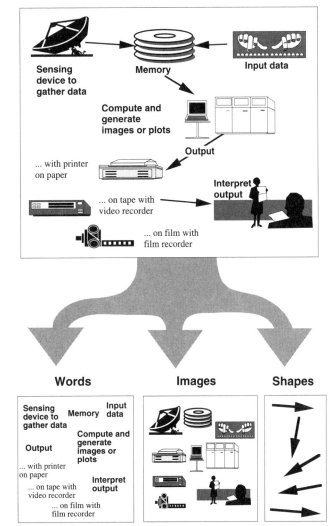

Functions of diagrams

Diagrams can serve several different functions:
A. Represent complex relationships
B. Make the abstract concrete
C. Show changes in time and branching
D. Show external, internal, and conceptual structure.

A. Represent complex relationships. Problems that occur when the number of novel elements and their connections go beyond the capacity of our short-term memory (→237) can be alleviated with diagrams. Example:

HOW TO APPROVE OR DISAPPROVE AN ORDER

IF credit limit is …	and IF pay experience is …	and IF special clearance has been obtained …	THEN …
OK			approve order
questionable	favorable		approve order
not favorable	not favorable	yes	approve order
not favorable	not favorable	no	return order

B. Make the abstract concrete. The brain's concept-creating and operating system is very flexible, enabling us to create models of relevant phenomena at many different levels of abstraction. Spoken or written prose and a variety of context markers enable us to describe most of these models quite easily. Diagrams help us organize and manage problems and issues that arise when the elements are highly abstract. Example:

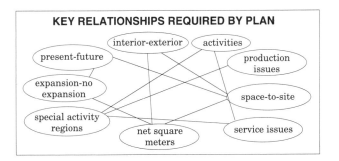

KEY RELATIONSHIPS REQUIRED BY PLAN

C. Show changes in time and branching. Language arranged in conventional sequential prose sentences that follow one after another in paragraphs has inherent difficulty representing segmented sequences of descriptions or functions, and has even more difficulty when there is branching involved. Example:

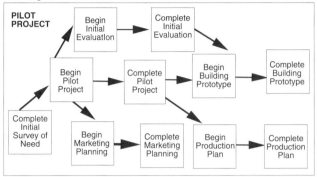

D. Show external, internal, and conceptual structure. Both realistic structures and those that cannot be seen (either because they are inaccessible or because they are conceptual) are often more effectively communicated with diagrams than with prose descriptions.

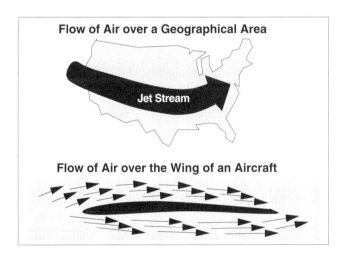

Why diagrams are superior

In an article called "A Diagram is (Sometimes) Worth 10,000 Words," Herbert Simon and Jill Larkin conclude, "A diagram can be superior to a verbal description for solving problems because:

- Diagrams can group together all information that is used together, thus avoiding large amounts of searching for the elements needed to make a problem-solving inference.

- Diagrams typically use location to group information about a single element, avoiding the need to match symbolic labels.

- Diagrams automatically support a large number of perceptual inferences, which are extremely easy for humans."

Richard E. Mayer and Joan K. Gallini add that diagrams "help learners build runnable mental models" that portray "each major state that each component can be in and the relations between a state change in one component and state changes in other components."

Diagrams are better representations of knowledge

Simon and Larkin assert that the advantages of diagrams are "computational" in nature. In other words, "diagrams can be better representations not because they contain more information, but because the indexing of this information can support extremely useful and efficient computational processes." As we shall see in this section, there are a fair number of different types of diagrams, each of which has a distinct syntax and semantics that must be learned, just as the syntax and semantics of a natural language must be. Once learned, diagrams enable the user to solve problems or, in Simon and Larkin's terms, to perform "efficient computational processes" with them.

Caution: Not every diagram is superior

But not every diagram is worth 10,000 words. Diagrams must be specifically developed to support computational processes. Any group of diagrammatic elements can be placed together in some sort of figure that resembles a diagram. But mere placement does not ensure that the elements are accurately combined and organized.

"Similarly, although every diagram supports some easy perceptual inferences, nothing ensures that these inferences must be useful in the problem-solving process. Failing to use these features is probably part of the reason why some diagrams seem not to help solvers, while others do provide significant help," write Simon and Larkin. Both the Mayer and Gallini and the Simon and Larkin studies reinforce the idea that, although diagrams have important communicative functions, not all of the ideas always should be put on the same diagram. Rather, groups of diagrams are often necessary to get all of the points across.

Semantic Analysis of Diagrams

A full semantic analysis of all kinds of diagrams has yet to be accomplished. The scheme I propose on these 2 pages is intended as a preliminary outline for such an analysis. Once all of a diagram's components are spelled out, it becomes immediately obvious that there is a lot going on even in a relatively simple diagram like this one. It suggests that there is much more than meets the eye to constructing and interpreting diagrams and that a considerable learning process is necessary. What is also suggested by this analysis is that often we use too little text, when more text should actually be used to make the information more immediately accessible to the general reader.

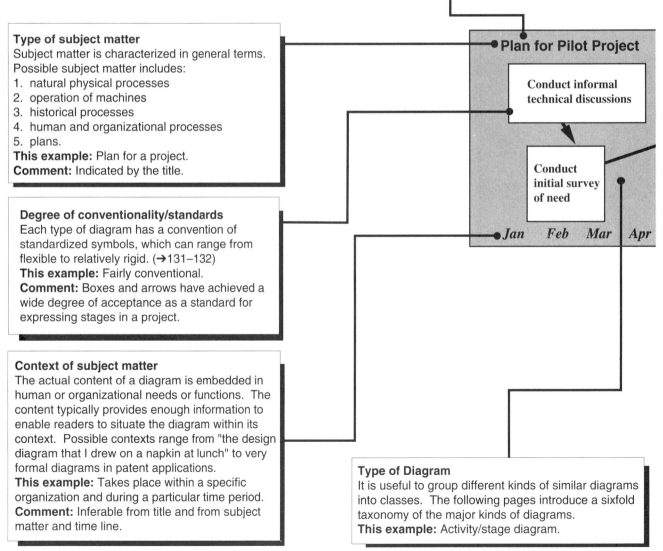

Point of view
Point of view is often implicit and not commented upon in any of the verbal discussions that accompany diagrams. The reader is frequently left to decipher whether a diagram contains static structural or organizational features or whether it illustrates some kind of dynamic. Point of view, however, is frequently inferable from the title and sometimes from the visual elements. Some points of view include:
1. a general idea for a process, plan, or procedure
2. a repetitive set of stages in a project (i.e., a cycle)
3. a specific plan, or process, procedure for a specific organization.
This example: Specific project for specific parts of an organization.
Comment: Indicated by the title.

Type of subject matter
Subject matter is characterized in general terms. Possible subject matter includes:
1. natural physical processes
2. operation of machines
3. historical processes
4. human and organizational processes
5. plans.
This example: Plan for a project.
Comment: Indicated by the title.

Degree of conventionality/standards
Each type of diagram has a convention of standardized symbols, which can range from flexible to relatively rigid. (→131–132)
This example: Fairly conventional.
Comment: Boxes and arrows have achieved a wide degree of acceptance as a standard for expressing stages in a project.

Context of subject matter
The actual content of a diagram is embedded in human or organizational needs or functions. The content typically provides enough information to enable readers to situate the diagram within its context. Possible contexts range from "the design diagram that I drew on a napkin at lunch" to very formal diagrams in patent applications.
This example: Takes place within a specific organization and during a particular time period.
Comment: Inferable from title and from subject matter and time line.

Type of Diagram
It is useful to group different kinds of similar diagrams into classes. The following pages introduce a sixfold taxonomy of the major kinds of diagrams.
This example: Activity/stage diagram.

Plan for Pilot Project

Conduct informal technical discussions

Conduct initial survey of need

Jan   Feb   Mar   Apr

Temporal aspect
How is time presented in the diagram? Is the temporal aspect the present, the past, a kind of ideal nontemporal point of view? Temporal aspects include:
1. time past (e.g., a diagram illustrating a historical point of view)
2. no specific time (e.g., a diagram that shows how a process works in general)
3. time future
This example: Specific future.
Comment: Inferred from title. Time is divided into chunks indicated by the boxes connected by arrows. The units of time are specified on bottom of diagram. The diagram shows time connections between stages (one has to happen after the other) and specification of general times of expected occurrence of the tasks, but no specific specification (e.g., a deadline or target date).

Locational aspect
In some diagrams, the location of the processes, procedures, and plans are important and specifically indicated on the diagram (usually by words, but sometimes by VLicon elements).
This example: None shown.
Comment: Partial locational information could be inferred by someone familiar with the organization.

Level of detail
The degree to which the components are named, described, or represented is another focus of analysis. The level of detail flows from the specific communication needs of the diagram.
This example: Names of activities.
Comment: Indicated by words in individual boxes.

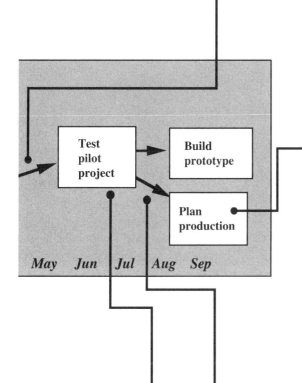

Context of document (→191–192)
The document is different from its subject matter and has its own context. It is important to specify the location and role of the diagram within the larger context of the document and its presentation: An exhibit in a report, for example, is different from a slide in a series for a visual presentation.
This example: Not specified.
Comment: May be a one-page handout or a diagram drawn on a whiteboard, but only the author and anyone else who was present at development would know. Some diagrams contain the name of the author, the date, and other identifying contextual information.

Semantic rules observed
The results of semantic analysis are frequently represented as rules. I present several categories of diagrams with straightforward rulelike descriptions in order to illustrate the kind of semantic rules that can be formulated about visual language. (→128–131) In many other places in this book, however, I prefer to use less formal presentation.
This example: Words specify name of event. Arrows indicate what event is followed by what next event. Boxes provide boundaries for name of event.
Comment: A variety of assignments of meaning are possible for any visual element. Assignment is inferred in this diagram because no key is provided.

Types of Diagrams

The following 4 pages describe 6 major classes of diagrams that a theory of semantics must address. These diagrams represent the fundamental ways in which we look at the structure and process of events and activities. Although they do not present all possible diagram types, they offer a wide variety, sufficient for our exploration of semantic features.

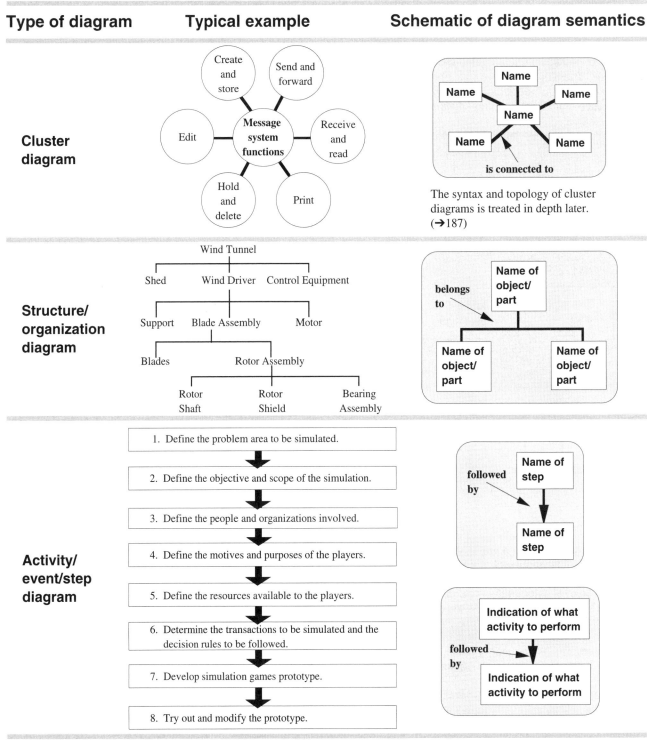

Type of diagram	Typical example	Schematic of diagram semantics
Cluster diagram		The syntax and topology of cluster diagrams is treated in depth later. (→187)
Structure/ organization diagram		
Activity/ event/step diagram		

Semantic content of words

Semantic content of visual elements

Words may
- name objects or parts of objects
- describe the object
- describe functions
- indicate location
- and perform many other similar descriptive functions

Lines may convey a variety of meanings, such as
- connected to
- related to
- associated with

Icons or illustrations can represent objects, parts of objects, locations, etc.

Overall combination of verbal and visual elements portrays the structure of what can be called semantic space of the subject matter.

Lines may convey
- is divided into (for physical things)
- is a part of
- reports to (for organizations)

Words may
- name objects or parts of objects
- describe functions or physical structure

Icons or illustrations can represent objects, parts of objects, locations, etc.

Overall combination of verbal and visual elements shows division of elements into subcategories and/or the merger of subcategories into groups.

Words may
- name the steps to be performed
- indicate the activity to be performed
- locate events
- describe functions
- and perform many other similar descriptive functions

Arrows may convey
- next
- followed by
- possibly followed by

Icons or illustrations can describe or locate an event.

Overall combination of visual and verbal elements portrays a sequence. Branching is permitted, that is, more than one step, activity, or action may come from a preceding step.

Three more types of diagrams are described on next page.

Types of Diagrams (continued)

Type of diagram	Typical example	Schematic of diagram semantics

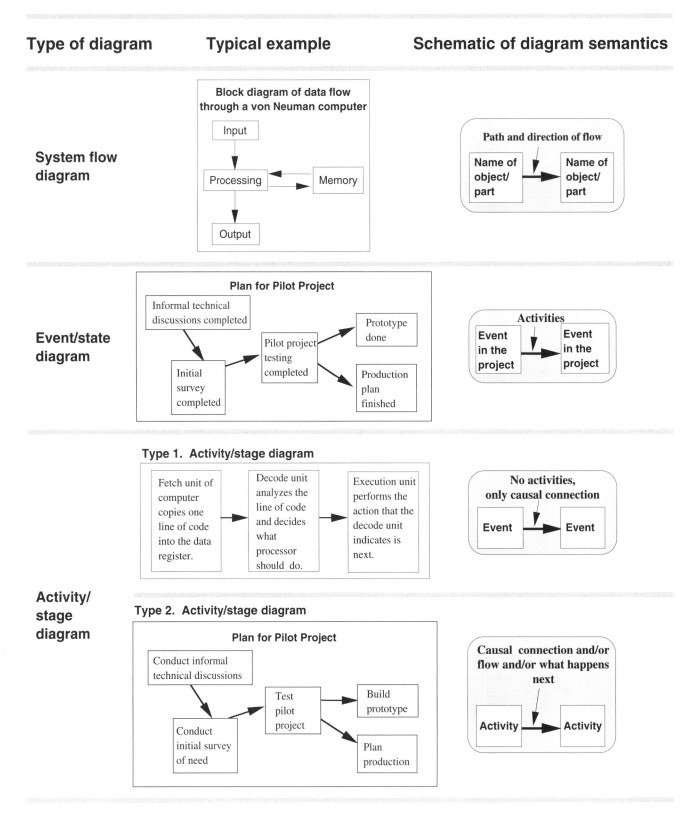

System flow diagram

Block diagram of data flow through a von Neuman computer

Input → Processing ⇄ Memory → Output

Path and direction of flow
Name of object/ part → Name of object/ part

Event/state diagram

Plan for Pilot Project

Informal technical discussions completed → Initial survey completed → Pilot project testing completed → Prototype done / Production plan finished

Activities
Event in the project → Event in the project

Activity/ stage diagram

Type 1. Activity/stage diagram

Fetch unit of computer copies one line of code into the data register. → Decode unit analyzes the line of code and decides what processor should do. → Execution unit performs the action that the decode unit indicates is next.

No activities, only causal connection
Event → Event

Type 2. Activity/stage diagram

Plan for Pilot Project

Conduct informal technical discussions → Conduct initial survey of need → Test pilot project → Build prototype / Plan production

Causal connection and/or flow and/or what happens next
Activity → Activity

Semantic content of words

Semantic content of visual elements

Words may
- name objects or parts of objects
- describe the object
- describe functions
- indicate location
- and perform many other similar descriptive functions

Arrows may represent actual or possible
- path or direction of flow of information, control, action, or decision

Icons or illustrations may describe or locate the object or part.

Overall combination of visual and verbal elements portrays the system components and its paths of flow. Branching is possible in this format.

Words may
- indicate beginning or end of event
- locate events
- describe functions
- and perform many other similar descriptive functions

Arrows represent
- processes
- activities

Icons or illustrations may describe or locate events.

Overall combination of visual and verbal elements portrays the system states or events in the system, but not the activities that produce the states or events. Branching is possible in this format.

Words may
- name events (usually instantaneous events or time durations that are treated as instantaneous)
- describe the event
- describe functions
- locate the event
- and perform many other similar descriptive functions

Arrows may represent
- causes
- next
- followed by
- possibly followed by

Icons or illustrations may describe or locate events or participants.

Overall combination of visual and verbal elements portrays the sequence of system activities. Branching is possible in this format.

Words may
- name events
- describe events
- locate events
- describe functions
- and perform many other similar descriptive functions

Arrows may represent
- next
- followed by
- possibly followed by

Icons or illustrations may describe or locate event.

Overall combination of visual and verbal elements portrays the sequence of system activities. Branching is possible in this format.

Types of Highly Standardized Diagrams

Semantics depends on stable meanings that communities create for themselves. We now turn our attention to the question of such highly standardized meanings in diagrams. Our examples come from computing, a discipline in which various diagrammatic inventions have been developed into software programs that aid analysts in the portrayal of data-processing systems.

The diagrams on this page are borrowed from the schema produced by James Martin and Carma McClure, who have summarized the semantics of diagramming for data processing. They propose an eightfold classification based on levels of detail from corporatewide to detailed planning for software code; they illustrate their classification with diagrams taken from a variety of sources. Each of the systems is highly standardized.

Data (structure)

Classification (Martin and McClure)	Name and definition	Example
Strategic overview of corporate data	**Entity–relationship diagram** An entity is something real or abstract in an organization about which data is stored. An entity–relationship diagram shows the relationships between different kinds of entities and the data that are connected with them at a high level of detail.	
Detailed logical data model	**Data structure diagram** A data structure diagram shows the associations between data items at a high level of detail.	
Program-level view of data	**Warnier–Orr diagram** A Warnier–Orr chart represents program structures, reports, or data structures with multiple sets of parentheses.	
Program usage of data	**Michael Jackson diagram** The Jackson diagram represents program and data structures hierarchically with tree structures.	

Even though the diagrams on this page and the highly standardized diagrams of other communities are developed to service specialized purposes, many of them eventually enjoy broader use—evidence of the synthesis and integration that visual language encourages.

Activities (process)

Classification (Martin and McClure)	Name and definition	Example
Strategic overview of corporate functions	**Decomposition diagram** A decomposition diagram breaks the activities and functions of an organization into levels of detail.	
Logical relationship among processes	**Action diagram** An action diagram lays out a specific set of steps and decisions required to accomplish a function.	
Overall program structure	**HIPO diagram** Represents a hierarchical input–process–output structure as performed by computer software.	
Detailed program logic	**Decision table diagram** A decision table presents a detailed level of program execution in the form of an if-then table.	

For the decomposition diagram example:

Publishing Division	Sales	Field sales Direct mail	Plan mailings Buy new lists Update old lists
	Finance		
	Operations		

For the action diagram example:

```
validate personnel file
    validate file header
    validate file body
        check name
        check address
            if errors
            go to error recovery
            else
            go to validate personal data
```

For the HIPO diagram example:

	INPUT	PROCESS	OUTPUT
Update Personnel File	add new name address phone ss # employee class	1. create new record 2. validate new information 3. add new information	print new additions to personnel file report

For the decision table diagram example:

HOW TO APPROVE OR DISAPPROVE AN ORDER

IF credit limit is …	and IF pay experience is …	and IF special clearance has been obtained …	THEN …
OK			approve order
questionable	favorable		approve order
not favorable	not favorable	yes	approve order
not favorable	not favorable	no	return order to sales dept.

When Vocabularies Intersect

Diagramming is one of the primary vocabularies of visual language. Although it has origins in specialized disciplines, all but its most highly standardized "dialects" are understandable to the casual reader. As diagrams emerge from the individual disciplines in which they originate and become part of the general vocabulary of visual language, they encounter other visual language vocabularies. The intersection and merging of different visual vocabularies is part of the definition of "tight integration."

Two of the more interesting confluences in recent years are between diagramming and cartoon conventions and between computer interface iconography and cartooning. These conjunctions work—that is, enable effective communication—because each of the vocabularies involved is compatible with the other.

Cartoons and business diagramming merge

Business ideas are increasingly being communicated with the help of cartoon conventions. The example here shows the rapidity with which a document travels up the corporate organization chart. The example combines cartoons, diagrams, and lifelike illustrations into one efficient communication unit.

Cartoons in scientific diagrams

The merging of cartoon and diagrammatic conventions is dramatically illustrated in an article on cellular suicide that appeared in *Science* magazine in 1995.

What is interesting for our present study is the appearance of cartoonlike elements in the diagram accompanying the article. (I have redrawn part of the diagram, omitting the detailed genetic information.) When cartoon vocabulary appears in the most sober of scientific magazines, the integration that characterizes visual language has surely become mainstream.

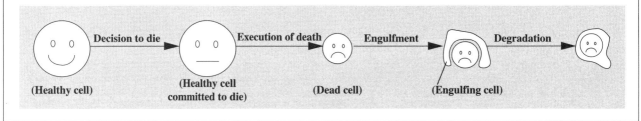

Cartoon conventions and computer interfaces

As computer interfaces become more complex, designers have turned more often to cartoon conventions to enhance usability and ease the learning process. Why cartoons? Because they are friendly and familiar to the vast majority of us. The next section explores in more detail what the cartoon vocabulary has to offer.

Speech balloon

The speech balloon convention appears as a pop-up element in computer interfaces, in particular on the Macintosh computer, where they are used to explain the meaning of icons and other components of computer functionality that are not readily intuited. This use of the speech balloon on a computer operating system, millions of which are sold around the world in a single year, has contributed to the integration of cartoon vocabulary into mainstream communication.

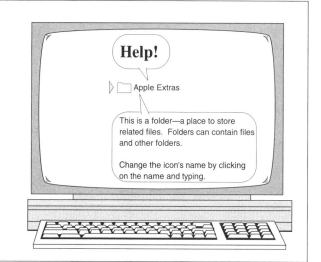

Iconization of cartoons

Cartoon-style representations are well suited for use as icons in software interfaces. Such iconized cartoons, combined with the use of other conventions of cartooning, show the degree to which software designers have taken advantage of the rich vocabulary of cartoon conventions to achieve their communicative intent.

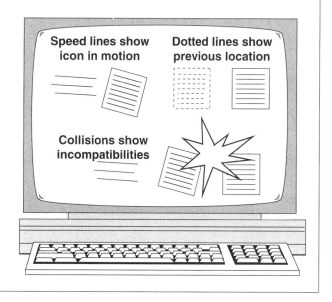

Cartoon Conventions

We have seen how diagramming vocabulary is central to visual language. A 2nd, complementary vocabulary, comes from a quite different arena—cartooning. Cartoons (and comic books) have swept rapidly around the globe in this century. What started as an invention of individual artists has gradually converged, stabilized, and become standardized, and is now being merged with diagrams and other branches of visual language vocabulary and syntax. Cartoons are understood by people of all ages in many, if not most, countries. The increased use of cartooning conventions is an important part of the development of an integrated, global visual language.

Panels and time/space representation

Cartoonists have developed the use of panels of different sizes, shapes, and patterns to represent the passage of time and the changing dynamics of actions (➔153–154), as well as changes of location and point of view. The panels control the reader's focus and path through the story and are divided in rough correspondence with the way we divide time into chunks of days, hours, minutes, and so forth.

Chunks of time

The basic convention is that one panel represents one duration of time in some space from some point of view. I should note in passing that this division of time into overt chunks is similar to that found in diagrams of process and movement (➔171–172), as well as in the steps of procedures (➔169–170).

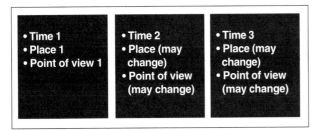

Flow of time

Generally, passage of time is represented from left to right, top to bottom.

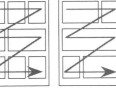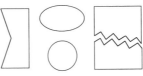

On occasion, one can find in some documents deliberate violation of this convention.

Often, cartoonists use a wider panel to indicate a longer amount of time, although such a panel sometimes represents simply a wide-angle view of a scene.

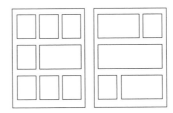

Expressive shapes and sizes

Panels express a variety of conventional feelings or moods through variations in size and shape. These conventions have come to be understood through repeated use.

 Rectangles usually indicate present time and are the standard view.

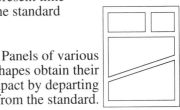

Panels of various shapes obtain their impact by departing from the standard.

A flashback to past time is sometimes indicated by a rectangular cloud panel.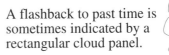

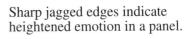 Sharp jagged edges indicate heightened emotion in a panel.

Rounded edges (like the outline of a cloud) often indicate that the entire scene is taking place in thought.

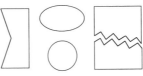 Other shapes add variety to the expressive vocabulary. These often do not have a specific verbal equivalent.

Sometimes the absence of panel outlines can convey the idea of unlimited space.

Physical phenomena

Another vocabulary that cartooning contributes to visual language involves the representation of natural or physical phenomena. The elegant simplicity of these conventions enables communicators to refer to natural phenomena without employing elaborate photographic or artistic images.

Events happen in the world that cartoonists try to capture with the simplest of drawings.

Conventionalized expressions are used to capture some of these phenomena, which are often not actually visible (e.g., vibration), visible only fleetingly, or impossible to see.

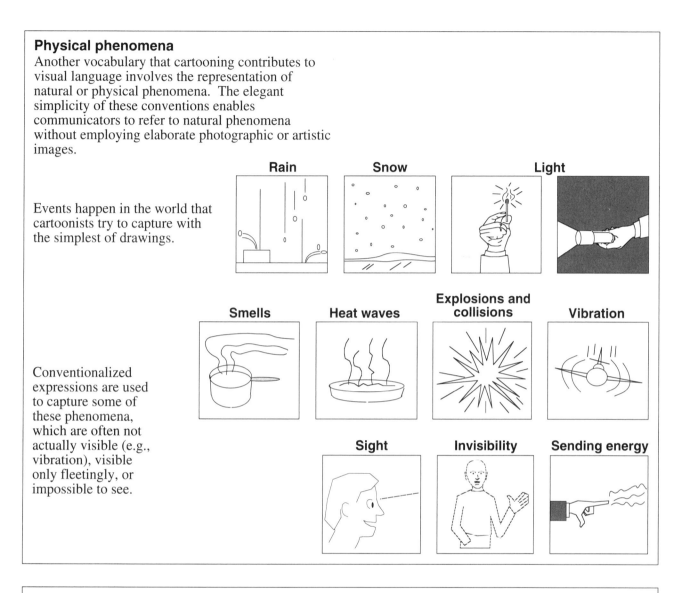

Motion

Cartoons have contributed the convention of the motion or speed line to visual language vocabulary. These lines express the direction, mode, and intensity of movement. (→171–172) Speed lines and other indications of motion are not visible in nature, of course, but in art they have become understood as conventions.

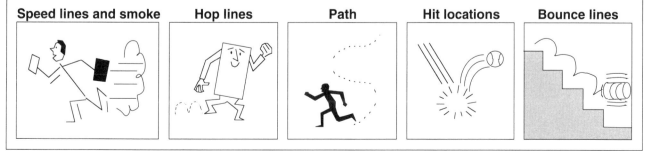

136

Cartoon Conventions (continued)

The inventiveness of cartoonists is not limited to expressions of time, space, motion, or natural phenomena. Cartoonists have developed visual conventions to express various and subtle human experiences and ideas.

Cartoon conventions have brought expressive gestures into visual language. The use of gestures in cartoon panels has emerged as a visual language vocabulary for use in icons or VLicon elements.

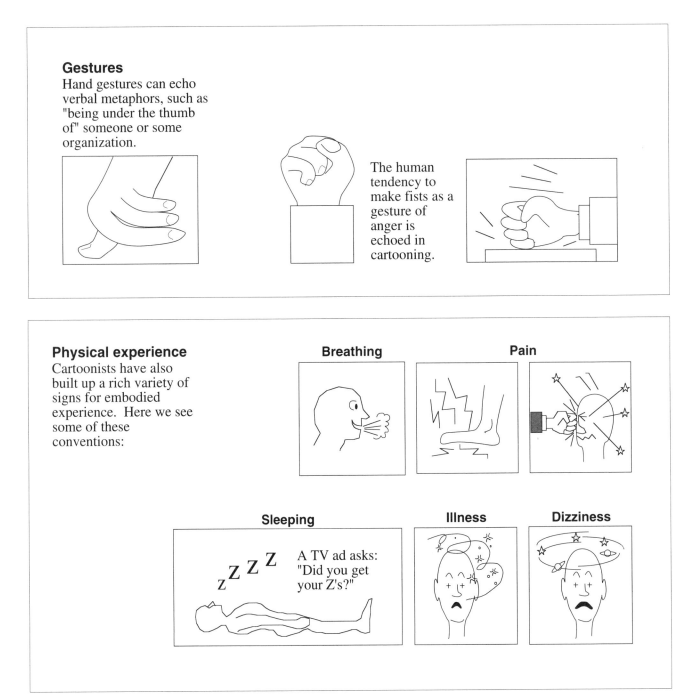

Gestures
Hand gestures can echo verbal metaphors, such as "being under the thumb of" someone or some organization.

The human tendency to make fists as a gesture of anger is echoed in cartooning.

Physical experience
Cartoonists have also built up a rich variety of signs for embodied experience. Here we see some of these conventions:

Breathing

Pain

Sleeping

A TV ad asks: "Did you get your Z's?"

Illness

Dizziness

Speech balloons

The content, size, and form of the speech balloon convey emotions and subtle expressions. For example, boldface frequently expresses loudness. The speech balloon has been extended to include a huge variety of moods and ideas.

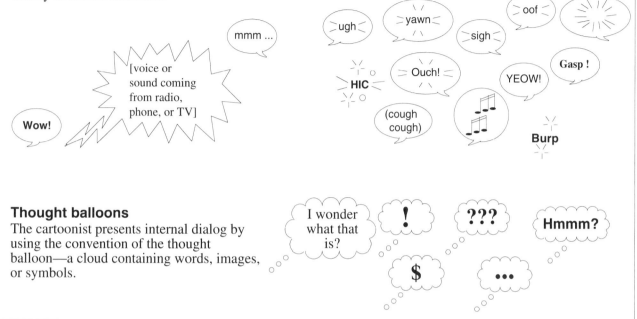

Thought balloons

The cartoonist presents internal dialog by using the convention of the thought balloon—a cloud containing words, images, or symbols.

Metaphor sources for cartoon ideas

Cartoons frequently present visual versions of the metaphors we encounter in speech.

Having an idea

A light went off in his head as he thought of a brilliant new idea. The metaphor is based on the idea that gaining new understanding is like going from darkness into light.

Love

The physical heart has become a universal metaphor for love. Cartoonists have picked up this symbol and use it to represent both thought and emotion.

Explosive thought

Ideas are like weapons; they can explode in your head. These metaphors provide a source for visual representations of thought.

Emotional Expression and Faces

Universal emotional expression

Psychologist Paul Ekman has researched the crosscultural expression of emotions. It seems that people in all cultures around the world thus far observed share a common interpretation of facial expressions depicting basic human emotions. Cartoonists around the world also use substantially similar techniques to show emotion. Here is a small sampling of the many possible emotional expressions now available in the vocabulary of visual language.

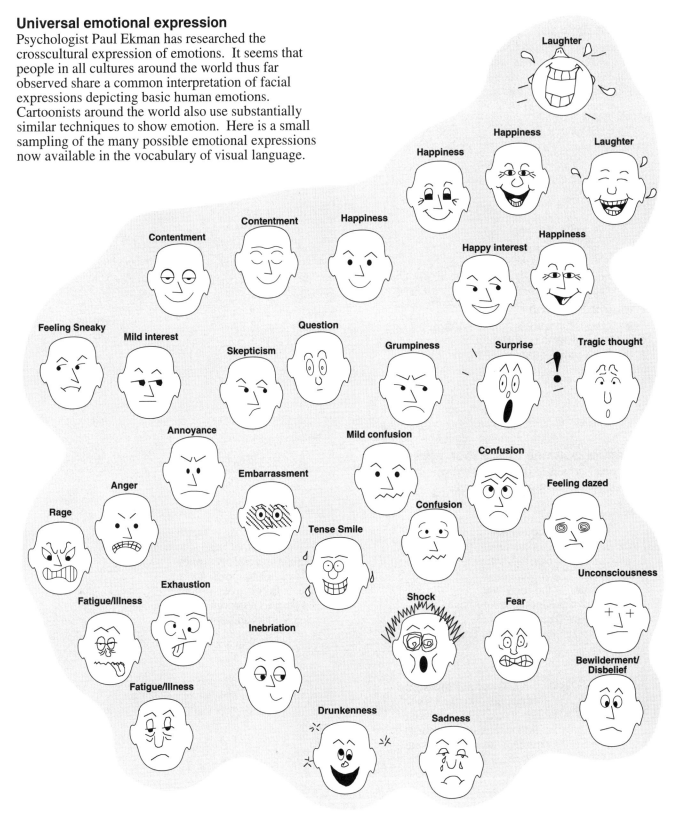

Conventional emotional expression

Cartoon conventions provide an even wider variety of emotional expressions. Many of these expressions have emerged through visual adaptation of verbal metaphor (➜113), although some, such as the "confusion marks" illustrated below, are of unknown or unclear origin.

Anger
"Breathing fire" and "so angry that smoke came out of his ears" are likely verbal sources of this visual metaphor.

Surprise
"He was so surprised his hair stood straight up on his head" is very likely the verbal source of this visual metaphor.

Hateful thoughts
"His eyes threw daggers."

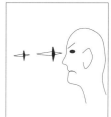

Pop-eyed surprise or fear
"I was so surprised my eyes almost popped out of my head."

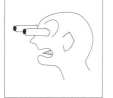

Pain
"He was hit so hard he saw stars."

Agitation
Agitation is frequently shown by facial expression plus lines to suggest head movement.

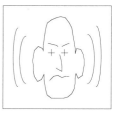

Innocence or goodness
A takeoff from religious paintings, the halo expresses innocence and beneficence.

Dark thoughts
"He was so morose you could see a black cloud over his head."

Worry
The expression of extreme concern, worry, or fear is frequently accomplished by showing sweat.

Frazzled nerves
"My nerves were jangled," or, "It was as if I was hit by a jolt of electricity."

Confusion
Sometimes a conventional symbol is adopted together with an expression to indicate a particular feeling.

Emanating anger
One of the most common augmentations to an expression is a variety of punctuation marks to indicate angry expletives.

Typography in Comics

Standard typography manipulates the size and form of letters for expression; boldface and italics are the most widely used for emphasis. Cartoonists have gone beyond this norm, often making the letters very large to indicate loudness of sound and to convey visual impact.

Verbal-visual onomatopoeias

Indeed, cartoonists have invented a sublanguage that is both verbal and visual, with special vocabularies to express many sorts of phenomena, thoughts, and actions. They "show" sounds by dramatizing them typographically and by adding a variety of visual elements (such as explosions) to the words. These verbal–visual onomatopoeias have spread from cartoons to graphic novels and advertising.

These typography conventions are becoming more frequently used on TV and on film; they are often intermixed with still photography and movies to make a particular point. As the barriers between words and images continue to break down, the integration of cartoon-based words and photography (or realistic illustration) is likely to result in a whole new genre of visual language.

What kinds of sounds

Natural sounds

141

can be shown?

Sounds created by human technology

tick   tick   tick   tick   tick
tock   tock   tock   tock

Sounds of explosions

BANG

Sounds of collisions, motors, and horns

VAROOM   BEEP   HONK   BAM   POW   RRRRR

RRING

Action without sounds

Pat
Pat

Animal sounds

CHOMP!   CHEEP   RAARRRR!   WOOF   Meow

The Vocabulary of Space

Space is more than an abstract location within which action takes place. It has powerful associations and an emotional impact on how we interpret what we see. As creatures who have always lived in a three-dimensional world, we carry strong expectations about horizon lines, size of objects, and other features of three-dimensionality. As creatures who look out of the front of our heads through a masklike frame, we always have a locational point of view. In other words, we see something from some position. As creatures who can move about in space, we can take different points of view—looking upon a scene from above, from below, from nearby, or from far away.

Many of the most powerful examples of visual language rely on spatial vocabulary. Camera angles, the size of the subject within the frame, the composition of the dominant visual shapes within the frame, and movement (➜171–172) all provide possibilities for conveying meaning.

Vocabulary from film studies

The study of art and film provides many of the distinctions with which visual language communications can be designed and critiqued. In the two-dimensional world (that is, paper or audiovisual screens) that we communicate with, using the vocabulary of space requires understanding the effects of seeing the world through frames (which screens and pages are). The vocabulary cataloged on these pages illustrates the extensiveness and influence of space on our communication habits.

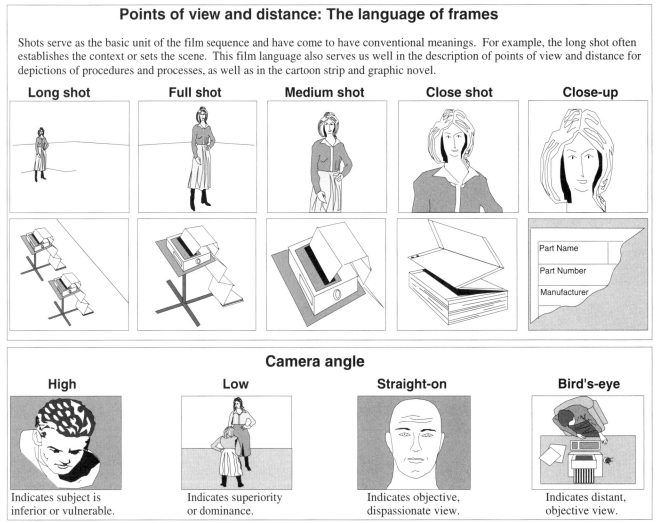

Points of view and distance: The language of frames

Shots serve as the basic unit of the film sequence and have come to have conventional meanings. For example, the long shot often establishes the context or sets the scene. This film language also serves us well in the description of points of view and distance for depictions of procedures and processes, as well as in the cartoon strip and graphic novel.

Long shot	Full shot	Medium shot	Close shot	Close-up

Part Name

Part Number

Manufacturer

Camera angle

High	Low	Straight-on	Bird's-eye
Indicates subject is inferior or vulnerable.	Indicates superiority or dominance.	Indicates objective, dispassionate view.	Indicates distant, objective view.

Placement of the subject in parts of the frame

"Mise-en-scene" is a theater term referring to the placement of persons and objects within the frame of the stage to help convey the story. Visual language users readily adapt the dynamic, three-dimensional vocabulary of mise-en-scene to static, two-dimensional presentations.

For example, looking at the different placement of the subject in the frames below, the reader begins to project meaning onto the scenes even without further context or knowledge of the narrative of which they might be a part.

Placement in frame

Subject at left or right edge is often perceived as weak relative to the subject at center.

Subject at top is often seen as dominant, powerful.

Subject at bottom is frequently perceived as submissive, weak, vulnerable.

Invasion of close personal space indicates threat or dominance.

Close personal space can also indicate intimacy.

Subject tilted laterally within frame suggests instability or disorientation.

Isolated subjects convey more visual weight than grouped subjects.

Subject squeezed into tight frame conveys claustrophobia or entrapment.

Subject with much space in frame suggests freedom.

Subjects on opposite sides of screen are distantly related or perhaps antagonists.

Subjects in center are closely related.

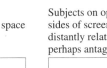

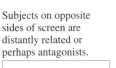

Visual masses balanced relative to center provide feeling of stability or serenity.

Visual masses can be out of balance to emphasize action.

Compositional Distinctions

Compositional distinctions are another type of visual language semantics. These principles originate with artists, who use them to compose pictures and to design layouts. The principles can be regarded as semantic in nature because each principle has particular interpretations attached to it, although they are somewhat more fuzzily defined than ordinary semantics for verbal language.

Compositional principles represent a vocabulary of distinctions that artists often use to convey what they call "visual ideas." Each characteristic influences the overall impact that a composition has, just as points of view and placement of a subject in a frame (➔143–144) do. Visual language enjoys the subtleties of layers of expression. The schema of opposites on these pages catalogs a taxonomy of purely visual semantic ideas developed by Donis Dondis. (The drawings are my own.)

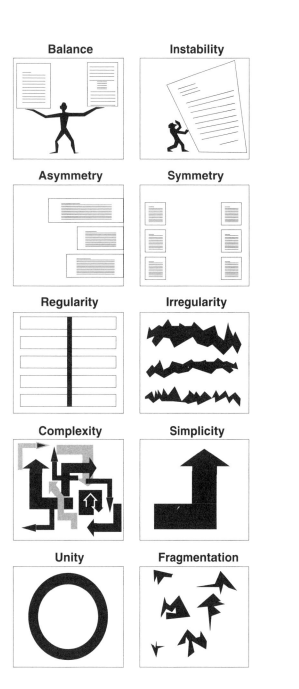

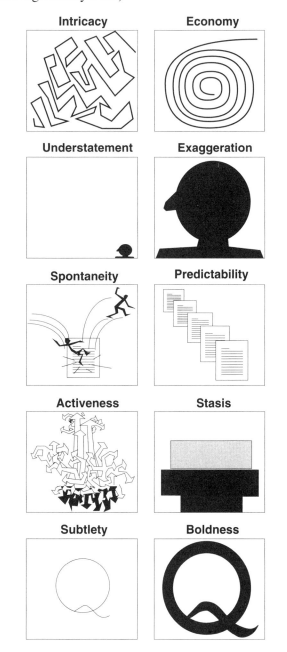

Many of these ideas could be represented as a continuum rather than as a series of polar opposites. For example, consistency and variation form a continuum that begins at total consistency, includes almost consistent, largely consistent, somewhat consistent, and ends up with total variation.

Artists emphasize that both the composition as a whole and its individual elements have characteristics that "say something" to the reader. The levels of semantical content that can be imbued in a visual language presentation via compositional principles greatly expand the communicative power of a given communication unit.

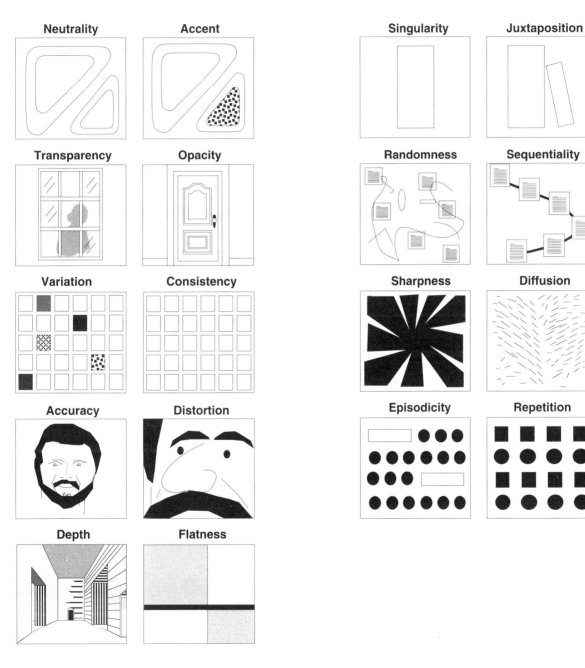

146

Associative Interpretation of Lines

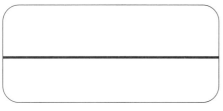

A single line placed horizontally across a blank piece of paper seems most often to suggest a horizon. This is because human perception is conditioned to recognize the meeting point between earth and sky. The purely visual features of lines, the empty space they configure around them, and the composition of components around them contribute to the esthetics and richness of communication values in visual language.

A number of observers have called attention to the ability of lines to convey different kinds of emotional feeling.

Such meanings are probably learned and thus culturally conditioned. Nonetheless, if most lines do convey feeling as such, then we must acknowledge that all visual language will express emotion, albeit sometimes at a relatively low level of intensity. What stories, hence, what semantics, do lines contain? Here, I combine the suggestions of three observers, a filmmaker (Herbert Zettl), an architect (Omar Faruque), and a cartoonist (Scott McCloud), on the semantics of lines by themselves.

Horizontal

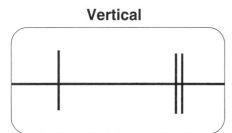

Visual effect: vast open space, suggesting lakes, oceans, open fields, passive, timeless.
Emotion: earthy, satisfying, calmness, tranquility, rest, stability.

Diverging

Visual effect: expanding, increasing, reaching out, progressive separation.
Emotion: earth defying, adventurous, dynamism.

Converging

Visual effect: reducing, decreasing, focusing, spatial depth, illusion of perspective and distance.
Emotion: closure, satisfaction, resolution.

Vertical

Visual effect: gravity, stability; 2 vertical lines "together oppose each other."
Emotion: proud, strong stately, noble, exciting, extra energy, dynamic.

Progression

Visual effect: waves advance and recede.
Emotion: progression, direction.

Retreat

Visual effect: concave.
Emotion: retreat.

Concave

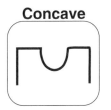

Visual effect: recessed, cut in, molded, sense of containment.
Emotion: inviting, protecting, shelter-giving, warm, gentle.

Convex

Visual effect: expanding, pressing.
Emotion: repelling.

Radial

Visual effect: light, energy, petals of a flower, center to fringe, central concentration of energy.
Emotion: vitality at center received by fringe.

Rising

Visual effect: mountain peaks, tall buildings, rising, tapering upward, dynamic, changing.
Emotion: improvement, attainment, success, optimism, progress, hope.

Falling

Visual effect: converging downward.
Emotion: falling, sinking, degeneration, defeat, pessimism.

Active and dynamic

Visual effect: motion, quick changes of direction, fast movement, sharp, acute angles, lightning, electricity, forceful curvilinear movements.
Emotion: chaos, out of control.

Smooth, refined

Visual effect: undisturbed dunes, seascapes, spotless, smooth, details evoke refinement.
Emotion: delicate mood.

Rough, brutal

Visual effect: irregular lines, sharp points, roughness, crack, breaks, animal teeth, continuous directional changes, jagged.
Emotion: hardness, brutality, unwelcoming, severe, exciting, energetic.

Static and fixed

Visual effect: point at center of square or circle, uniform space around, focus, stability, bilateral symmetry, no tension, no imbalance.
Emotion: static emotion.

Structural stability

Visual effect: stability, strength, structure, solidity.
Emotion: rational, conservative.

Irregular wavering

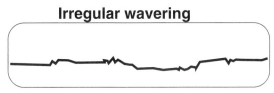

Visual effect: uncertainty, weakness.
Emotion: lacks confidence.

Rolling, wavering, meandering

Visual effect: wind, air, water, snow, sweeping, rolling curves.
Emotion: swelling, sliding, fluidity, casual, relaxed, interesting.

Abstract and Imaginary Spaces

The combination of powerful computer graphics and scientific and mathematical imagination has created a huge array of abstract and imaginary spaces. As they become more familiar, all of these spaces become accessible as places in which thoughts can be expressed visually. Many of the new abstract or imaginary spaces are expertly suited to "house" the complex ideas that we express with visual language.

Coordinate spaces

Through most of history, we had access only to the space provided by attempts to represent reality in perspective.

Abstract coordinate spaces are used today not only for scientific and mathematical purposes, but also as more general representation spaces for expression and communication.

Interiorness or exteriorness can be suggested by the Cartesian coordinate space, and the addition of a human figure, even in silhouette, gives context to the display.

The following abstract spaces can be used at different scales: as icons or VLicon elements to identify a kind of space, or as background in infographics to suggest particular moods or locations.

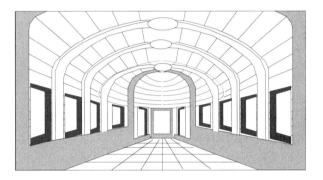

In the 17th century, Descartes developed the geometry and mathematics of the coordinate system, which allowed for representation of abstract ideas in both two-dimensional and three-dimensional space.

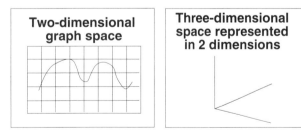

Two-dimensional graph space

Three-dimensional space represented in 2 dimensions

Abstraction and generalization from those spaces created other spaces in which to think about abstract concepts.

One-point perspective space

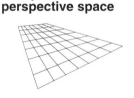

Two-point perspective space

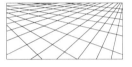

Three-dimensional interior space

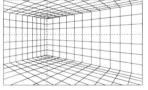

Three-dimensional exterior space

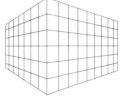

Abstract spherical (or global) space

Tilted one-point perspective space

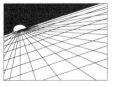

Abstract multiple-plane space

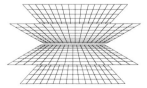
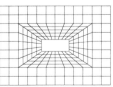

149

Imaginary and scientific spaces

Our experiences with television, science fiction books and movies, mathematical instruction, and computer games provide more sources for spaces in which we can visually represent information. Science fiction abounds with worm holes and warp-speed drives through them.

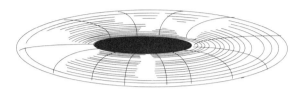

Television repeats scenes of astronauts floating in space, without referents except for the distant stars.

As children play games, they fly through virtual reality space

or experience the extraordinary underwater ocean space.

Using space for visual problem-solving

Three-dimensional scientific visualization space. Scientific visualization techniques use abstract space in sophisticated displays, for example, to display in 3 dimensions the ocean's temperature gradients.

Wireframe displays. Coordinate space bent in appropriate ways has become literally the framework for developing physical objects on a computer. The so-called wireframe displays are created for objects such as this aircraft, and then surface colors and textures are applied by the graphic computer.

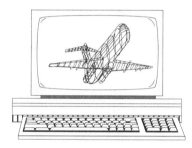

Abstract diagram space. Abstract space facilitates diagramming, especially in terms of a diagram's ability to make visible complex thought. Using abstract space for a diagram makes available all the aspects of space (where things are, movement, etc.) as part of the metaphoric vocabulary of the diagram.

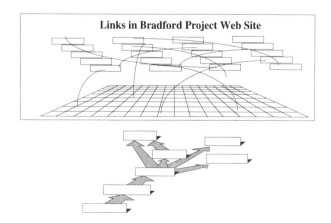

Image Constancy and Slices of Space-Time

In prose narrative, time most often appears as a sequence of discrete events tied together by time words such as "then," "next," "later," "the following day," and so on. Visual language is able to represent time-ordered sequences of events much more efficiently by the use of panels, which are understood to indicate that changes in time and/or location have taken place.

The panel readily provides the "contextual" information of location, time, and point of view, a task that traditionally results in tediously long and inadequate prose text.

The division of time into panels enables a reader to look from one panel to the next and realize that time has passed, even though no verbal elements are present to reinforce the notion. For people who enjoy high exposure to visual culture, the process is instantaneous and automatic.

Space-time slicing and sequencing
Look at the following 3 panels:

We tend to see these panels as a sequence that tells a brief narrative. There are 3 space-time slices:
(1) the offer (of something) represented by the outstretched hand,
(2) the thought of approval illustrated with cartoon conventions, and
(3) the handshake indicating agreement.

The space between the panels—called gutters by cartoonists—indicates the change of space and time.

The panels are a "general indicator that time and space is being divided. The durations of that time and the dimensions of that space are defined more by the contents of the panel than by the panel itself," says McCloud.

One further unique aspect to space-time slicing in visual language is that a panel most often shows both a distinct location and a passage of time. Additionally, each space-time panel can be said to have a particular point of view. Even so, we generally have the cognitive ability to "close the gap" from panel to panel in order to create meaning.

Thus, in the following 2 panels, even though the point of view has changed, the location is different, and apparently time has passed, we are able to understand that the 2 panels are related in a narrative way.

We put the panels together and "mentally construct" what McCloud calls a "continuous unified reality."

Our ability to create meaning out of visual space-time slices is facilitated by 2 cognitive phenomena— image constancy and closure.

Image constancy and closure

Despite great variation in the images on the eye that represent a given object in the world, the object looks much the same to us. It appears to be about the same size despite the changes in the size of its images (size constancy), to have much the same shape despite changes in the shape of its images (shape constancy), and to have much the same orientation (tilted, upright, upside down) despite changes in how its images are oriented on the retina (orientation constancy). It also appears to be located in much the same direction in relation to ourselves and other objects despite where on the retina its image is located (constancy of direction or position constancy), and much the same lightness, or shade of gray, despite changes in the intensity of light reaching the eye from its surfaces (lightness constancy).

Irving Rock, perceptual psychologist

im • age con • stan • cy /n/

The perceptual capability that enables humans to recognize objects and backgrounds in the visual environment as continuous even when they are actually seen from many points of view and under a huge variety of conditions.

Image constancy is related to the Gestalt principle of closure (➜75–76), which states that humans tend to make perception as good as possible, to see a whole instead of parts, whenever possible. Thus, if we glance at a television screen and see a sequence of images such as these

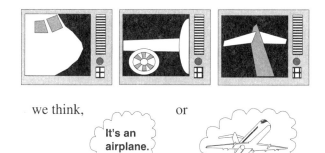

we think,   or

Image constancy is an unconscious, automatic, and incredibly fast process. To perceive even a simple object, humans use conceptual models that are built up over time to interpret the world based on experience. Image constancy processes help us fill in all the changes of points of view and conditions and put all the information together into a continuous reality and narrative. When image constancy involves situations instead of objects, it is called closure.

clo • sure /n/

In psychology, perception of incomplete figures or situations as though complete by ignoring the missing parts or by compensating for them by projection based on past experience.

Similar in different media

Storyboards for films, diagrams, and comic strips all rely on image constancy and closure to facilitate transitions between panels. Static visual language media divide up time and space into panels containing static images, which are interpreted reliably as showing change and motion.

The media of motion, such as video and animation, actually show the motion and change, but these media also have punctuation techniques, such as cuts, that indicate changes in time and place.

Cuts can convey a variety of changes. They can continue action, reveal detail, change locale, change point of view, show simultaneous events, establish sequential rhythm, and intensify action. Very fast cuts enable time compression.

Similar in different types of communications

The conventions of gutters and panels come to visual language from the vocabulary of cartooning (➜135–142), but they are relied upon in other areas of visual communication as well. The assumptions of space-time slicing, of the use of panels (sometimes called frames), of image constancy, and of closure also appear in diagrams.

Look at this example:

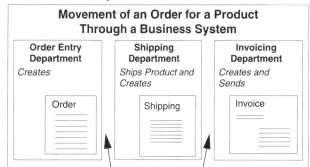

Changes of time and space

Sometimes an arrow replaces the gutter between panels in a diagram to represent passage of time. Whichever convention is used, the interpretation is similar; some change of space-time framing has taken place.

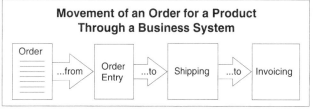

Transitions in Space-Time

Not only does the gutter between panels indicate space-time changes, but the contents of the panels enable us to make inferences about such transitions. Scott McCloud has suggested a sevenfold taxonomy of such transitions, which I illustrate on these pages with my visuals.

These pages also illustrate how our examination of semantics of visual language transitions borders on an analysis of visual language in motion. In video and animation similar transitions happen between scenes. Thus, it is apparent that the emerging semantics discussed here in relation to static presentations of visual language apply to video and animation as well.

1. Moment-to-moment transitions

Moment-to-moment transitions
- have very short intervals of time between panels, and
- usually show the same person (subject) from the same point of view in each panel.

McCloud notes that these types of transitions "require little closure" for readers to establish meaning.

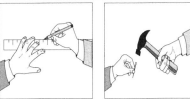

2. Action-to-action transitions

Action-to-action transitions
- show "a single subject (person) in distinct ... progressions" of tasks or actions, and
- may or may not show a subject from the same point of view in each panel.

McCloud suggests that for static media these transitions require moderate closure.

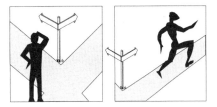

These 2 pairs of panels show transitions by presenting actions somewhat related by figures, or parts of figures identifiable as the same figure, thus providing continuity (closure) yet indicating a space-time transition.

3. Subject-to-subject transitions

Subject-to-subject transitions
- show more than one person (subject)
- often show a subject from different points of view.

McCloud suggests that these transitions require considerable reader closure to create meaning.

These 4 panels show 3 members of an audience thinking about what the presenter is about to write on the easel. This is a transition in which the addition of verbal components to the visual will aid in precise interpretation.

153

4. Scene-to-scene transitions

Scene-to-scene transitions
• may have short or long periods of time and space between panels
• may show same or completely different subjects from quite different points of view.
McCloud comments that these transitions often require deductive reasoning, and hence require a great deal of closure.

This example shows a transition from office planning to accomplishment of the plan in the warehouse. Like subject-to-subject transitions, scene-to-scene transitions also often require verbal elements to clarify what the proper interpretation is.

5. Aspect-to-aspect transitions

Aspect-to-aspect transitions
• usually keep time at very short intervals between panels
• suggest that the eye is scanning the scene and pausing momentarily on one or another parts or aspects.
These transitions usually don't require a great deal of closures.

This example shows the eye focusing on different details in a bedroom.

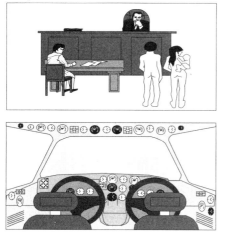

6. Non-sequitur transitions

Non-sequitur transitions
• may portray any-time, any-place transitions,
• usually offer "no logical relationship between panels whatsoever" and, according to McCloud, require almost total reader-supplied closure.

This example shows transition between a scene in a courtroom and in an aircraft cockpit in someone's dream. Only the dreamer knows the connection, although accompanying verbal elements may help the reader understand certain of the connections.

Punctuation in the Media of Motion

Representation of motion and change is the forte of video and film media. But they also divide time into chunks. Just as static media use gutters and frames (→151–152) to convey the semantics of time, the media of motion use a variety of devices to punctuate sequences in a film. These changes in space, time, and viewpoint use transitions similar to those used by static media.

The simplest transition is the cut, in which one scene or viewpoint is closed and another is introduced. Other kinds of transitions can be thought of metaphorically as forms of punctuation, each of which is coming to have a customary meaning.

Dissolve

A dissolve provides a smooth transition (on a continuum between fast and flow), links intervals in time or distances in space, interconnects rhythms of events, and can support a nostalgic mood.

Fade

A fade provides clear and definite finish (fade out) or beginning (fade in) and separates scenes. Variations include fade to white or some other color.

Wipe

The wipe indicates a definite ending or beginning, usually of a sequence; is often faster than a fade and enables movement to next scene in sequence; and is not a final ending. Sometimes the wipe is made to black or white. Illustrated is what is sometimes called an action wipe or a push-off, in which a scene comes in from the left as the other scene disappears as a wipe. Wipes can be up, down, right, left, and of many different colors.

Other effects

The electronic equipment used in video production enables a director to punctuate scenes with over 200 different effects, some of which are illustrated here. All of the following achieve a somewhat similar effect—a closure of the scene, which can convey a variety of feelings, depending upon the speed and the type of motion. The "barn door" cut, for example can have a squeezing effect. The "iris" cut can convey a sense of increasing distance.

Venetian blind

Barn door

Checkerboard

Iris

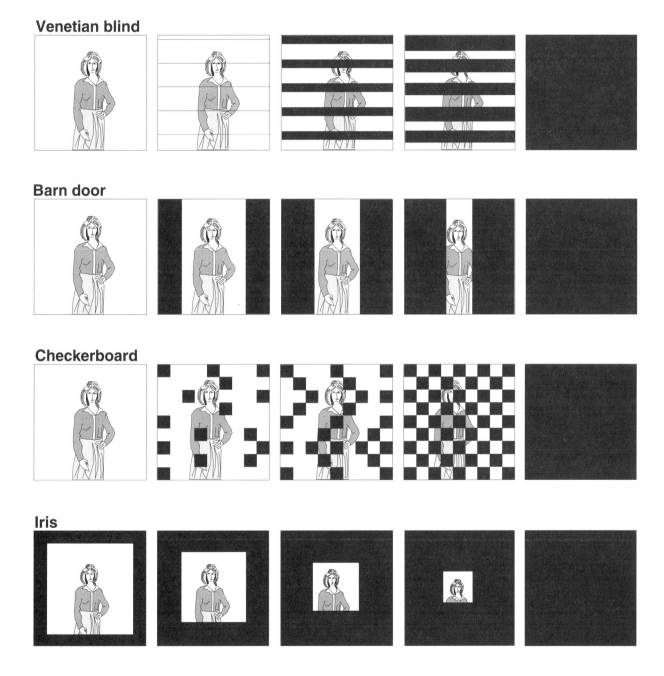

Chapter Summary

This chapter has made a case for semantic analysis of visual language by showing some of its major vocabularies as well as many of the kinds of integration possible. As a particular kind of information graphic and/or mural, the infoscape is well suited to represent large quantities of complex information. The infoscape on this page makes use of nearly all the characteristics of visual language semantics discussed in this chapter in order to communicate a complex set of ideas and relationships. It shows how such large, complex, semantic integrations achieve what is possible with visual language.

The Bradford Project

Overview
The Bradford Project is the flagship project of our next 5-year company plan. This infoscape shows the major project stages (as floating platforms) and their interconnections.

Status
Presently we are in the crucial phase of building the initial prototype. We expect that the prototype will be completed within 2 quarters.

Initial Beta Test
Marketing has already completed contacts with key customers to perform initial beta tests.

Patent Application Process

Patent Search

Key Vendors Planning

Special Safety Simulations

Legal Dept. Involved

Initial Prototype Beta Tests

Initial Prototype Built

Revised Pilot Project Approved

Offsite Critique Session

Pilot Project Approved

246

Percept/concept integration
The platforms of the infoscape, representing major activities in the project, float unaccountably in the air. The infoscape fuses concept (major activity) and percept (platform) (→95–96), and somehow we are able to suspend our judgment about certain physical laws.

Types of tight integration
At least 3 major types of tight semantic integration (→101–104) are represented in the infoscape. The platforms serve to chunk time, thereby serving a framing function; the text for each stage of the project provides labels for the visual illustrations of each stage; and the visual elements at each stage reinforce the meaning of the words.

Spatial time flow
Time flows in a directed fashion but not as a straight line (→115–116, 167–168). Here the arrows can be translated "leads to."

157

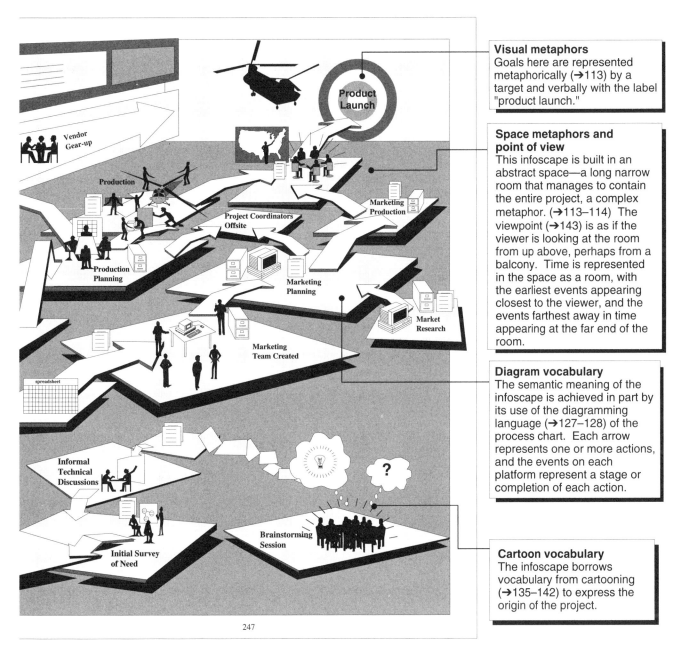

Visual metaphors
Goals here are represented metaphorically (→113) by a target and verbally with the label "product launch."

Space metaphors and point of view
This infoscape is built in an abstract space—a long narrow room that manages to contain the entire project, a complex metaphor. (→113–114) The viewpoint (→143) is as if the viewer is looking at the room from up above, perhaps from a balcony. Time is represented in the space as a room, with the earliest events appearing closest to the viewer, and the events farthest away in time appearing at the far end of the room.

Diagram vocabulary
The semantic meaning of the infoscape is achieved in part by its use of the diagramming language (→127–128) of the process chart. Each arrow represents one or more actions, and the events on each platform represent a stage or completion of each action.

Cartoon vocabulary
The infoscape borrows vocabulary from cartooning (→135–142) to express the origin of the project.

Within the image:

Product Launch

Vendor Gear-up

Production

Project Coordinators Offsite

Marketing Production

Production Planning

Marketing Planning

Market Research

Marketing Team Created

spreadsheet

Informal Technical Discussions

Brainstorming Session

Initial Survey of Need

?

247

158

Chapter 5

Functional Semantics of Content

Visual language can handle many, if not most, of the heavy-duty information representation jobs in contemporary business, science, technology, and academic discourse. The process of applying a sense of order to such a wide range of communication events involves a two-level analysis of what I call functional semantics.

First level of analysis
First, I propose that visual language semantic functions be divided into those mainly pertaining to content (the subject of this chapter) and those associated with other rhetorical functions, such as navigation, organization, and influence (the subject of Chapter 6).

Second level of analysis
Within the discussion of these 2 categories, I examine how each individual function may be best performed when words and visual elements work together. The 2 key questions are: What functions do visual elements perform best? What do words do best? To illustrate how the visual language approach is frequently superior, I contrast it with an attempt to communicate particular functions with words alone.

Other functions
The catalog of semantic functions presented here and in chapter 6 is by no means exhaustive. Further categories will be developed and explored in later works.

func • tion • al   se • man • tics   /n/
The study of the purpose for the inclusion of each element in a visual language communication unit. Hence, the study of what job each unit is doing.

Contents of Chapter 5

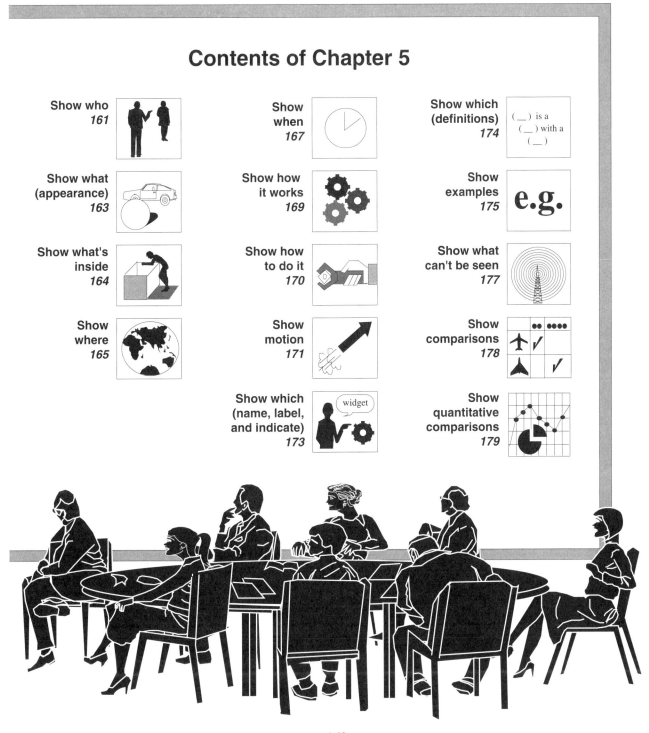

Show Who

Shows or tells about:
- **the person(s) involved**
- **their identity, appearance, emotions, attitudes, career, etc.**

The "show who" category is an excellent example of the division of labor in visual language. No verbal description of a person's face can compete with a photograph to describe or identify the individual. Words almost always compare unfavorably to an image when a detailed description of an individual is the goal.

For example, how would Shakespeare describe himself?

Bald … wears hair long … big eyes … slight mustache … an intelligent look … dispassionate as … as … words fail even me … forsooth … methinks I'll take up painting!…

Show the person(s) involved

Often we don't need to actually see Shakespeare or the specific person who is the subject of the communication in order to learn a lot of information. Nonetheless, we have normal human curiosity; people are interested in who is or has been involved, and we prefer to put faces with information.

Levels of "show who"

Our ideas of ourselves or of others are not exhausted by portraits, or by knowing what someone looks like. There are other aspects of selves that are important, for example, our roles in the world. Such aspects of personhood can be represented with images that at first glance might seem to be more appropriately classified under the category "show what." For example, in the case of Thomas Jefferson on these pages, the idea that he was a president is represented by an image of the White House. *Who* Jefferson was, in other words, is partially defined using images of *what* he was associated with.

President-Politician

Member, Virginia House of Burgesses, 1769–75
Governor of Virginia, 1779–81
Delegate, Second Continental Congress, 1775–76
Author of the Declaration of Independence, 1776
Secretary of State, 1790–93
Vice President, 1797–1801
Third President of the United States, 1801–09
Purchased Louisiana from France, doubling the size of the United States, 1803

Author

Jefferson wrote a book called *Notes on the State of Virginia,* which was the 1st description of the geography, government, and customs of the state.

Research administrator

Jefferson sent 2 army officers, Meriwether Lewis and William Clark, on an expedition (1804–06) to explore the Louisiana Territory and beyond in a search for a route to the Pacific Ocean. Other aims were scientific, and included identifying plants and animals and studying the customs of the Native Americans.

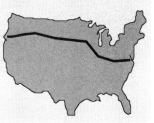

Educator

Jefferson was the founder of the University of Virginia, which was his major passion after he retired from government service. He regarded the university as 1 of the 3 chief accomplishments worthy of being mentioned on his tombstone.

Thomas Jefferson
1743–1826

Diplomat

In the delicate period after the War of the American Revolution, Jefferson was sent by the Continental Congress to be Minister to France, 1785–89.

Artist and architect

Jefferson was fascinated with the study of architecture, which he regarded as one of the fine arts. He continuously redesigned his own home at Monticello, as well as providing designs for the University of Virginia and other public buildings. He was also an accomplished violin player.

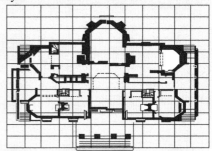

Scientist-Agronomist

Jefferson was a tireless experimenter with plant growing, collecting and importing many kinds from Europe. He was president of the American Philosophical Society, the 1st scientific organization in the United States, and an avid collector of palentological items. He also invented many practical items, including a device that enabled him to make copies of his correspondence.

Show What (Appearance)

- **Identifies**
- **portrays**
- **describes the appearance of physical objects**

Illustrations have been used for thousands of years to show how objects look and to portray their relationship to each other in the physical world. Usually they are regarded as superior to verbal descriptions alone of the same objects for most communicative purposes.

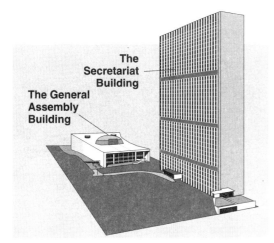

Point of view

Among the advantages of using illustrations instead of words is the ability to direct the viewer's or reader's attention from a precise angle, as shown in the examples below.

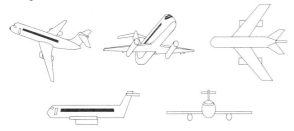

Parts

Using visual language, a communicator can also show situations that might otherwise be difficult to visualize, such as an aircraft split into parts.

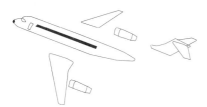

Background or context

Showing physical objects in their context, or against a background, conveys much more than words alone can.

It is difficult to convey the complexity of structure and texture of many objects with words alone. As a result, it is often more useful to portray the objects themselves rather than to attempt a verbal description. Here is the outside of a complicated physical object displayed through illustration.

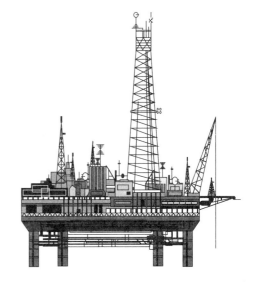

Would you rather use words or graphics to describe an oil rig? Ask yourself how many words it would take. You may very well agree with the old proverb that a picture is worth a thousand words. ... What better reason for the increasing proliferation of visual language?

163

Show What's Inside

Shows visible and invisible interiors of objects

Visual language allows for a more complete understanding of complex natural or constructed phenomena through the use of labeled cutaway drawings. These kinds of drawings permit us to look at what no human being ever literally "sees."

The inside of a missile silo is shown in the drawing below. The structure of the silo is invisible from any single position outside or inside. In this example, verbal elements label parts of the structure and describe their functions.

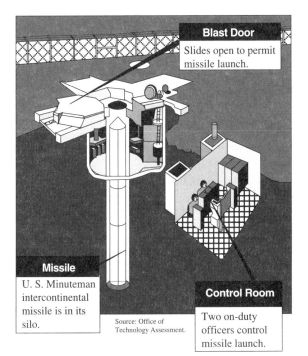

Blast Door
Slides open to permit missile launch.

Missile
U. S. Minuteman intercontinental missile is in its silo.

Source: Office of Technology Assessment.

Control Room
Two on-duty officers control missile launch.

Ghosted diagrams

Ghosted diagrams strip away the exterior surface of an object, as in this illustration of the inside of an airplane engine turbine. Rarely can prose by itself compete with visual language when the communication requirement is to show what's inside physical objects.

Cutaway diagrams

Cutaways cut into a physical object to show what the interior looks like at a particular point, as in this cutaway of the wing of an aircraft.

Wireframe diagrams

Invented to show a framework structure of the basic parts, the frames may not always correspond to the exact internal structure, but rather allow a structure to be seen all the way through. Wireframe diagrams are used to simplify computer drawings upon which textures and colored surfaces are applied.

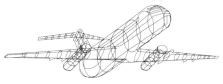

Cross-section diagrams

Invented during the standardization of engineering drawing, cross-sections show an object as if it had been sliced through with a knife and then viewed straight on, as in this cross-section of an aircraft body.

Visual enlargements of objects

Different scales on the same drawings provide the ability to show context as well as detail. Shown here are pop-ups, or pop-outs, of equipment in an office building. The verbal elements contribute vital labeling functions.

Schematic of network layout

File Server: Ultraminivac KX202

Workstation: Ultraminivac 4000

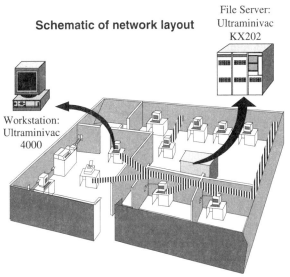

164

Show Where

Shows or tells locations of things in space

The very early appearance of maps in human communication history (→23) illustrates how important it was for our ancestors to convey ideas of location. These days, maps are always tight integrations of words and images, in which the visual elements do the major job of representing point-to-point homologies, and the words help interpret the abbreviations and name the locations.

As shown on these 2 pages, a whole vocabulary of visual language has been developed for different scales. This vocabulary is available for integration with other vocabulary sources, such as illustration, cartooning, and diagramming. Specific locations are generally shown by 1 of 3 methods: pointing (for exact position); shading, texture, or color (for a general idea); or lines (for boundaries).

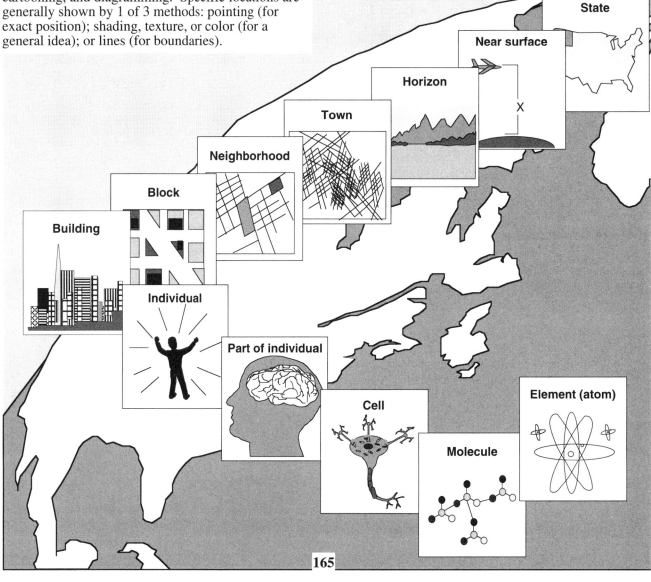

165

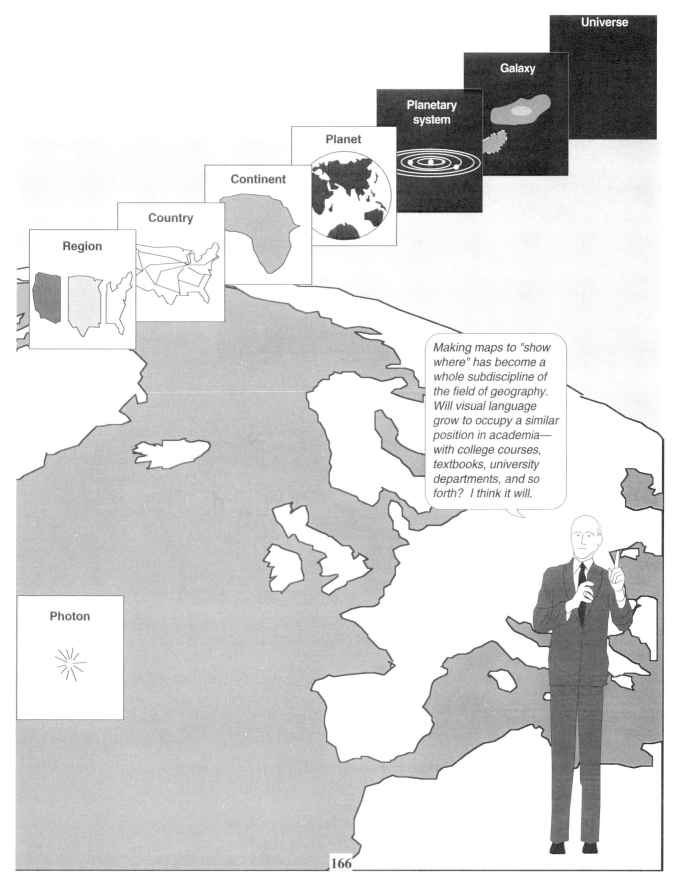

Show When

Shows or tells time:
- **general or specific**
- **as duration or as instantaneous events**

Obviously, prose provides compact and efficient ways of telling the time: "It's Tuesday," or "It's 10:15 a.m. on June 21, 1999." But to especially emphasize time factors, or show how time affects a complex arrangement (and for other reasons as well), visual expressions of time can be useful. An array of options for expressing time visually is available; many of them are shown below.

Clocks

Human beings have used clocks to measure time for centuries. Images of clocks, from iconic to realistic, from analog to digital, are some of the easiest ways to show time visually.

Calendars

Particular dates can be shown with calendars.

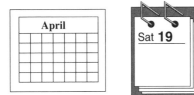

The passage of days can be shown by the removal of pages from a day-to-day calendar.

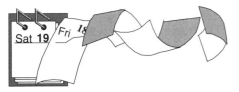

Sundials

Images of older timekeeping tools, such as sundials, are sometimes used for special effect or to make historical allusions.

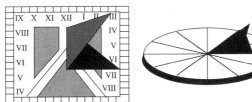

Icons for natural events

Our primary reference for time is the natural movement of the the sun, or the division between night and day, pictures of which immediately convey rough ideas about time of day.

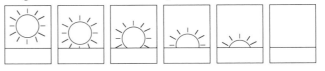

Images of the moon and sun, whether iconic or fanciful, can also indicate time.

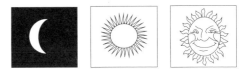

Seasonal images

In many parts of the world, seasons are easily identifiable by changes in the environment, and images showing these changes can be used to indicate time of year or transitions between times of the year.

The entire season of winter can even be represented iconically by a single snowflake or by a snowman.

Holiday images

All human societies have special days that come at a particular time of year. Images or icons associated with holidays can be used to suggest that time of year.

Weather images

Storms differ in duration, but seldom last longer than a few days. Because of this natural phenomenon, storm images can be used to convey a limited time frame as well as atmospheric conditions.

Abstract representations of time

Gantt charts and schedules. On a more abstract level, chunks of time can be represented as lines on graph paper through the use of various schedule conventions, like the Gantt (→41–42) chart.

Space between frames. Also on an abstract level, the space between frames in cartoons and certain kinds of diagrams implies the passage of time. Arrows are sometimes used in this gap to suggest movement. (→135)

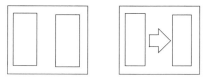

POPP (Project Organization Process Procedure) arrows. The POPP arrow is a name given to the arrangement of a set of cards or panels, each of which represents a chunk of time on a three-dimensional arrow. It has a multiplicity of uses, in that the diagram can represent a project, an organization moving through time, a set of stages in a process, or a set of set of steps in a procedure.

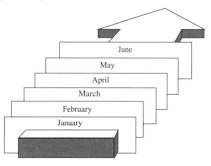

Time lines. A line to arrange historical events has become a standard kind of diagram.

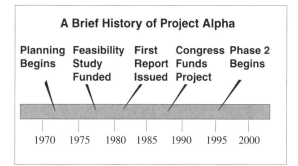

Time metaphors. Human beings have many different time metaphors, many of which can be treated visually. We go into more detail on visual metaphors about time in Chapter 4. (→115–116)

168

Show How It Works

Shows or tells about:
- **how a machine or human-made system works**
- **how a natural system or process works**

Diagrams showing how a machine or process works or operates comprise one of the most important realms of discourse in visual language. It is here that the ability of visual elements to portray complex interacting parts that change through time can facilitate a greater understanding than words alone.

I challenge the reader to write out in declarative sentences all of the information contained in the diagrams below and then compare the prose descriptions to the diagrams, using clarity, efficiency, and effectiveness as criteria.

The study of diagrams is dealt with more extensively as a complete vocabulary domain in several places in this book, notably chapter 4.

Example: Business process diagram

Example: Cycle chart

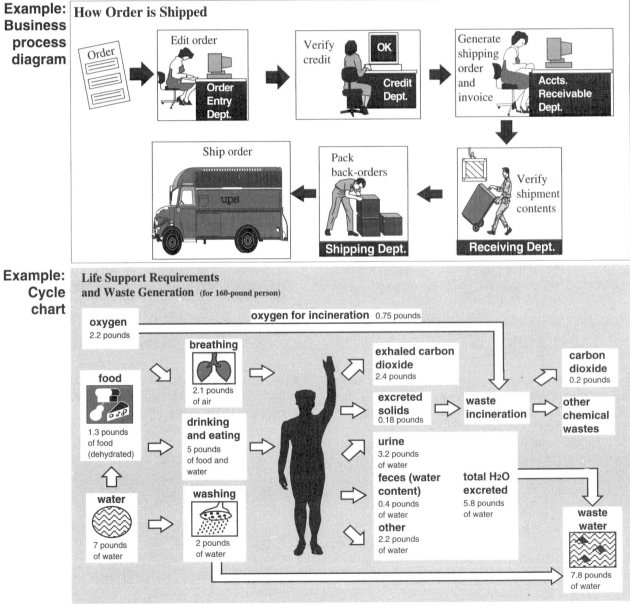

Show How to Do It

Shows or tells about accomplishment of specific steps in a task.

"How-to-do-it" visual language is increasingly used for the assembly of both consumer goods and industrial equipment.

How the course materials printing and shipping process works

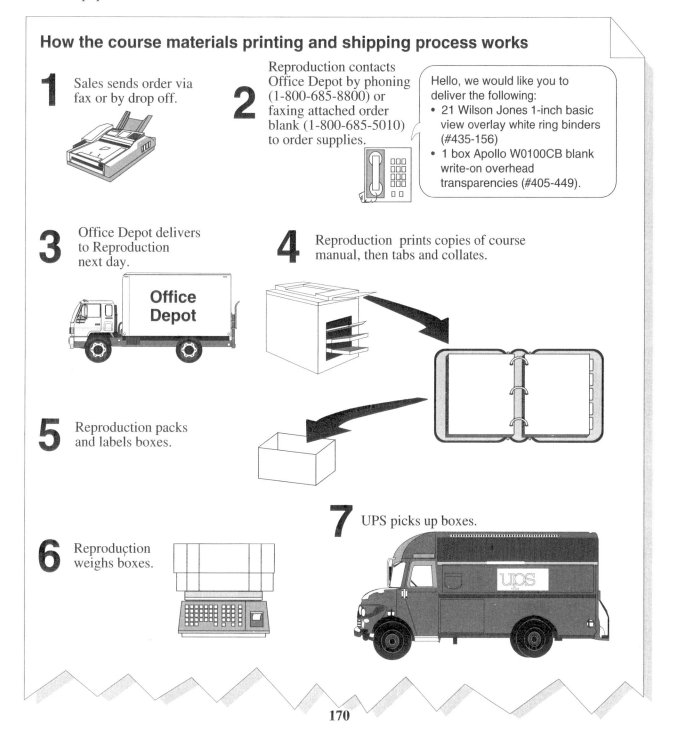

1 Sales sends order via fax or by drop off.

2 Reproduction contacts Office Depot by phoning (1-800-685-8800) or faxing attached order blank (1-800-685-5010) to order supplies.

Hello, we would like you to deliver the following:
- 21 Wilson Jones 1-inch basic view overlay white ring binders (#435-156)
- 1 box Apollo W0100CB blank write-on overhead transparencies (#405-449).

3 Office Depot delivers to Reproduction next day.

Office Depot

4 Reproduction prints copies of course manual, then tabs and collates.

5 Reproduction packs and labels boxes.

6 Reproduction weighs boxes.

7 UPS picks up boxes.

Show Motion

Shows or tells about the change in location of physical objects, which is perceived as movement

Lines to indicate paths of motion

Very likely the earliest attempts to express motion simply used a line and a point to show the path of motion. Today we still use that method:

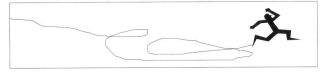

Origination, destination, environment, and direction of movement

Sometimes the line is changed to an arrow to show direction. Frequently, visual indication of the environment is added to the visual language unit to show origination, destination, or geographic area to scale. These indications may be drawn at various levels of abstraction.

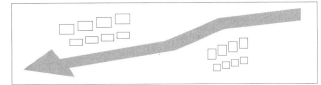

Positions of movement

We know that showing animals and people in positions of motion has conveyed the idea of motion from at least the time when the Lascaux cave paintings were created.

Multiple overlapping images and fuzzy outlines

Overlapping images and fuzzy outlines have also been used from early times to convey motion.

Natural phenomena in motion

A fixed portrayal of phenomena that we usually experience in motion can communicate the feeling of motion.

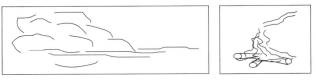

Similarly, showing objects in the control of natural laws such as gravity conveys the idea of motion.

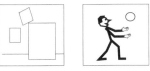

Distortion of natural motions

Cartoonists heighten the impression of motion by exaggerating natural shapes as they change. Animators use this "squash and stretch" technique to create motion that appears more natural and less rigid than when a fixed shape is moved from place to place.

Distortions in shape

Simple distortions in shape create a sense of imbalance that has the sensation of movement attached to it. (➔145)

One-point perspective

Images coming at a reader from one-point perspective affect our sense of balance to some degree. We tend to recoil internally from things coming at us.

Bursting out of frame

Motion effects are suggested by images bursting out of frame, as in these documents coming out of a screen.

Motion lines

Cartoonists have developed a series of conventions to show motion. Motion lines behind a figure and little puffs of smoke indicate "really fast."

Blurred figures or objects in foreground

When we see something moving very fast, we often experience it as blurred. Visual language can reproduce this experience to convey the meaning of rapid motion.

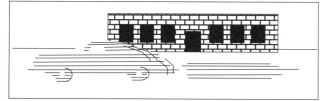

Blurred background

In movies, when our eyes are fixed on a rapidly moving object, we tend to focus our eyes on the object itself (which appears unchanged). The environment through which it is moving thereby becomes blurred.

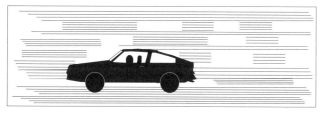

Arrows

Twisting, turning, or entwining lines and arrows engage the eye and force us to imagine movement.

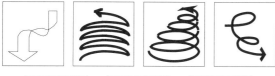

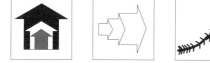

Dashed lines or compositions with lines

Even without arrow points, simple abstract compositions with dashed lines can convey the rhythm of movement.

Shading

Abstract shading can also indicate a kind of change, which can convey movement.

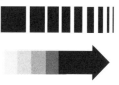

Pattern changes

Shading is similar to changes in pattern, which can also suggest movement.

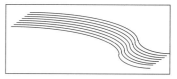

Fantastical and metaphorical uses

Visual language encourages playfulness so we would expect visual language speakers to express motion in a variety of metaphorical ways. (→113–122)

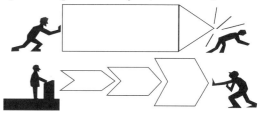

Motion in film

Finally, I should note that all of the examples showing motion in visual language on these pages are static. The ability to show motion in "movies" simply increases the expressive possibilities of visual language. Indeed, the strip of film itself has become an icon for movement.

Show Which (Name, Label, and Indicate)

Indicates distinctions and the conventional names for these distinctions

Situations in which readily portrayable objects need to be distinguished in terms of parts or functions take great advantage of visual language's integration of verbal and visual elements.

Example: Labeling equipment

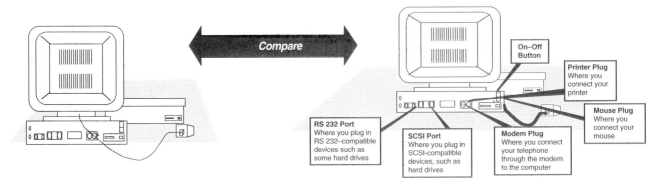

Compare

On–Off Button

Printer Plug
Where you connect your printer

Mouse Plug
Where you connect your mouse

RS 232 Port
Where you plug in RS 232–compatible devices such as some hard drives

SCSI Port
Where you plug in SCSI-compatible devices, such as hard drives

Modem Plug
Where you connect your telephone through the modem to the computer

Example: Labeling objects in an artificial environment

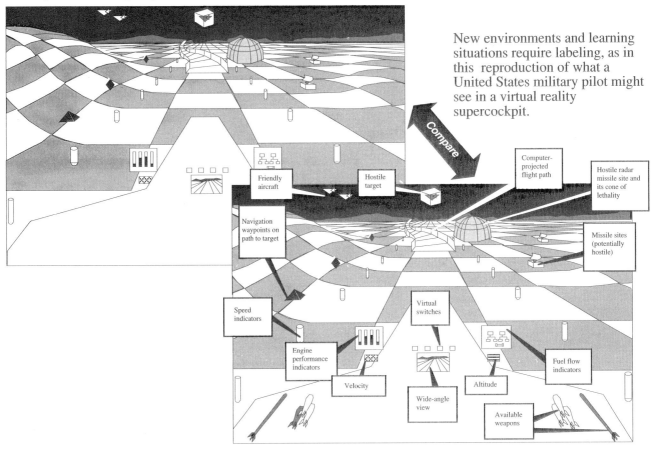

New environments and learning situations require labeling, as in this reproduction of what a United States military pilot might see in a virtual reality supercockpit.

Compare

Friendly aircraft

Hostile target

Computer-projected flight path

Hostile radar missile site and its cone of lethality

Navigation waypoints on path to target

Missile sites (potentially hostile)

Speed indicators

Virtual switches

Fuel flow indicators

Engine performance indicators

Velocity

Wide-angle view

Altitude

Available weapons

Show Which (Definitions)

(__) is a
(__) with a
(__)

**Shows or tells how to identify something
using words alone.**

Definitions are used to communicate abstract ideas
that cannot be pictured. Thus, they are almost entirely
verbal, except when they refer to picturable objects.
When a definition becomes very complex, however, a
graphic structure can help to display it. Here is an
example taken from law of graphical display of a
complex definition.

Example: Visual ordering of a complicated definition

Definition: Tort
Torts refer to "wrongful acts, injury or damage for which a civil action can be brought."

A Tort is …

    … one or more of the following types of acts:

Battery
or
False imprisonment
or
Malicious prosecution
or
Trespass to land
or
Interference to chattels
or
Interference with advantageous relations
or
Misrepresentation
or
Defamation

Type of act

    … and either or both …

Malicious intent
and/or
Negligence

**"Motivation and/or
irresponsibility of defendant"**

    … and …

Causal nexus (i.e., the wrongful act must
be the cause of the plaintiff's injury)

**"Proven connection between
defendant's wrongful act and
injury claimed by plaintiff"**

    … and either or both …

Consent
or
Reasonable risk by plaintiff
or
Privilege
or
Breach of contract

**"Agreements and
responsibilities of defendant
and plaintiff before and during
the act"**

174

Show Examples

Shows or tells about instances of a general category or idea

The example relationship is one of the easiest, most fundamental, and most unconscious human processes. Examples are integral to the ability to categorize, that is, to place a group of specimens into a single category by virtue of overall similarity to each other or to some prototype, or because of the presence of one or more properties or attributes.

Examples enable readers (or listeners) to more easily comprehend abstractions and incorporate them into their mental models. In some books, half or more of the text may be classified as examples. Examples can be expressed through words alone, but visual elements may aid comprehension. Generally, strictly visual examples perform the same purpose as verbal ones.

Example

This visual serves as an example of the principle being discussed. It conveys an idea quickly and reminds the reader of the details stated in the conceptual sentence at top.

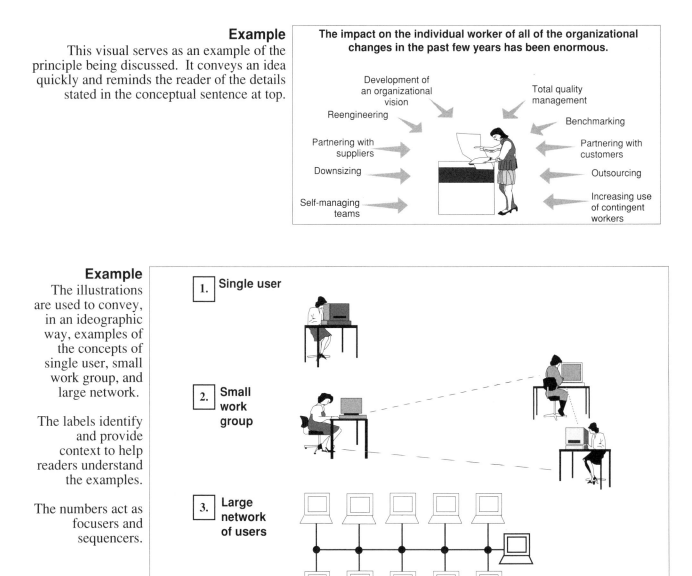

Example

The illustrations are used to convey, in an ideographic way, examples of the concepts of single user, small work group, and large network.

The labels identify and provide context to help readers understand the examples.

The numbers act as focusers and sequencers.

Example

Hypermedia permits the learner to move along links between related documents, video, and other media, a process illustrated here by a course in Shakespeare.

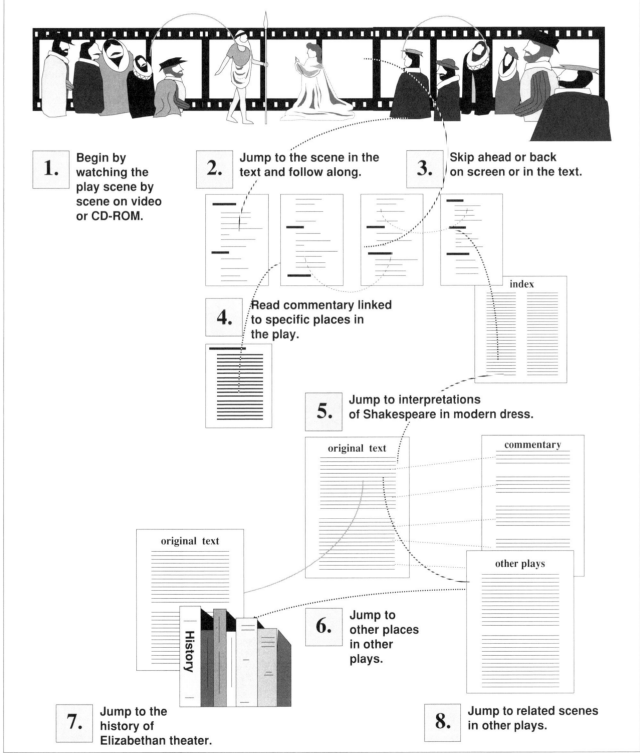

1. Begin by watching the play scene by scene on video or CD-ROM.

2. Jump to the scene in the text and follow along.

3. Skip ahead or back on screen or in the text.

index

4. Read commentary linked to specific places in the play.

5. Jump to interpretations of Shakespeare in modern dress.

original text

commentary

original text

other plays

History

6. Jump to other places in other plays.

7. Jump to the history of Elizabethan theater.

8. Jump to related scenes in other plays.

Show What Can't Be Seen

Shows or tells forces, relationships, and other influences that cannot be perceived with the naked eye

Invisible forces can only be seen by instruments or inferred from data collected by different observational procedures. They can, however, be represented with conventions of visual language. In addition, many conceptual ideas are invisible yet representable through visual means. Various shapes and lines can show radiation, relationship, force, and influence.

Example: Satellite transmission

Directed beams such as those in satellite transmission are often represented by lines, usually by a dotted or patterned line.

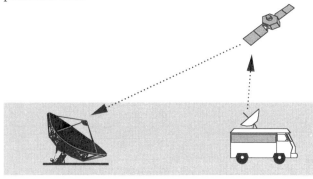

Example: Wave-form patterns of electromagnetic radiation

The example shows wave-form patterns of electromagnetic radiation displayed on a computer screen. Such patterns are obviously difficult to describe in purely verbal form. At the same time, however, they are largely meaningless unless accompanied by words that clarify the context.

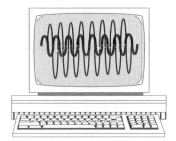

Example: X-Rays

Electromagnetic rays themselves are often represented with dotted lines, in contrast to the electromagnetic wave forms, which are generally shown on computer screens (see previous example).

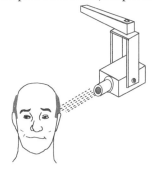

Example: Radio or television broadcast waves

Radio waves move out from the antenna in concentric circles.

Example: Weather patterns

Until the appearance of satellite photography, weather patterns could not usually be seen because of their large size. But they were nevertheless conceptualized and presented in diagrams based on inferences from data such as temperature and air pressure.

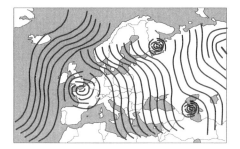

Show Comparisons

Shows or tells how things are similar and different

A fundamental quality of thinking is the ability to discriminate, that is, to show that something is different from, or similar to, other things. We are always comparing similarities and differences, on the micro level to identify properties, and on the macro level to sort things into classes.

In visual language, comparison is facilitated by the use of side-by-side alignment of words, shapes, and objects. Any property may be important for comparison. Size, for example, is frequently shown visually.

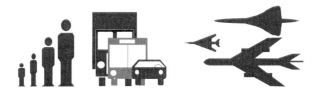

Tables and spreadsheets are most frequently used to show quantitative data comparisons.

Age and Skill

Age	Average skill level
21–25	15
26–30	35
31–35	10
36–40	25

Non-numerical tables permit easy comparison of nonquantitative factors.

Model	Transmission	Color
Sedan	manual, automatic	black, white, red, gray
Racer	manual only	red

Shapes can occupy the cells of the tables in order to show the presence or absence of a factor.

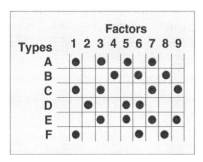

Other shapes can represent evaluations, as in the "+" and "-" in the following table.

Options	Factors					
	1	2	3	4	5	6
A	+	-	+	-	+	+
B	+	-	-	-	+	-
C	+	-	+	+	+	+
D	+	-	+	+	-	+

Images can appear in the headers and stubs of tables ...

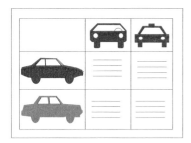

... or in the cells of tables.

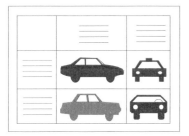

178

Show Quantitative Comparisons

Shows or tells how amounts, trends, proportions, etc., can be visually examined and compared

The portrayal of quantitative information forms a whole branch or vocabulary of visual language. Quantitative charts and graphs amplify the power to communicate numerical information such as percentage, quantity, trend, and rank, because they provide a comparative context against which to judge the importance of the information.

These pages catalog some of the most common types of graphs and charts. However, there are well over 100 major types of such charts, and some say there are over 1,000 possible variants—far too many to treat in detail except in a specialized treatise. Suffice it to say that they all qualify as tightly integrated, word–shape units of communication.

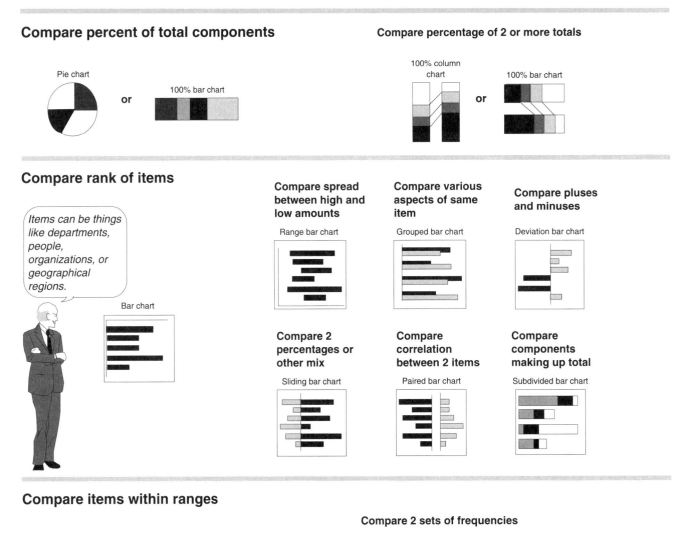

Compare percent of total components

Pie chart or 100% bar chart

Compare percentage of 2 or more totals

100% column chart or 100% bar chart

Compare rank of items

Items can be things like departments, people, organizations, or geographical regions.

Bar chart

Compare spread between high and low amounts

Range bar chart

Compare various aspects of same item

Grouped bar chart

Compare pluses and minuses

Deviation bar chart

Compare 2 percentages or other mix

Sliding bar chart

Compare correlation between 2 items

Paired bar chart

Compare components making up total

Subdivided bar chart

Compare items within ranges

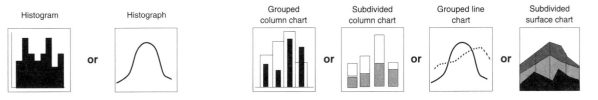

Histogram or Histograph

Compare 2 sets of frequencies

Grouped column chart or Subdivided column chart or Grouped line chart or Subdivided surface chart

Compare changes over time

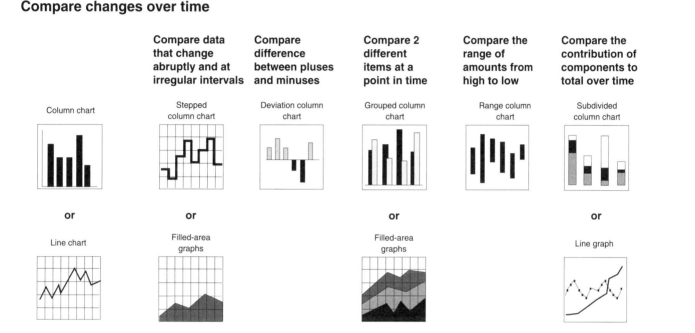

Compare data that change abruptly and at irregular intervals

Compare difference between pluses and minuses

Compare 2 different items at a point in time

Compare the range of amounts from high to low

Compare the contribution of components to total over time

Column chart

Stepped column chart

Deviation column chart

Grouped column chart

Range column chart

Subdivided column chart

or

or

or

or

Line chart

Filled-area graphs

Filled-area graphs

Line graph

Compare patterns of relationships between 2 or more variables

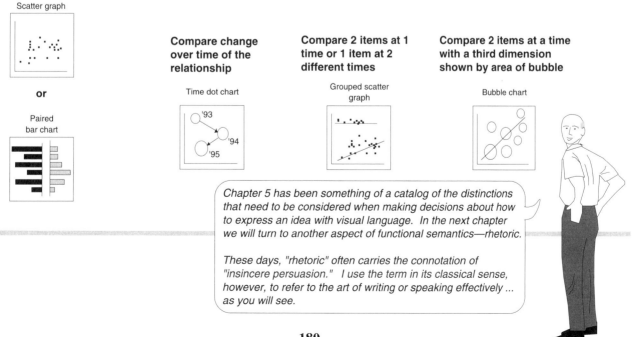

Scatter graph

or

Paired bar chart

Compare change over time of the relationship

Time dot chart

'93
'94
'95

Compare 2 items at 1 time or 1 item at 2 different times

Grouped scatter graph

Compare 2 items at a time with a third dimension shown by area of bubble

Bubble chart

Chapter 5 has been something of a catalog of the distinctions that need to be considered when making decisions about how to express an idea with visual language. In the next chapter we will turn to another aspect of functional semantics—rhetoric.

These days, "rhetoric" often carries the connotation of "insincere persuasion." I use the term in its classical sense, however, to refer to the art of writing or speaking effectively ... as you will see.

Chapter 6
Functional Semantics of Rhetoric

This chapter continues the discussion of functional semantics, which began in chapter 5 with a discussion of the functional semantics of content. This chapter focuses on rhetoric, which is defined as elements of documents that are used primarily for navigation and organization and that are intended to influence the reader's attitude in various ways.

Visual language provides integrated alternatives to strictly prose or strictly visual approaches to such rhetorical problems.

Two levels of analysis
I will again use a two-level analysis of functions. The first identifies and delineates the rhetorical functions themselves.

The second compares how each function may be best performed by words and visual elements working together. On occasion I will contrast this tightly integrated approach with attempts to communicate the same or similar messages with words alone.

Dual-use elements
As I have mentioned, more than one semantic function is often performed simultaneously by a single visual or visual-verbal element. This chapter provides examples of some of the more interesting dual-use elements.

func • tion • al   se • man • tics   */n/*
The study of the purpose for the inclusion of each element in a visual language communication unit. Hence, the study of what job each unit is doing.

rhe • tor • ic   */n/*
1. originally, the study of the means of persuasion in verbal discourse. **2.** the study of the methods and means of communication. **3.** recently has come to mean empty, false.

rhe • tor • i • cal   func • tions   */n/*
Those parts and properties of a communication unit that communicate directions, instructions, organizational messages, or emphasis and tone to a reader.

Contents of Chapter 6

Guide Readers Through Document

Shows or tells the reader how the document is organized and provides landmarks for maintaining orientation to the subject

see page > 5

"Navigation" is one of the most common current metaphors for thinking about how to get through masses of information. The term has been applied to large-scale online databases as well as to complex paper documents. Originally performed almost exclusively with words, information navigation now frequently uses visual language.

Visual language answers questions about where a reader is in a document or database. It is used to convey the locations of links and other references. It is also used to convey the structure of the document itself. These days, navigational elements such as these are quite frequently tight combinations of words, shapes, and images.

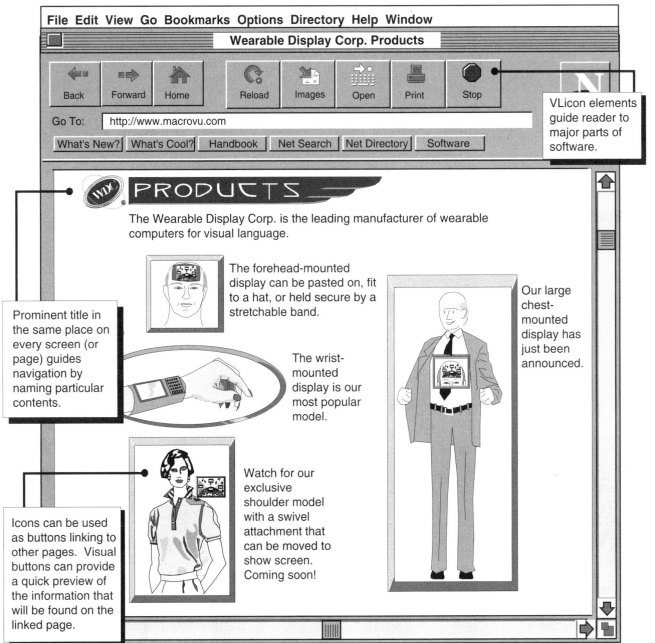

File Edit View Go Bookmarks Options Directory Help Window

Wearable Display Corp. Products

Back Forward Home Reload Images Open Print Stop

Go To: http://www.macrovu.com

What's New? What's Cool? Handbook Net Search Net Directory Software

VLicon elements guide reader to major parts of software.

PRODUCTS

The Wearable Display Corp. is the leading manufacturer of wearable computers for visual language.

The forehead-mounted display can be pasted on, fit to a hat, or held secure by a stretchable band.

Our large chest-mounted display has just been announced.

Prominent title in the same place on every screen (or page) guides navigation by naming particular contents.

The wrist-mounted display is our most popular model.

Icons can be used as buttons linking to other pages. Visual buttons can provide a quick preview of the information that will be found on the linked page.

Watch for our exclusive shoulder model with a swivel attachment that can be moved to show screen. Coming soon!

Example: Arrows and icons link pages in document

Traditional devices used to help readers understand the structure of the document and to guide them through it have always been both visual and verbal (e.g., isolating page numbers [the verbal element] in specific locations on a page [the visual element]). As the complexity of documents and subject matter has increased, new visual elements have been introduced to show in various ways linkages to other sections of a document. In this example, icons and arrows are used to guide readers to more information about the topic. In nonvisual versions, the links usually appear in phrases such as "for more information, see chapter 3." Of course, the tabs in this example also help readers navigate.

Example: Repetitive visual cues

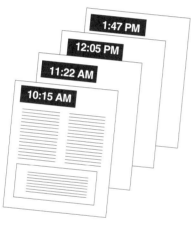

In a minute-by-minute scenario, the digital clock in the upper-left-hand corner of each page shows readers what time it is in the scenario and cues them that a new moment or event is taking place. Both the placement and the use of the digital clock image make this an effective visual language element. In a nonvisual version, words such as "At 10:15 a.m." would simply appear in the text with few or no visual orientation devices.

Example: Prerequisite chart

A map of the prerequisite arrangement of subject matter is a useful tool. In schematic form, this chart shows that *A* must be understood before *B, C,* or *D* can be learned. After learning *E,* the reader can go to *F* or *G*. In a more realistic chart, actual topics would be substituted for the letters.

Focus Attention

Shows or tells the reader that different areas of the page should be given special kinds of attention

Visual language writers undertake to direct the reader's eye. A class of visual elements called "focusers" has emerged, along with techniques for applying them, to facilitate management of reader's attention.

> **fo • cus • ers** /n/
> Small, discrete visual elements used to organize smaller areas of the page or display screen to attract readers' attention, if only for a momentary pause at a specific place, or to delineate a collection of objects or text.

Focusers are often used together with clustering and other devices (such as color) to serve the vital function of guiding the reader's eye.

Prose versions of focusers

In the absence of visual tools such as focusers, prose equivalents of focusers appear frequently in phrases such as:
- "This is important."
- "There are 4 of these."
- "The reader is advised to pay close attention to ..."
- "Notice ..." or "Note ..."
- "Examine ..." or "Watch for ..."

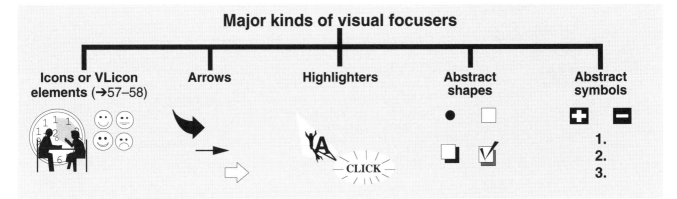

Major kinds of visual focusers

Icons or VLicon elements (→57–58)   Arrows   Highlighters   Abstract shapes   Abstract symbols

Example: Using arrows as focusers

In this schematic of a page on which arrows act as focusers, notice that the arrows make our eyes look at specific places. Because of the pattern of the blocks of text, the arrows also help cluster the information into eight chunks.

What are the Goals of the Project?

Example: Using abstract symbols as focusers

This schematic illustrates the use of symbols to:

1. act as focuser

2. convey some meaning (i.e., favorable ✚ versus unfavorable ▬ rating)

3. visually cluster (→187–188) elements on the page.

Note that all 3 functions are performed simultaneously.

Should We Buy the Equipment?

Example: Focusers on a Web page

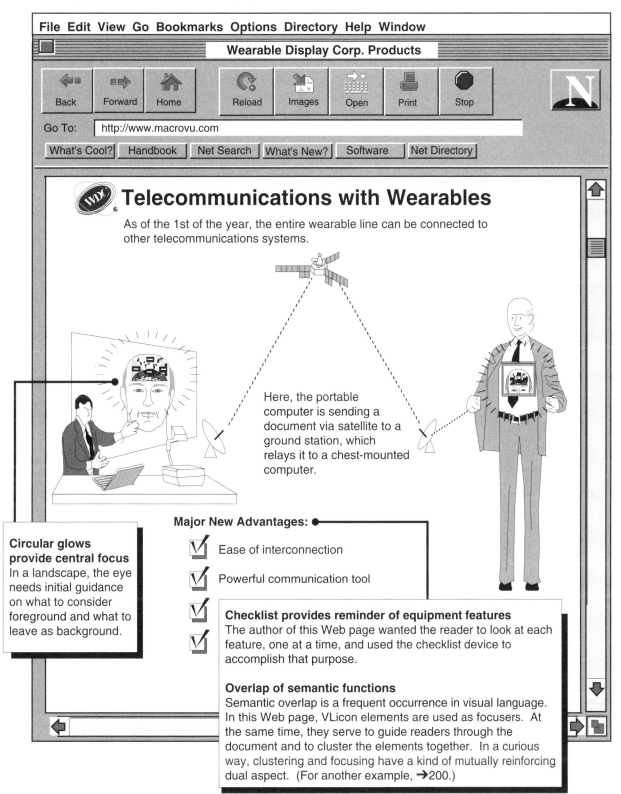

Cluster Visual and Verbal Elements

Shows or tells the reader what elements belong together or are connected in some way

Clustering is emerging as one of the most useful visual language techniques for managing complexity. The Gestalt perceptual principles that explain the effectiveness of clustering are discussed in depth in chapter 3. In short, however, cluster diagrams make use of Gestalt principles such as proximity, which describes how elements that exist in close physical relationship to one another can be easily understood, without conscious effort, to be related.

Chunking for short-term memory

The necessity of clustering in part results from the limitations of human short-term memory. (→237) Chunking enables us to overcome those limits by allowing us to see several bits of information as if they were one chunk. For example, on the facing page, we see each of the cluster diagrams as a single unit, as well as being able to focus in on single elements.

Prose treatments

Even prose does not escape clustering, as exhibited in the variety of purely prose ways to express the grouping of ideas:
- "All of the following belong together …"
- "Can be grouped …"
- "Can be divided into …"
- "Fit the following categories …"
- "Are connected by …"
- "Have been organized into …"

Major types

The two-dimensional rendering of clusters yields a limited number of kinds of devices, a topic that is treated more extensively in chapter 3. Here we provide only a reminder to the reader of the major types of cluster diagrams.

clus • ter /n/ /v/
1. /n/ any one of the shapes used to group other words, shapes, and images. **2.** /n/ the use of clustering has produced a branch of diagrams called cluster diagrams. (→127) **3.** /v/ the use of shapes and assemblies of shapes to group visual and verbal elements on a page or display screen.

Example: Mandalas radiate information out from central point

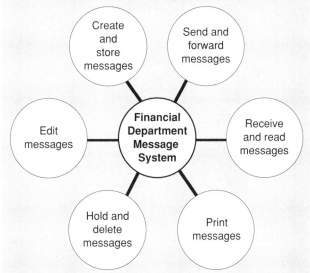

Major types of visual clustering devices

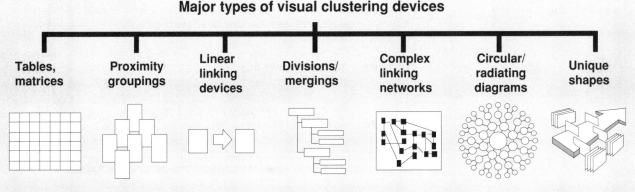

| Tables, matrices | Proximity groupings | Linear linking devices | Divisions/ mergings | Complex linking networks | Circular/ radiating diagrams | Unique shapes |

Example: Treelike structures show classification, division, choices, and mergings

Simple organization and structure charts can be thought of as one form of clustering. They group similar units together based on size and shape and connect them with lines to show specific relationships.

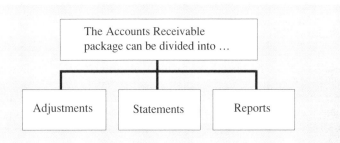

Example: Unique shapes and proximity produce cluster diagrams

Sometimes different clustering devices can be used in conjunction with one another. In this example, the up and down arrows function to separate out or divide elements. At the same time, the way they are placed on the page clusters the messages into a group.

In addition, the learned meaning of the unique shape of the arrows reinforces the concepts of "increase" or "decrease" (➔98) that are presented or implied by the words.

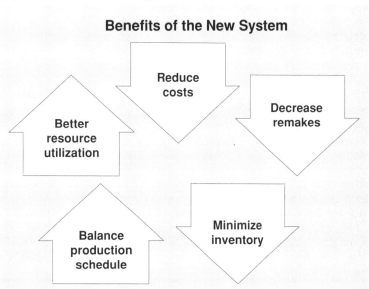

Example: Three-dimensional shapes

Initially created for the two-dimensional world, clusters have recently graduated to the world of 3 dimensions. Virtual reality and other computerized graphic programs enable creators to design "spaces" that organize complex concepts and relationships.

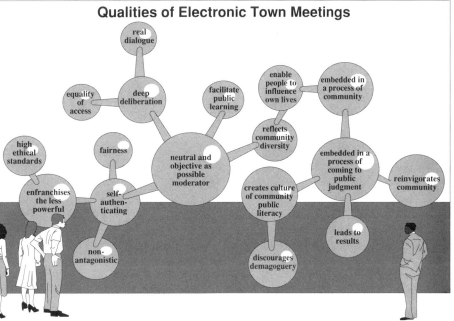

Organize Overall Page (or Screen) Design

Shows or tells the reader how the major parts of a page or screen are organized

Document designers have long manipulated blocks of text in a variety of ways to bring a sense of visual order to pages of print and to computer display screens. Empty, or "white" space, pure shapes, and other visual elements are also used to organize overall page design. These visual elements group, link, delineate, and show relationships; they also guide the eye and focus attention. In short, they organize the overall page design to help the reader manage information. The discipline of page layout and document design is part of a distinct field, which is sometimes called information design. (➔237–238) The most common design tools for page organization are surveyed on these pages.

Evolution of page design

Before books evolved into their present form, a process that began in the 12th century, nearly all text was run together in one long chunk. Gradually, however, book designers began using shapes, blocks of text, and other visual elements to group (i.e., to separate and link) and to organize ideas on the page. These page design techniques are some of the earliest examples of the tight integration of words and visual elements that is much more common today.

Blocks of type for columns and paragraphs

Among the earliest and most frequently encountered methods of chunking, or grouping, information is the division of text into paragraphs and columns.

The dependence of prose communication on paragraphs as a primary organizational tool has caused prose to suffer from lack of precision in its organization. The absence of frequent, systematic, and informative headings in paragraphs makes rapid scanning for key ideas more difficult, as does the fact that there is little agreement as to exactly what a paragraph consists of—about the only element common to all paragraphs is the white space between them. The labeling and display of structured information blocks with systematic headings has begun to solve this problem.

Prose treatments

Various rhetorical devices are used in writing to divide text into comprehensible units and to aid the reader in organizing them.

Organizing for the reader
- "I will take up 3 topics in this chapter …"
- "My first topic is …"

Itemizing parts of the topic
- "I call this concept …"
- "There are 4 subparts, each of which has a catch phrase …"
- "The next thing I will take up is *x,* which in the jargon of the field is known as *y.*"

Calling attention to parts of the discourse
- "I call this topic …"
- "First, I want to introduce …"
- "Now I will give you some background on …"
- "Let me summarize what I've stated so far …"
- "Next …"
- "Thus …"

Clustering the topics
- "I am going to put this topic in a four-by-four matrix. The left axis is …"
- "This is really a hierarchy or outline. I'll describe it for you …"
- "The network of beginning and ending events is pretty complicated, but if we take it slowly we can get the picture."

Visual shapes, shading, white/gray space

Boxes (or sidebars) on a page of text have become great favorites of designers for separating out a specific topic from the main flow of the text. Modern readers of magazines have become accustomed to reading in chunks and understanding that it is their task put together information from different sidebars, captions, and parts of the text.

Other shapes, such as the ellipsis and rectangles below, can be used to divide a block of text from the rest of the page. Such shapes take advantage of the Gestalt principle of common regions (➔75–76) to guide the reader's eye.

Document designers use white space to provide a background against which the foreground of the text is set off, manipulating the Gestalt principle of proximity. (➔75–76)

Some critics charge visual language with using too little white space, which they say results in a "crowded" look. I suspect that this criticism will fade after the current transition period from prose to visual language is completed.

Titles, headings, and subheads

Headings and titles on pages provide the reader with guideposts for scanning and browsing, as well as visually breaking up the text. However, relevance and consistency are required if such headings are to truly aid the reader. In particular, headings that merely seduce the reader by offering a juicy advertising message rather than a succinct summary of content do more harm than good, particularly in a world of information overload.

Grids

In this century, document designers have emphasized the use of an underlying grid or framework to organize pages. Grids provide a kind of predictability (and, hence, reliability) to the form of the page. Predictability, it is asserted, reassures readers and possibly also conveys a metamessage of objectivity. Current graphic design guidelines often require communication units to be smaller or larger than their importance warrants in order to fit the grid. Such requirements can easily result in distorted content and meaning. Full visual language uses grids somewhat less frequently than current graphic design guidelines suggest in order to facilitate the required integration.

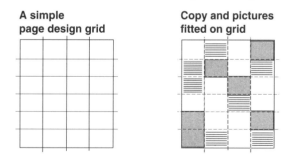

A simple page design grid   **Copy and pictures fitted on grid**

Specific clustering devices

A great many more clustering and focusing devices are relied upon heavily by document designers to accomplish page design and organization. This is another instance of dual-use elements: For example, a cluster diagram can be used on a page both to connect related elements and to imbue the page as a whole with an organized structure. Some of these devices, including the ones listed below, are treated elsewhere in this book. (➔77–80)

Show Context of Concepts

Orients the reader to the situation and the document in which the current message plays a part

Many prose phrases signal the need for or the description of context:
- "We must understand this in terms of …"
- "In the context of …"
- "Against the background of …"

With visual language, context can be, at least in part, instantly communicated via the visual elements that are a part of the page or display screen.

Example: Showing the context of a computer system

Visual elements can be used to show how other subunits fit into a larger conceptual or physical scheme. Visual illustration of the interconnection of 2 networks in a company provides the context for understanding the details of the complex idea of "our company's 2 networks."

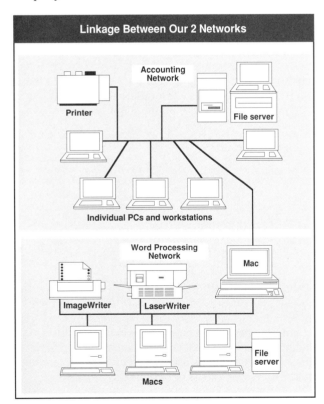

Linkage Between Our 2 Networks

Accounting Network

Printer

File server

Individual PCs and workstations

Word Processing Network

Mac

ImageWriter   LaserWriter

File server

Macs

This book frequently makes use of this context-providing function. For example, the discussion of information murals in Egypt (→26) included this illustration. The size of the tourists looking at the mural communicates, at first glance, its tremendous size. No further textual context is necessary.

And again, in this book's discussions of VLicon elements as they are used in computer interfaces, the examples are always situated on drawings of computer screens. Thus, at first glance, the reader has complete information about the VLicon element's context—it appears on a computer screen, not on a book page.

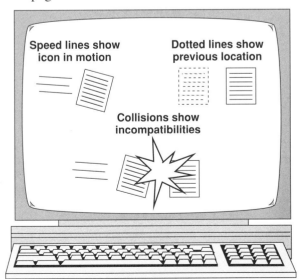

Speed lines show icon in motion

Dotted lines show previous location

Collisions show incompatibilities

Context can be thought of as a web of linked relationships that together enable the reader to understand the communication unit. The schematic diagram on this page catalogs many of the questions whose answers help determine context. Of course, not every question is answerable for every communication unit. The flip side is also true: The questions listed here by no means exhaust the possibilities where investigation of context is concerned.

Context of the subject matter

- What are the major questions asked?
- What are the major ways the subject matter is organized?
- What are the major components and how do they fit together into larger wholes?
- Who has an interest in the subject and why?

Context of the organization

- Stakeholders of organization
- Issue history
- Professional discipline
- The setting (i.e., purpose of presentation)
- Previous work done in this area and published or distributed
- Relation to the rest of the organization's mission and current niche in the organizational ecology.

Context of the document

- Title of document
- Table of contents
- Index
- Introduction by author stating purpose/audience
- Title on page itself
- Pages preceding and following
- Titles and subheadings
- Overview of chapter/section
- Links to other pages
- Glossary

Context of the reader

- How does this fit into my life?
- What are my objectives?
- What do I need to know to understand this?
- What are the relationships, forces, tasks, and so forth that bear on this issue?
- What does that mean for me?

Context of the interactive system

- Where am I?
- Where have I been?
- What can I do next (including where can I go next)?
- If I do any of these things, what will happen?
- What just happened?
- What is happening now?
- What equipment is being used?

Visual representation of context proves to be a difficult puzzle. Any readers who find a solution are encouraged to share it!

Provide Lightness, Humor, and Irony

Shapes attitudes of readers

The humorous or ironic view is often the main attraction in visual language communications like editorial cartoons. Often humor can be used to set a tone, or to leaven an otherwise rather dull presentation of subject matter. Like other forms of impact, humor can occur in both pure prose and in visual art without words.

Sometimes the words are neutral (or nonhumorous), and the addition of humorous visual elements creates the humor. On the other hand, the visual elements may be neutral, and the words add the lightness and humor. Of course, both may reinforce each other in enhancing the lightness of the message.

Example: Visual reinforces verbal

In this example, the visual elements reinforce the verbal elements' lighthearted treatment of the subject of information browsing.

Browsing as grazing
Some observers have described information grazing—a kind of slow-motion browsing in which the user simply meanders along, munching on whatever information is at hand.

information*uuuuuuuuuuuuuuuu*

Example: Humorous commentary

In this example, the verbal element provides a factual distinction. The communication unit as a whole becomes a commentary about moving through large amounts of material when the humorous visual is added.

Browsing is skimming, usually quickly, over large amounts of text to find regions of interest. We distinguish browsing from referencing, which is the search for very specific information or places that are known to exist.

ZAP!   ZING!   wow!

Example: Unusual juxtapositions

In this example, motivation is illustrated by its opposite, in a kind of whimsical visual comment on the otherwise neutral verbal definition.

Motivational awareness is defined as the ability to monitor motivation in learning so as to conduct learning under the best circumstances possible.

z Z Z Z

Example:
Lightness reinforces impact

In this example, the visual and verbal elements reinforce each other to strengthen the impact. Either element on its own would contain less meaning than is contained in the combination of the 2 into a single communication unit.

What do you think of the air pollution in the city today?

Example:
Neutral visual reinforces verbal humor

In this example, the verbal phrase creates the strong impact. The picture of the lion is neutral, but, with the verbal phrase, begins to appear as if it is a picture of a lion that might have eaten a lazy lion hunter, and, thus, contributes to the humorous impact of the message.

There are no lazy veteran lion hunters.

Example:
Irony

In this example, the visual element is used to have a strong ironic impact upon the reader. We all have had some experiences with so-called customer service departments like this one.

Customer Service Department

How may I help you?

You did WHAT with the disk drive?

Increase Impact

Uses visual techniques to emphasize certain aspects of the message

In prose, readers often encounter attempts by writers to increase the impact of the message and influence judgment. These phrases exemplify such attempts:
- "I can't make this point strongly enough."
- "Despite what you imagine, the facts are ..."
- "I don't want to shape your opinion, but ..."
- "Let me emphasize ..."
- "I want to underline this ..."
- "Pay attention to this next part."

Similar rhetorical moves are made in visual language. Sometimes the visual elements are primarily neutral, and the verbal elements add the impact. In other communication units the verbal elements are neutral, and the visual elements provide the impact. The next 4 pages explore the vocabulary of visual impact.

Overlap in rhetorical functions

Trying to tease out and classify the different kinds of impact is difficult because sometimes a given visual element can be classified as performing more than one function. Performing multiple functions is particularly common when the function is to increase impact. For example, a communicator may choose to increase impact through the use of humor. One criterion that connoisseurs of visual language use to assess elegance is the presence of multiple functions in one element of a communication unit—when the communication unit performs more functions with less ink.

Abstract or three-dimensional shapes. Using purely abstract visual elements to add emphasis works primarily because it manipulates foreground and background elements. A variety of methods exist to make something stand out from its background.

In a general sense, unusual or three-dimensional shapes surrounding, enclosing, holding, or supporting the verbal elements add extra visual impact.

Compare the presentation below with the presentation at the top of the next column. The words in the 2 versions are the same.

> **The benefits of the new system include ...**
>
> Patient registration information readily available
>
> Shared information accessed by all hospital stations
>
> Bed availability status known instantly
>
> Paperwork reduced

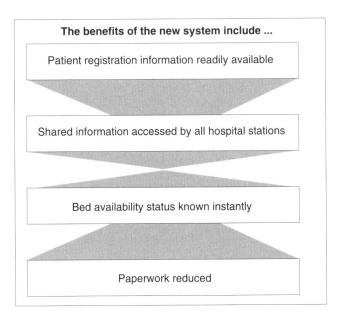

This example provides a striking comparison of the relative impact of a list of words displayed without visual devices (except for the list format) and the same words displayed inside a set of shapes that burst out three-dimensionally. Clearly, it is the visual element that provides the extra impact.

Contrast. Making an element in the foreground different from the background in one or more ways increases impact: for example, light colors on dark background or white on black. Compare the relative impact of these pairs of VLicon elements:

Frame. Because of the Gestalt principle of common region (➔75–76), any kind of line or lines around an object or area makes it stand out from the background.

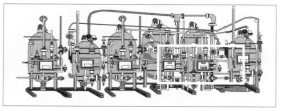

Detail. Showing the element to be emphasized in greater detail than the surrounding objects attracts the eye. Human beings seem to be wired to look first at interesting texture or detail.

Sharpness. Clear outlines and shapes stand out from a background of fuzzy, vague elements.

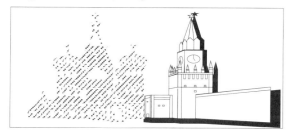

Size. Sheer size differences can create significant emphasis, usually on the larger figure or on the contrast between 2 or more figures.

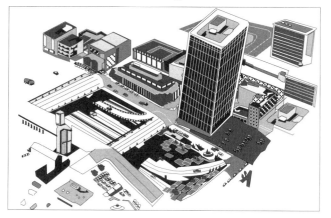

Shape. An unusual or irregular shape surrounding an element attracts the eye and increases impact.

White space. White (or other background color) space around the element to be emphasized will make it stand out from its surroundings. "White space is not wasted space," says the classic design maxim.

Front. If the element to be emphasized is put in front of the other elements, it will usually stand out from its surroundings to command initial attention.

Motion. If the display medium permits animation or live action, the object to receive more attention can be shown in motion.

New products

Arrows. Conventionally, arrows either point at important elements to bring them into focus or are important elements in themselves.

196

Increase Impact (continued)

Strong shadows. The eye is more attracted to elements that have shadows.

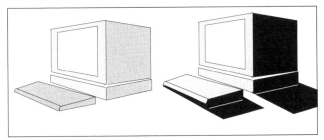

Perspective. In one-point perspective, the eye is drawn to the vanishing point.

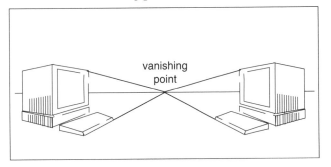

Silhouettes. Another form of visual contrast that increases impact is placement of one element in silhouette in a scene that is otherwise conventionally depicted.

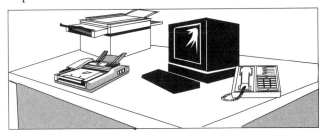

Human Figures. The eye is immediately attracted to human figures. We seem to have an instantaneous kind of curiosity about figures that look like us. Thus, any time a figure remotely resembles a human figure, it focuses attention and may add emphasis and impact in the area in which it is located.

Visuals contrasting with text. Our brains are programmed to notice changes. In a sentence of text, VLicon elements or small illustrations stand out by way of contrast and can be used to increase the impact of the point. This is an example of a more general observation: The only thing of its kind stands out from the rest.

oooooooooooooooXooooooooooooooo

This same principle applies to illustrations placed among larger blocks of text, where they serve as reinforcements, not substitutions. (→101)

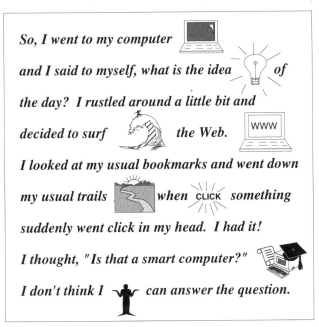

Unusual angle or visual juxtaposition.
Representations in which subjects are seen from an unusual point of view (as in the view from above) or in which 2 elements are juxtaposed in an unfamiliar way (as in the hand coming out of the computer) can add impact to a message.

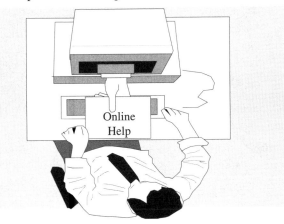

Exaggeration. Making some element oversized or out of place immediately attracts the reader's eye and conveys an attitude. The visual elements in the following example convey a sardonic view of the relatively neutral verbal message.

Some large Web sites use scrolling with few suggestions or signs to tell you where you are or where you are going. It is easy to get lost and it takes considerable mental effort to keep going under such circumstances.

Upper left location. Elements in the upper left corner in Western cultures attract attention to themselves, all other things being equal.

Central locations. The center of a communication unit is also likely to be a visual focus, all other things being equal.

Combinations. Putting together any 2 or more of the techniques for increasing impact described in these 4 pages can magnify effect: (1) framing the object, (2) using human figures, (3) using an unusual shape, and (4) placing it in the middle of the page, for example, should *guarantee* impact.

Manipulate and Operate

Shows or tells the reader how to make something happen to the
- **navigation**
- **point of view**
- **subject matter**
- **outside environment**

Visual language connects to the wider world of interactive computer interfaces in fascinating and only recently emerging ways. Visual language can be used, not only to aid navigation (➔183–184) by guiding readers, but to communicate to users how they may take action—to operate on and manipulate—what is displayed.

The World Wide Web is rife with examples of visual language that tells the reader to manipulate or operate (➔200). First, however, let us examine some examples from other areas of communication. In all of these cases, using visual language to communicate is clearer and more efficient than using words or visual elements alone.

Overlapping functions: An aesthetic principle

This is a good place to point out one of the aesthetic principles that is developing along with the emergence of visual language: Combining several semantic functions in one visual or visual-verbal element is both efficient and pleasing to those who appreciate simplicity and elegance. The arrow used in Web browsers for the "forward" and "backwards" commands is a convenient example. The arrow both guides readers and suggests that they operate (i.e., go forward or backward); thus, the 2 functions overlap. (For more on overlapping functions, ➔186.)

Example: Computer application toolbars

Comprised of icons or VLicon elements, application toolbars show the user what action options are available. Such actions include "draw" (manipulating the subject matter), "print" (the outside environment), and "magnify" (point of view).

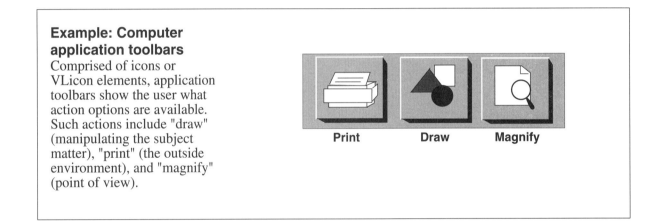

Print   Draw   Magnify

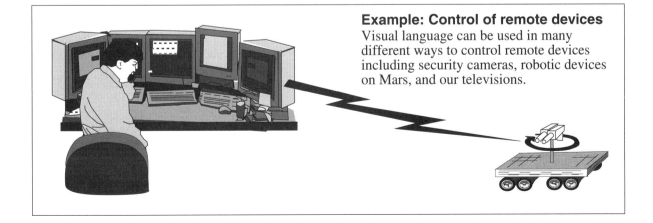

Example: Control of remote devices

Visual language can be used in many different ways to control remote devices including security cameras, robotic devices on Mars, and our televisions.

The navigation buttons encourage the reader to move forward and backward through a site or group of sites.

File Edit View ... Help Window

Wearable Display Corp Products

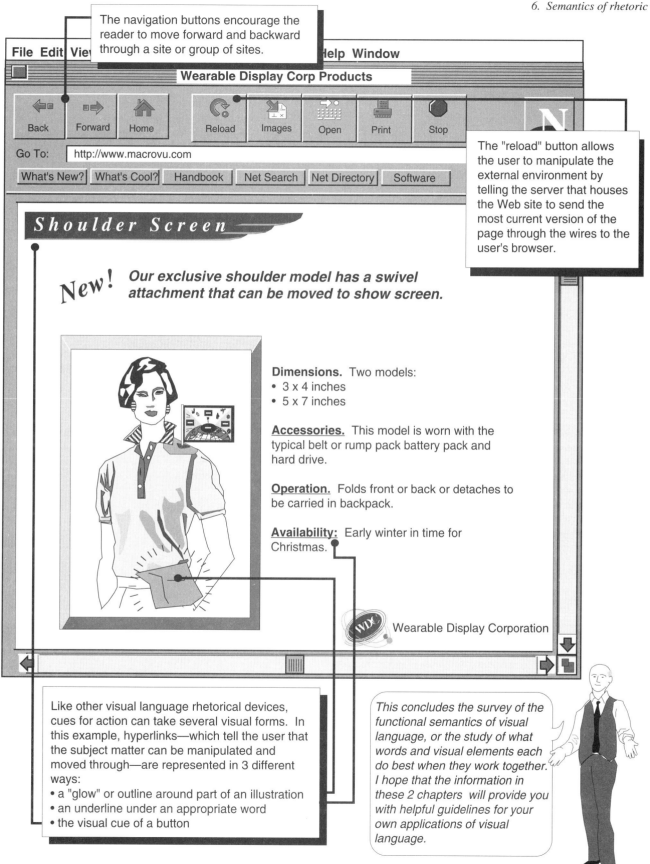

Back   Forward   Home   Reload   Images   Open   Print   Stop

Go To: http://www.macrovu.com

What's New?   What's Cool?   Handbook   Net Search   Net Directory   Software

The "reload" button allows the user to manipulate the external environment by telling the server that houses the Web site to send the most current version of the page through the wires to the user's browser.

Shoulder Screen

New! **Our exclusive shoulder model has a swivel attachment that can be moved to show screen.**

Dimensions. Two models:
• 3 x 4 inches
• 5 x 7 inches

Accessories. This model is worn with the typical belt or rump pack battery pack and hard drive.

Operation. Folds front or back or detaches to be carried in backpack.

Availability: Early winter in time for Christmas.

Wearable Display Corporation

Like other visual language rhetorical devices, cues for action can take several visual forms. In this example, hyperlinks—which tell the user that the subject matter can be manipulated and moved through—are represented in 3 different ways:
• a "glow" or outline around part of an illustration
• an underline under an appropriate word
• the visual cue of a button

This concludes the survey of the functional semantics of visual language, or the study of what words and visual elements each do best when they work together. I hope that the information in these 2 chapters will provide you with helpful guidelines for your own applications of visual language.

Chapter 7

Pragmatics of Visual Language

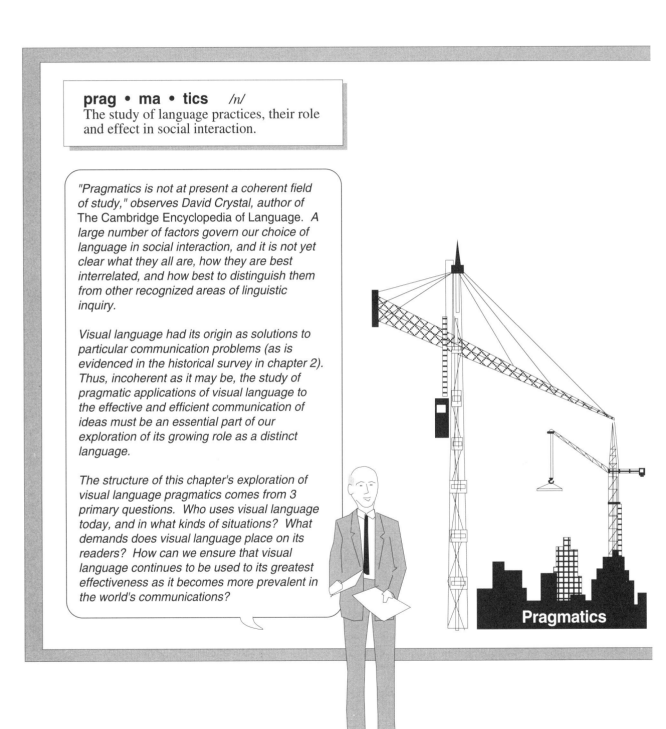

prag • ma • tics /n/
The study of language practices, their role and effect in social interaction.

"Pragmatics is not at present a coherent field of study," observes David Crystal, author of The Cambridge Encyclopedia of Language. A large number of factors govern our choice of language in social interaction, and it is not yet clear what they all are, how they are best interrelated, and how best to distinguish them from other recognized areas of linguistic inquiry.

Visual language had its origin as solutions to particular communication problems (as is evidenced in the historical survey in chapter 2). Thus, incoherent as it may be, the study of pragmatic applications of visual language to the effective and efficient communication of ideas must be an essential part of our exploration of its growing role as a distinct language.

The structure of this chapter's exploration of visual language pragmatics comes from 3 primary questions. Who uses visual language today, and in what kinds of situations? What demands does visual language place on its readers? How can we ensure that visual language continues to be used to its greatest effectiveness as it becomes more prevalent in the world's communications?

Pragmatics

Contents of Chapter 7

Social Context: Where Has Visual Language Become a Basic Communication Tool?

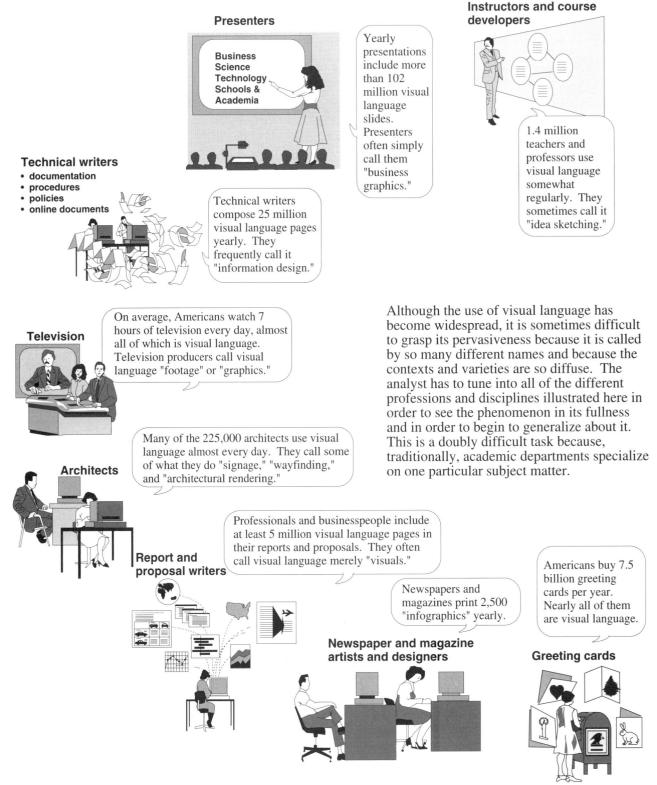

Presenters

Business
Science
Technology
Schools &
Academia

Yearly presentations include more than 102 million visual language slides. Presenters often simply call them "business graphics."

Instructors and course developers

1.4 million teachers and professors use visual language somewhat regularly. They sometimes call it "idea sketching."

Technical writers
- documentation
- procedures
- policies
- online documents

Technical writers compose 25 million visual language pages yearly. They frequently call it "information design."

Television

On average, Americans watch 7 hours of television every day, almost all of which is visual language. Television producers call visual language "footage" or "graphics."

Although the use of visual language has become widespread, it is sometimes difficult to grasp its pervasiveness because it is called by so many different names and because the contexts and varieties are so diffuse. The analyst has to tune into all of the different professions and disciplines illustrated here in order to see the phenomenon in its fullness and in order to begin to generalize about it. This is a doubly difficult task because, traditionally, academic departments specialize on one particular subject matter.

Architects

Many of the 225,000 architects use visual language almost every day. They call some of what they do "signage," "wayfinding," and "architectural rendering."

Report and proposal writers

Professionals and businesspeople include at least 5 million visual language pages in their reports and proposals. They often call visual language merely "visuals."

Newspapers and magazines print 2,500 "infographics" yearly.

Newspaper and magazine artists and designers

Americans buy 7.5 billion greeting cards per year. Nearly all of them are visual language.

Greeting cards

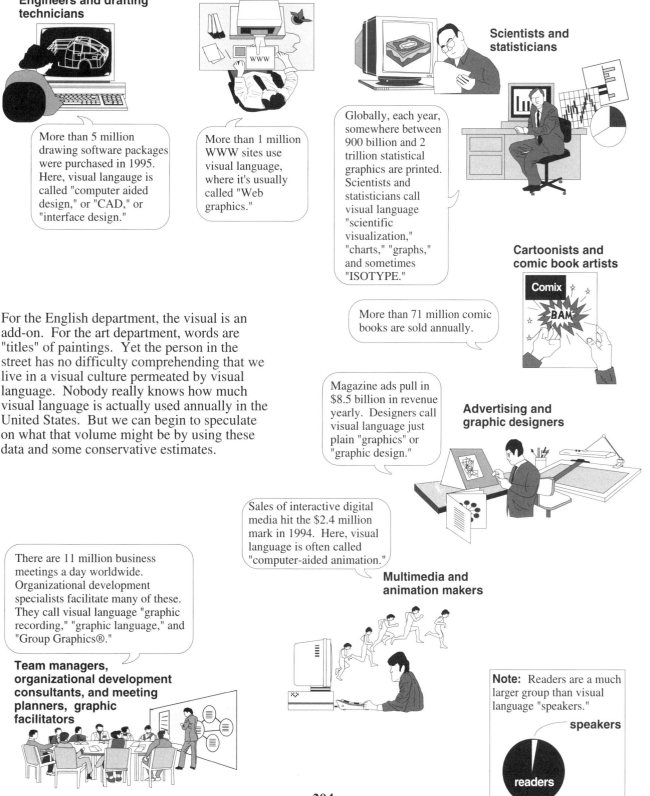

For the English department, the visual is an add-on. For the art department, words are "titles" of paintings. Yet the person in the street has no difficulty comprehending that we live in a visual culture permeated by visual language. Nobody really knows how much visual language is actually used annually in the United States. But we can begin to speculate on what that volume might be by using these data and some conservative estimates.

Visibility and Accessibility of Complex Issues

Increasingly, we are called upon to resolve complex issues and problems. Often it is difficult for a group to come to a common understanding of just what the problems are, let alone develop a process for working together toward their resolution. Using visual language to cooperatively construct an information mural that displays the multiplicity of aspects of the issue on the table encourages a group of problem solvers to stay focused (literally) on the issue as a whole, rather than on those subsets of a particular problem that each individual will tend to emphasize. Visual representation of all aspects of an issue greases the brainstorming process; interconnections or hidden components may be discovered that might have remained hidden had the group members been faced with keeping all the information straight in their heads or in awkward prose reports. Furthermore, keeping the model on display can help keep the group on track as it works toward a resolution.

O.K. Now we've got this group's ideas displayed. We've modeled the dangers inherent in democratic process in the ongoing struggle for power between majority party and opposition and its effect on minority group problems within the state.

As we can all see, the temptation for the majority party is to blame the minority groups. The opposition, in turn, is frequently tempted to object that the majority party is letting the country be broken up. At times, either the majority or the opposition or both resist(s) the temptation to place blame, in which cases the problem is somewhat alleviated. Nonetheless, the process that we have modeled is an ongoing potential danger for any democratic country with a sizable minority ethnic group. We have also modeled the consequences of such struggles. We can all see that, often, the negotiated agreement, at the end of what may be 20 or 30 years of struggle, simply leads back to restoration of ethnic minority rights.

We now agree on the problem. Would the group like to turn its attention to discussing what can be done to prevent this problem from getting worse?

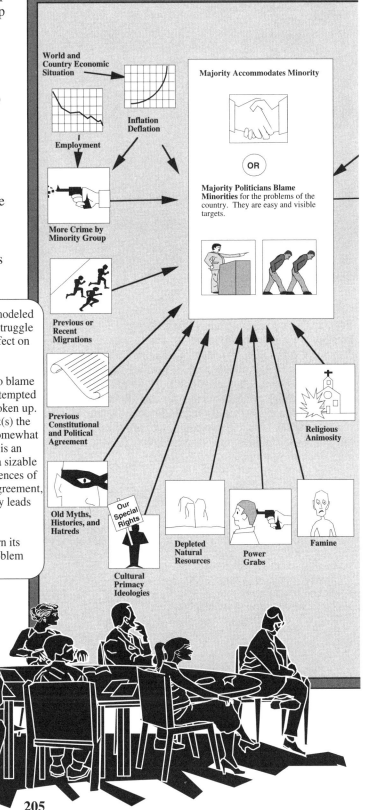

A Model of Majority–Minority Conflict

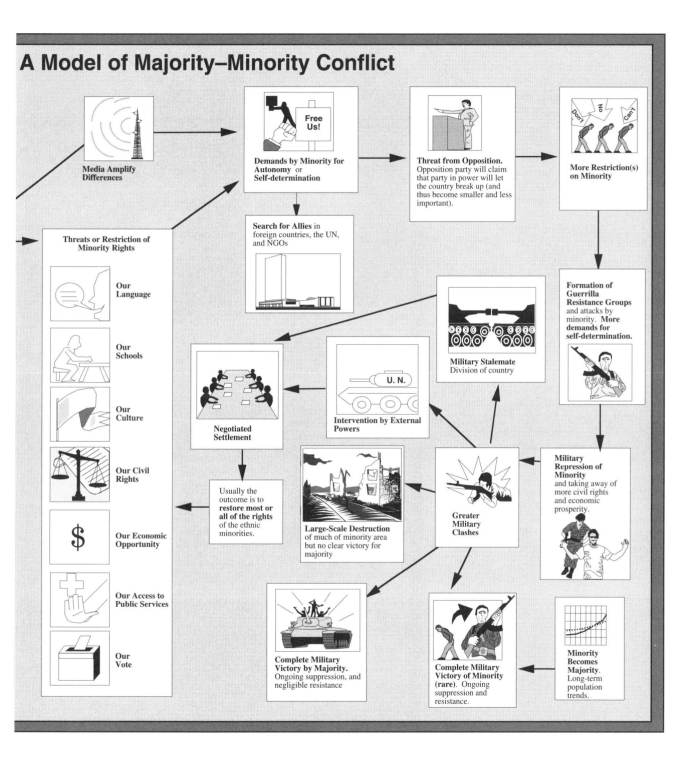

Illumination of Cross-Boundary Issues

The problems we face today seem to be growing more difficult to resolve. The most often-mentioned driver of this phenomenon is increasing complexity. When we talk about complexity, we usually mean the presence of tight interconnections between the social, political, and economic systems within which we lead our lives, and which we are accustomed to thinking of as discrete arenas. In fact, they are deeply intertwined.

In problem-solving situations, too often there is only token acknowledgement of such linkages, as opposed to an attempt to integrate the interconnections into problem definitions and solutions. Too often, a group will examine just one sector, ignoring the cross-sector influences. We may look at the economy or at the public policy issues but neglect to keep in mind the long causal loops between sectors. Without a way to simultaneously keep track of all the data from all the sectors, we disregard the linkages, and our discussions suffer as a result.

Visual language, displayed on information murals, computer screens, or paper, can be used to keep the larger picture at the forefront of any crossboundary discussion.

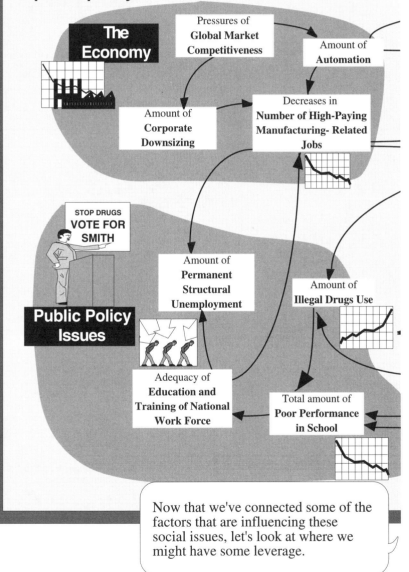

Where is the problem located? In the economy? With parents? Among children? In public policy?

The Economy

Pressures of **Global Market Competitiveness**

Amount of **Automation**

Amount of **Corporate Downsizing**

Decreases in **Number of High-Paying Manufacturing- Related Jobs**

STOP DRUGS
VOTE FOR SMITH

Amount of **Permanent Structural Unemployment**

Amount of **Illegal Drugs Use**

Public Policy Issues

Adequacy of **Education and Training of National Work Force**

Total amount of **Poor Performance in School**

Now that we've connected some of the factors that are influencing these social issues, let's look at where we might have some leverage.

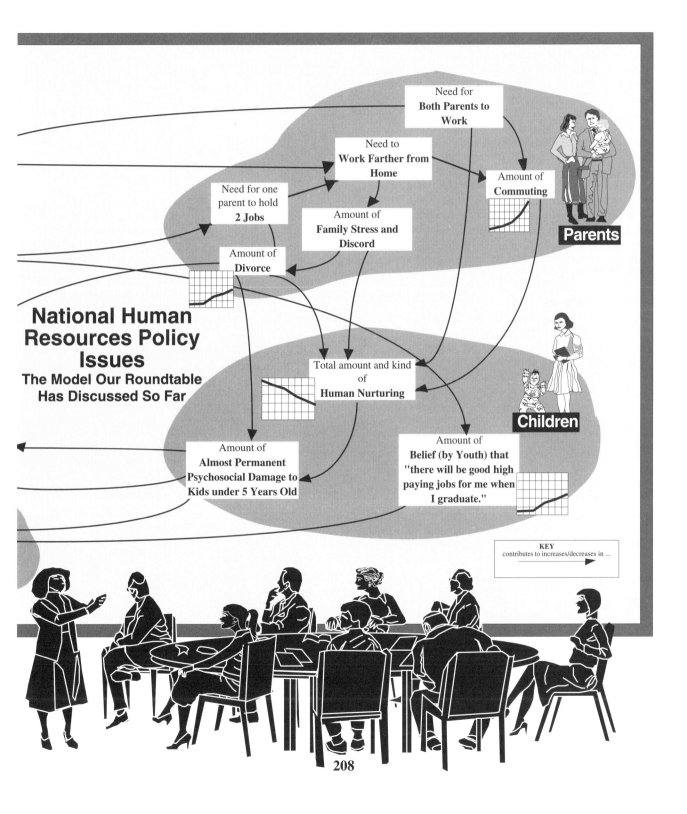

National Human Resources Policy Issues
The Model Our Roundtable Has Discussed So Far

Need for **Both Parents to Work**

Need to **Work Farther from Home**

Need for one parent to hold **2 Jobs**

Amount of **Commuting**

Parents

Amount of **Family Stress and Discord**

Amount of **Divorce**

Total amount and kind of **Human Nurturing**

Children

Amount of **Almost Permanent Psychosocial Damage to Kids under 5 Years Old**

Amount of **Belief (by Youth) that "there will be good high paying jobs for me when I graduate."**

KEY
contributes to increases/decreases in ...

Exploring Deeper Connections and Feelings

Another result of the nature of the cross-boundary environment in which a lot of problem-solving activity takes place is that the problems we address increasingly require the participation of individuals from many different cultures, professions, and civilizations. Success requires each group to find a common language with which they can understand their differences, share visions of the future, adopt common symbols, and empathize with others' difficulties.

Visual language positively impacts the intitial dialogue phase of a problem-solving session, in which participants each get enough "air time" to express the depth of their feelings about the issue on the table. Visual language recording of group members' remarks both legitimizes them by making them a permanent part of the group's visual landscape, and enhances the results of such conversations by making connections between points of view and by highlighting main themes.

Reproduced here are the graphic results of the initial phase of such a discussion. The diagram may be incomprehensible to someone who did not participate in the discussion, but it can help group members form important bonds when they see how their different contributions connect.

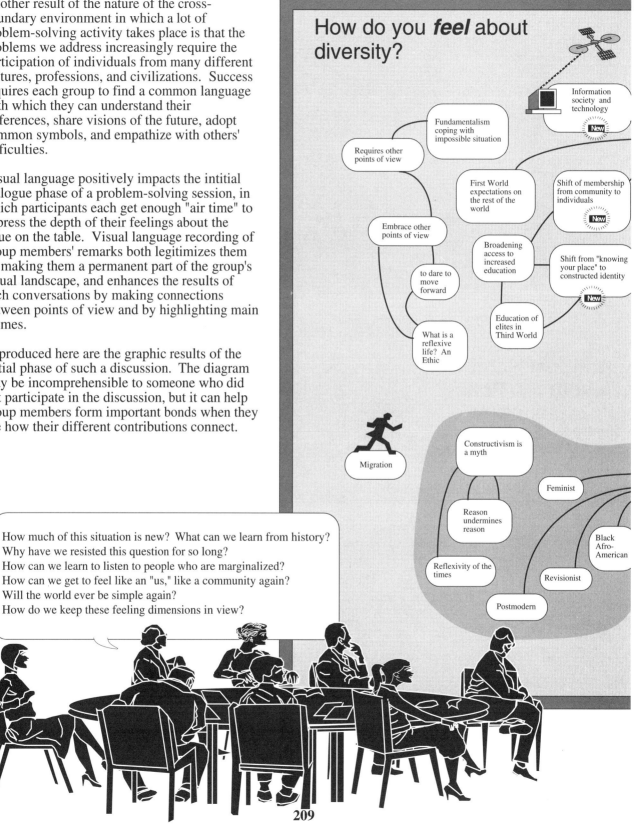

How do you *feel* about diversity?

Information society and technology
New

Fundamentalism coping with impossible situation

Requires other points of view

First World expectations on the rest of the world

Shift of membership from community to individuals
New

Embrace other points of view

Broadening access to increased education

Shift from "knowing your place" to constructed identity
New

to dare to move forward

What is a reflexive life? An Ethic

Education of elites in Third World

Migration

Constructivism is a myth

Feminist

Reason undermines reason

Black Afro-American

Reflexivity of the times

Revisionist

Postmodern

How much of this situation is new? What can we learn from history?
Why have we resisted this question for so long?
How can we learn to listen to people who are marginalized?
How can we get to feel like an "us," like a community again?
Will the world ever be simple again?
How do we keep these feeling dimensions in view?

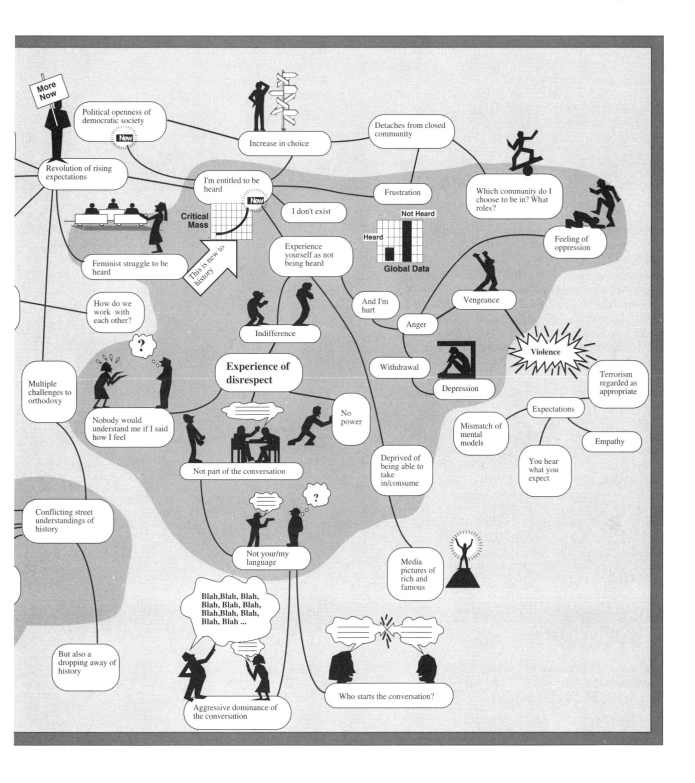

Displaying Problem Analysis

Problem analysis is often complicated by factors such as the existence of multiple points of view and the need to simultaneously examine physical data and invisible relational information.

In such situations, organized visual displays of the relationships and factors that inform the problem are a useful tool.

Over time, literally hundreds of such diagrammatic displays have been developed in different professions and academic disciplines to analyze specific problems. A number of these diagrams, organized by their commonalities, are cataloged here.

Cluster diagrams

Represent abstractly the relationships between elements and are easily modified to express different concepts. Cluster diagrams have a grammar based on similarity, proximity, position, and other Gestalt perception principles.

Area

Point-to-point homologies, along scale, allow displays of relative volumes) and direct semantic

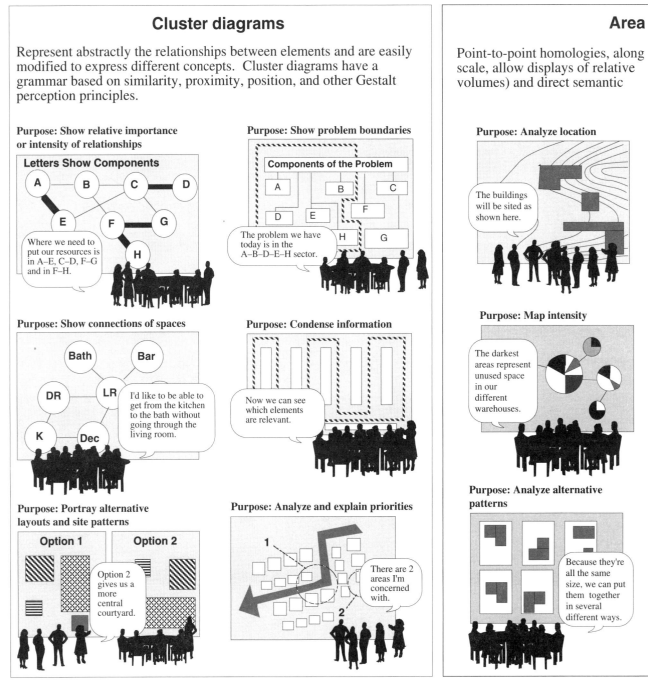

Purpose: Show relative importance or intensity of relationships

Letters Show Components

Where we need to put our resources is in A–E, C–D, F–G and in F–H.

Purpose: Show problem boundaries

Components of the Problem

The problem we have today is in the A–B–D–E–H sector.

Purpose: Analyze location

The buildings will be sited as shown here.

Purpose: Show connections of spaces

I'd like to be able to get from the kitchen to the bath without going through the living room.

Purpose: Condense information

Now we can see which elements are relevant.

Purpose: Map intensity

The darkest areas represent unused space in our different warehouses.

Purpose: Portray alternative layouts and site patterns

Option 1 Option 2

Option 2 gives us a more central courtyard.

Purpose: Analyze and explain priorities

There are 2 areas I'm concerned with.

Purpose: Analyze alternative patterns

Because they're all the same size, we can put them together in several different ways.

211

diagrams

with explicit or implicit sizes (e.g., widths, areas, or read-out.

Purpose: Discover trends

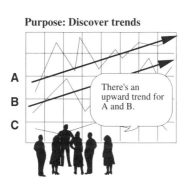

Purpose: Show volume and direction of flow

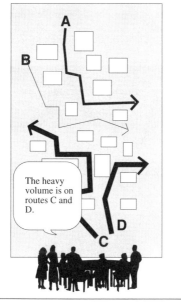

Matrices

Tabular syntax displays information for side-by-side comparison.

Purpose: Classify problems, compare relationships, and show solutions

Purpose: Compare options

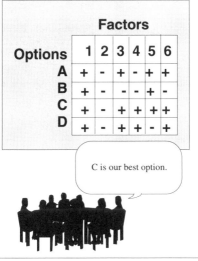

Network diagrams

Branching syntax connects and displays time-linked or logically linked information for portrayal of choices or alternative scenarios.

Purpose: Analyze decisions

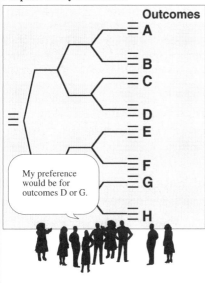

Purpose: Show event precedence and critical event paths

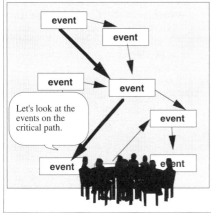

Creative Problem Solving

Most people attack problem solving only within their own brains, without ever representing any part of the problem-solving process outside their own craniums. Even teachers of creative problem-solving courses frequently miss the value than can be gleaned from visually representing solutions or parts of solutions as they emerge. Such externalization gives the mind more stable, albeit interim, data with which to work. Creativity is not a linear process. It has many loops and feedbacks, the productivity of which depend on initial and continual externalization of the creative problem-solving process.

The American graphic designer and educator Robert McKim (→48) introduced the distinction between producing complete pieces of art, the work of artists, and using visual tools in creative thinking,—which the rest of us can do profitably without much training in art. McKim used his insights into the value of externalizing thinking to develop an approach, which he pioneered at Stanford University's school of engineering in the 1970s, that teaches the acquisition of quick-and-dirty visual tools for thinking—not for presenting information. His book *Experiences in Visual Thinking* condenses his ideas on creative visual-language thinking into a process called Express-Test-Cycle (ETC), which I illustrate on these 2 pages.

Advantages of externalized thinking

- **Provides sensory nourishment.** "Direct sensory involvement with materials provides sensory nourishment—literally 'food for thought.'"
- **Promotes serendipity.** "Thinking by manipulating an actual structure permits serendipity—the happy accident, the unexpected discovery."
- **Produces sense of immediacy.** "Thinking in the direct context of sight, touch, and motion engenders a sense of immediacy, actuality, and action."
- **Provides object for critical contemplation.** "Externalized thought structure provides an object for critical contemplation as well as a visible form that can be shared with a colleague or even mutually formulated."
- **Encourages right-hemisphere thinking.** "The intense sensory/spatial involvement of externalized thinking fires up the right hemisphere of the brain; it is a marvelous antidote for thinking that has become locked up in words and symbols."

Robert McKim

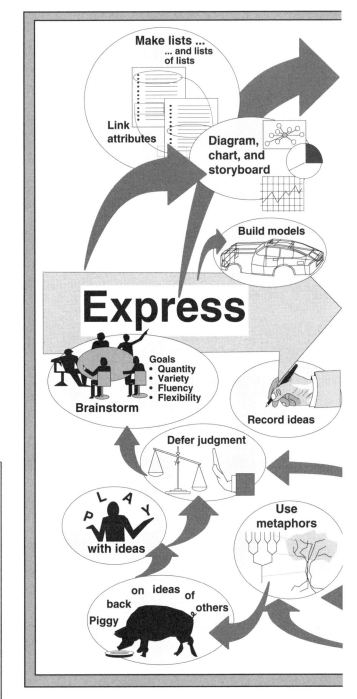

213

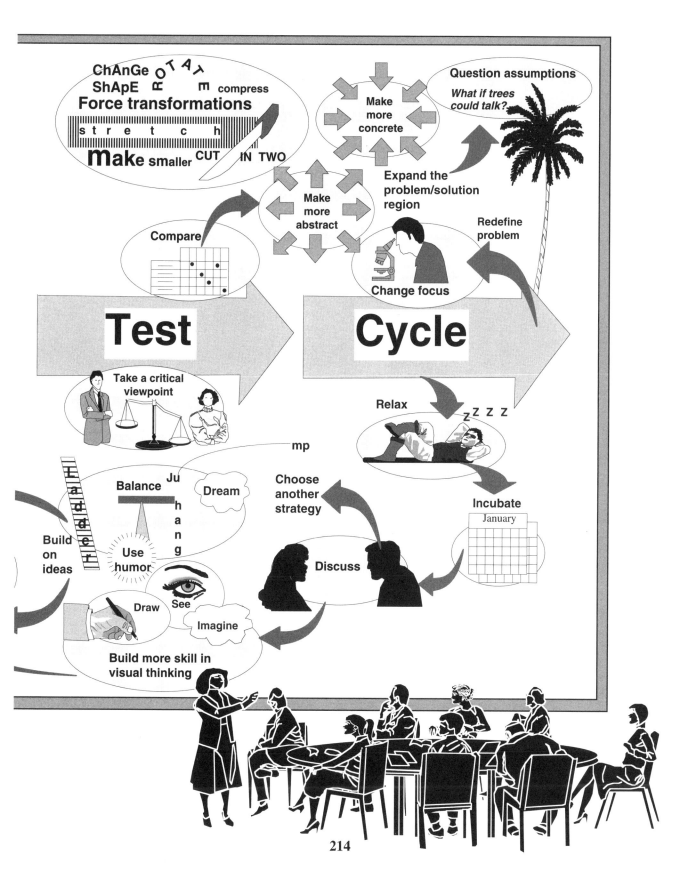

Making Group Process Visible

In addition to its applicability to the substance of problem-solving situations, visual language has been shown to facilitate underlying group dynamics as well. Meeting recorders can use visual language to track the dynamic group process, providing a quick, ongoing progress report of where the group stands. Better understanding of the process helps keep the group on track, keeps morale up during difficult stretches, and encourages individual members to remain mindful of the group as a whole.

The Team Performance Model outlined on these pages was developed by Allan Drexler, an organizational development specialist, and by David Sibbet, a pioneer in developing the pragmatics of visual language for facilitating group process. Sibbet's set of group-process frameworks, called the Group Graphics® keyboard, corresponds to the 7 stages. The keyboard analogy refers to the fact that some or all of the 7 stages can take place within each larger stage of the group process.

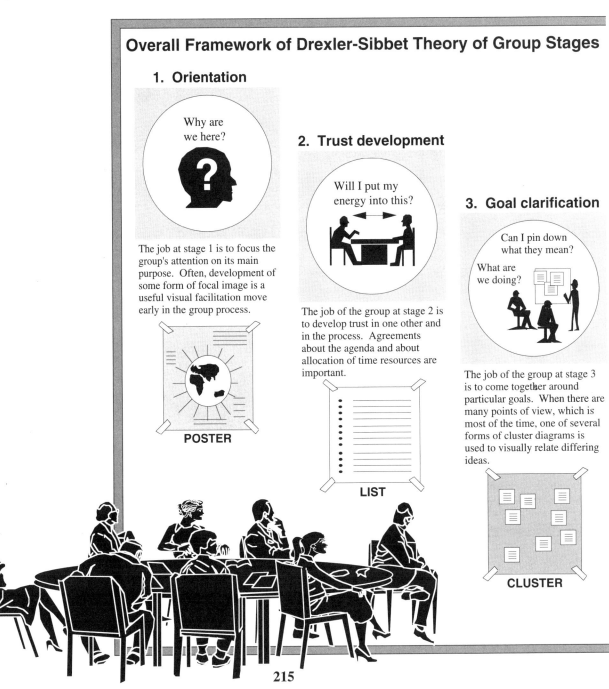

Overall Framework of Drexler-Sibbet Theory of Group Stages

1. Orientation

Why are we here?

The job at stage 1 is to focus the group's attention on its main purpose. Often, development of some form of focal image is a useful visual facilitation move early in the group process.

POSTER

2. Trust development

Will I put my energy into this?

The job of the group at stage 2 is to develop trust in one other and in the process. Agreements about the agenda and about allocation of time resources are important.

LIST

3. Goal clarification

Can I pin down what they mean?

What are we doing?

The job of the group at stage 3 is to come together around particular goals. When there are many points of view, which is most of the time, one of several forms of cluster diagrams is used to visually relate differing ideas.

CLUSTER

As the group moves from the early stages of getting acquainted to tackling nitty-gritty problems, their ability to return to a shared understanding of the process and where they are—provided by the visual recorder—supports full participation, systems thinking, and group memory, and paves the way for productive work.

There is a considerable difference between the use of visual language in broadcast mode (such as I am doing in this book) and the generation of visual language during group problem solving. In the group there is greater simplification, fewer words on the information mural, and, in general, less formality. The fact that the communication unit is created in front of the group during discussions provides the context and compensates for this simplification. To make such visual language units comprehensible to persons not present at the discussion requires the addition of supplementary visual and verbal elements.

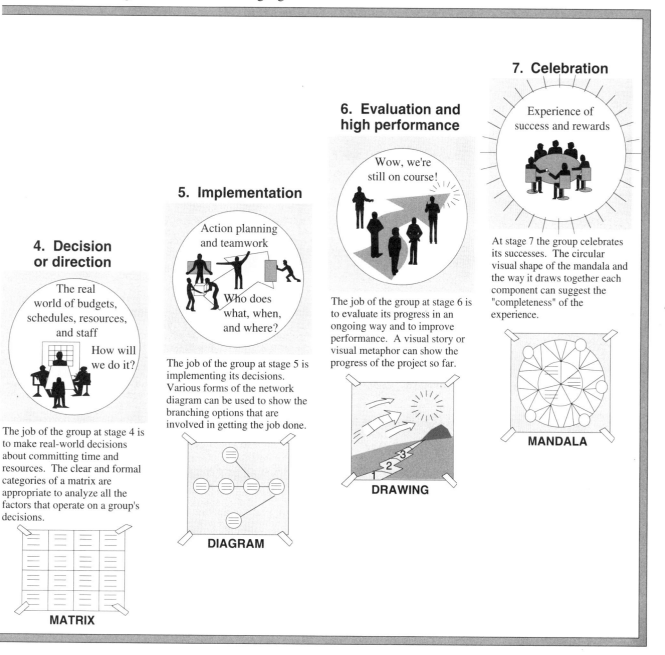

4. Decision or direction

The real world of budgets, schedules, resources, and staff

How will we do it?

The job of the group at stage 4 is to make real-world decisions about committing time and resources. The clear and formal categories of a matrix are appropriate to analyze all the factors that operate on a group's decisions.

MATRIX

5. Implementation

Action planning and teamwork

Who does what, when, and where?

The job of the group at stage 5 is implementing its decisions. Various forms of the network diagram can be used to show the branching options that are involved in getting the job done.

DIAGRAM

6. Evaluation and high performance

Wow, we're still on course!

The job of the group at stage 6 is to evaluate its progress in an ongoing way and to improve performance. A visual story or visual metaphor can show the progress of the project so far.

DRAWING

7. Celebration

Experience of success and rewards

At stage 7 the group celebrates its successes. The circular visual shape of the mandala and the way it draws together each component can suggest the "completeness" of the experience.

MANDALA

Presenting Multiple Points of View

Many of the perennial political and philosophical problems that we face are ill-structured problems. Ill-structured problems are defined as complicated and complex, ambiguous, highly interconnected, and often alogical, illogical, or multivalued. They are problems about which there are 2 or more viewpoints from the very start of discussion.

Comparison of such multiple points of view is always useful, and always difficult. A textual document can present each point of view separately and in great detail, or briefly and in comparison with other points of view—but it cannot do both at once.

Visual representation of the structure, history, and current status of a debate can provide some structure to a problem that is otherwise ill-structured by presenting multiple points of view in close connection with one another.

The example on this page is an excerpt from a series of 7 argumentation analysis maps that chart the history of the debate around whether computers can, or ever will be able to, think. The entire series includes more than 800 arguments, rebuttals, and counterrebuttals from more than 385 contributors.

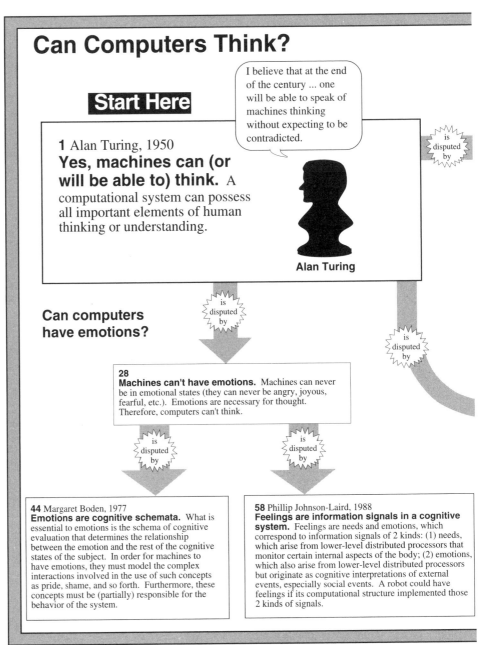

Can Computers Think?

Start Here

I believe that at the end of the century ... one will be able to speak of machines thinking without expecting to be contradicted.

1 Alan Turing, 1950
Yes, machines can (or will be able to) think. A computational system can possess all important elements of human thinking or understanding.

Alan Turing

is disputed by

Can computers have emotions?

is disputed by

is disputed by

28
Machines can't have emotions. Machines can never be in emotional states (they can never be angry, joyous, fearful, etc.). Emotions are necessary for thought. Therefore, computers can't think.

is disputed by

is disputed by

44 Margaret Boden, 1977
Emotions are cognitive schemata. What is essential to emotions is the schema of cognitive evaluation that determines the relationship between the emotion and the rest of the cognitive states of the subject. In order for machines to have emotions, they must model the complex interactions involved in the use of such concepts as pride, shame, and so forth. Furthermore, these concepts must be (partially) responsible for the behavior of the system.

58 Phillip Johnson-Laird, 1988
Feelings are information signals in a cognitive system. Feelings are needs and emotions, which correspond to information signals of 2 kinds: (1) needs, which arise from lower-level distributed processors that monitor certain internal aspects of the body; (2) emotions, which also arise from lower-level distributed processors but originate as cognitive interpretations of external events, especially social events. A robot could have feelings if its computational structure implemented those 2 kinds of signals.

Can computers have free will?

2
Computers can't have free will. Machines only do what they have been designed or programmed to do. They lack free will, but free will is necessary for thought. Therefore, computers can't think.

is disputed by

11 Alan Turing, 1950
Machines can exhibit free will by way of random selection. Free will can be produced in a machine that generates random values, for example by sampling random noise.

is disputed by

is disputed by

free will: The ability to make voluntary, unconstrained decisions. Freely made decisions are independent of the influence of such deterministic factors as genetics (nature) and conditioning (nurture).

Can computers be creative?

12
Randomization sacrifices responsibility. Machines that make decisions based on random choices have no responsibility for their actions, because it is then a matter of chance that they act one way rather than another. Because responsibility is necessary for free will, such machines also lack free will.

is disputed by

97
Computers can never be creative. Computers only do what they are programmed to do; they have no originality or creative powers.

is supported by

106 Douglas Hofstadter, 1995
The ELIZA effect. The ELIZA effect is a tendency to read more into computer performance than is warranted by their underlying code. For example, the computerized psychotherapy program ELIZA (see "ELIZA," Chart 2, Box 34) gives apparently sympathetic responses to human concerns, but in fact is only utilizing a set of canned responses.
Note: The ELIZA effect was recognized and described by ELIZA's creator Joseph Weizenbaum, though he didn't give it that title.

is disputed by

105
Computers have already been creative. Computer models that exhibit creativity or at least some component of creativity have already been developed.

is supported by

108 Phillip Johnson-Laird, 1988
The jazz generator. The jazz generator produces chord sequences and uses them to improvise chords, bass-line melodies, and rhythms.

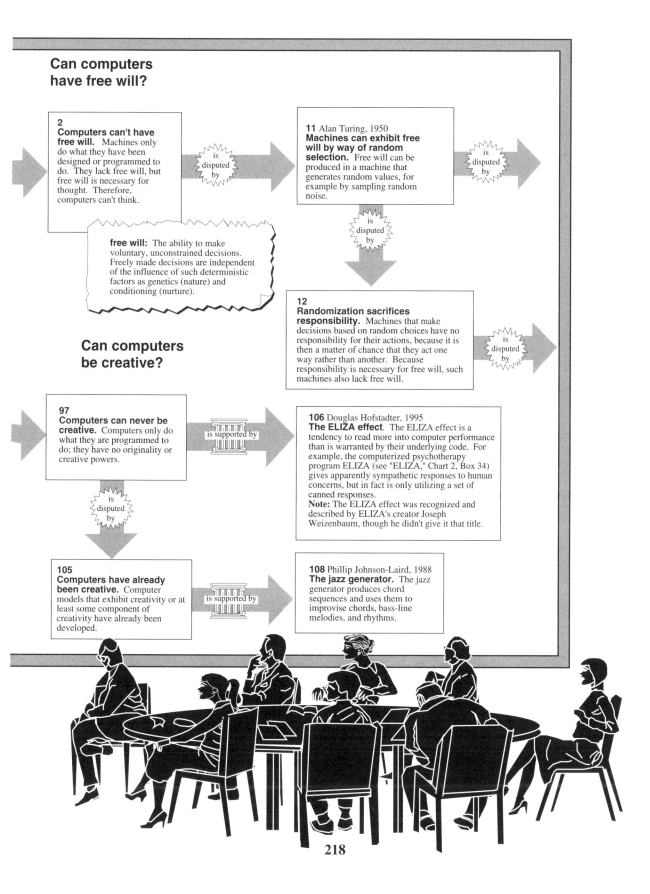

218

Facilitating Cross-Cultural Communication

It is in the very nature of cultures to be different from one another. One major source of such differences is the presence of underlying sets of assumptions that vary from culture to culture. When these assumptions remain unspoken, unheard, and unacknowledged, they can serve as barriers to attempts at crosscultural communication or problem solving.

By virtue of its ability to bring such assumptions to the surface of a group's communication process, visual language facilitates cross-cultural communication. Once different sets of cultural assumptions—about approaches, processes, definitions, goals, values, and so forth—are made visible in a permanent way that the group can return to as needed, the group can explore its different meanings, implications, constraints, and similarities.

The example on this page illustrates part of the results of a study that attempted to facilitate cross-cultural communication between 2 groups of people working in the same company—operators and engineers. The study is the work of Edgar Schein of MIT, who has studied organizational cultures for many years. Schein observed that communication difficulties between the several distinct cultures operating within most organizations were a major roadblock to corporate learning. Schein wrote, "Until executives, engineers, and operators discover that they use different languages and make different assumptions about what is important, and until they learn to treat the other cultures as valid and normal, organizational learning efforts will continue to fail."

219

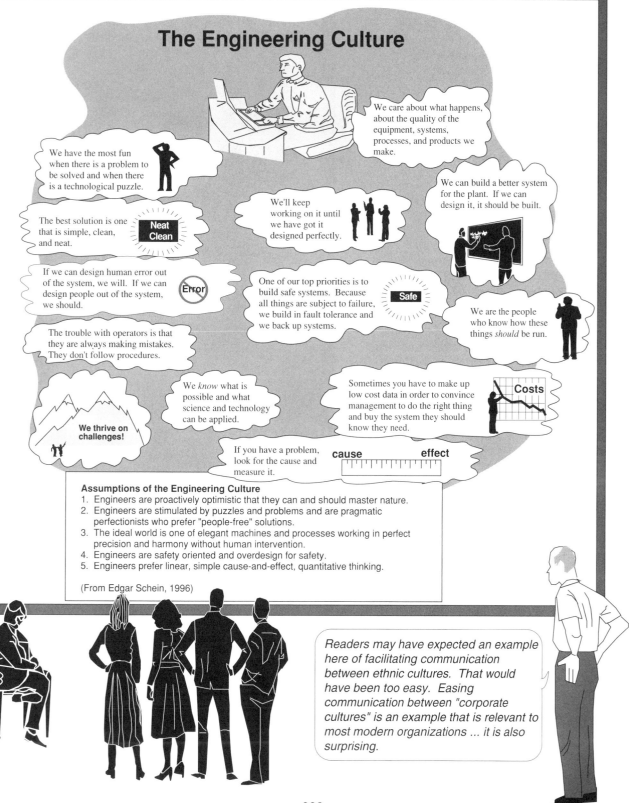

The Engineering Culture

We care about what happens, about the quality of the equipment, systems, processes, and products we make.

We have the most fun when there is a problem to be solved and when there is a technological puzzle.

We can build a better system for the plant. If we can design it, it should be built.

The best solution is one that is simple, clean, and neat.

Neat Clean

We'll keep working on it until we have got it designed perfectly.

If we can design human error out of the system, we will. If we can design people out of the system, we should.

Error

One of our top priorities is to build safe systems. Because all things are subject to failure, we build in fault tolerance and we back up systems.

Safe

We are the people who know how these things *should* be run.

The trouble with operators is that they are always making mistakes. They don't follow procedures.

We *know* what is possible and what science and technology can be applied.

Sometimes you have to make up low cost data in order to convince management to do the right thing and buy the system they should know they need.

Costs

We thrive on challenges!

If you have a problem, look for the cause and measure it.

cause   effect

Assumptions of the Engineering Culture
1. Engineers are proactively optimistic that they can and should master nature.
2. Engineers are stimulated by puzzles and problems and are pragmatic perfectionists who prefer "people-free" solutions.
3. The ideal world is one of elegant machines and processes working in perfect precision and harmony without human intervention.
4. Engineers are safety oriented and overdesign for safety.
5. Engineers prefer linear, simple cause-and-effect, quantitative thinking.

(From Edgar Schein, 1996)

Readers may have expected an example here of facilitating communication between ethnic cultures. That would have been too easy. Easing communication between "corporate cultures" is an example that is relevant to most modern organizations ... it is also surprising.

Facilitating International Communication

In multilingual situations, visual language has a capacity to bring cultures together in a way that favoring one spoken language over another does not. Multinational corporations and government agencies find visual language especially important because it provides a common language for the conference room.

How might visual language facilitate international communication? We live in an increasingly visual world. And even when native languages are not shared, exposure to visual culture often is. Further, the increasing integration of text and visual elements —which has been facilitated by the graphic computer, television, animation, and international scientific, technical, and commercial communications (such as advertising)—is doing more to internationalize visual language.

In a multilingual context, documents composed in visual language make sense, especially from a translator's point of view, because they are easier to translate. There is always less text in a visual language composition than there is in straight prose (20–30 percent less, according to recent studies), because the images and the shapes provide much of the information, as well as a lot of the context.

How might visual language facilitate international communication?

The frequent use of **illustrations** makes possible nearly instant recognition of physical objects.

Budget
$

The widespread use of **icons** on close to 100 million computer screens worldwide has brought to light their potential to serve in other arenas as visual signposts and navigational devices that need little translation.

Agenda

IN

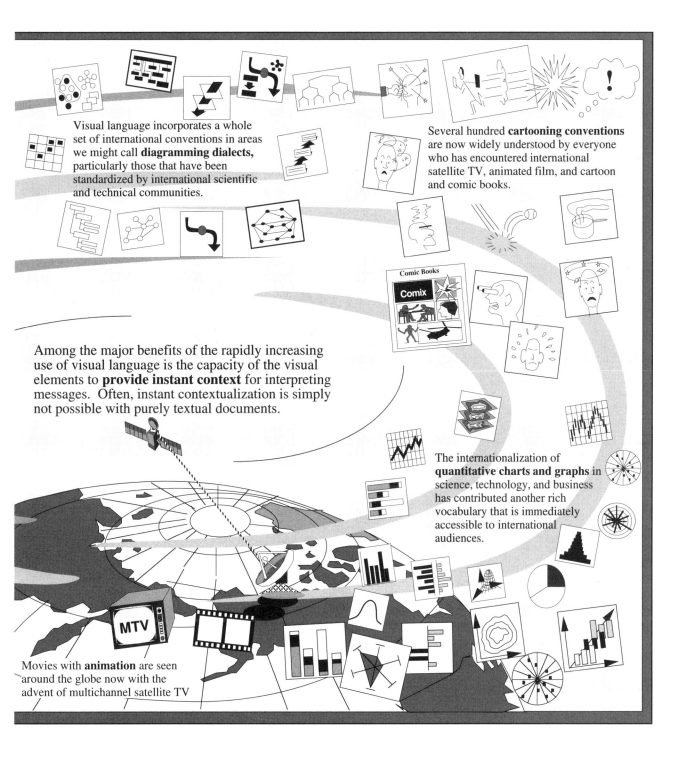

Visual language incorporates a whole set of international conventions in areas we might call **diagramming dialects,** particularly those that have been standardized by international scientific and technical communities.

Several hundred **cartooning conventions** are now widely understood by everyone who has encountered international satellite TV, animated film, and cartoon and comic books.

Comic Books

Comix

Among the major benefits of the rapidly increasing use of visual language is the capacity of the visual elements to **provide instant context** for interpreting messages. Often, instant contextualization is simply not possible with purely textual documents.

The internationalization of **quantitative charts and graphs** in science, technology, and business has contributed another rich vocabulary that is immediately accessible to international audiences.

MTV

Movies with **animation** are seen around the globe now with the advent of multichannel satellite TV

222

Multilevel, Multimodal Reading Process

Visual language communication units are both more demanding for readers and more immediately comprehensible. Because multiple levels of visuals, text, and concepts are combined, they require readers to spend more time in analysis and synthesis in order to come away with the full meaning of the communication.

At the same time, the presence of familiar visual images provides a point of immediate entry and understanding that often bypasses conscious evaluation. This multimodal reading process is the subject of this section.

Mix of metaphorical and literal communication
Visual metaphor (e.g., the signpost) and verbal metaphor (e.g., "backbone network") are mixed with literal text.

Bottlenecks on the World Wide Web

ISP modems clogged. When too many customers dial in at the same time, the number of modems available can dramatically [   ]cess and download times. With some providers you [   ]usy signals 30 percent of the time. Most of the ISPs in [   ]d States are connected with each other, as opposed to [   ]backbone, and delays occur during the transfer of [   ]on from carrier to carrier. ISPs create yet another [   ]hen they sell accounts to more customers than they [   ]al bandwidth to handle, which is a common fall-out [   ] pricing wars.

Backbone capacity struggles to keep up with message load. The fiberoptic lines that comprise the pathways of the backbone are fast, but they are continuously pushed to capacity because of increased use. For example, MCI's monthly Internet traffic has been tripling yearly for the last 3 years and is now about 330 terabytes.

Layers of commentary
The reader of this diagram is required to understand that the outer ring of text is a layer of commentary on the diagram contained within the ellipse, and, of course, that the commentary in this and other shadowed boxes is yet a 3rd layer of commentary.

Implicit Relationships
Often in these types of complex infographics, a major goal of the message is to show the relationships involved, which may not be explicitly described in words. For example, readers are required to interpret that the lines of connection between major components may be two-way connections. And they are required to understand that the signal goes either of 2 ways from the modem.

Insufficient bandwidth in company gateways. The connection between the company intranet and the external Internet is provided by the gateway computer. Companies often do not supply enough bandwidth for employees to connect to all the different sites on the Internet that they want to.

Satellites
Commercially owned, low-orbit satellites for wireless data transmission.

ACCESS "R" US

Internet service provider (ISP) ISP has a rack of modems that accepts multiple simultaneous incoming calls. Receives call and processes request, passing the connection to its leased line link to a computer on the Internet backbone. It simultaneously accepts multiple, incoming calls from subscribers who dial in at their convenience.

Gateway
Connects an intranet or LAN to the external Internet. All requests from the internal system must pass through the gateway to reach the outside.

Intranets
Internal corporate-wide networks based on the Internet and Web technology.

Local Area Networks (LAN)
Groups of computers connected to each other by cables and often then connected to the Internet by linking to a host computer or another network.

Browser interface & software
Software tool to access and view Web pages. May be text-only or graphical.

Nonoptic fiber internal nets. Some internal company nets give poor performance because they lack optic fiber. But many company intranets have optic fiber or advanced coaxial cable that will handle data up to 50 times faster than the standard 28.8 modem.

Modem
Dial-up device that connects the computer to the ISP via local- and long-distance phone lines. Modems convert digital information to analog signals transmitted by phone lines.

Point of View
Portrayal of the back of a woman's head suggests the presence of a user and subtly also suggests a starting point.

Slow modems. Modem-based transfer of information can be long and inefficient. The capacity of handling incoming bandwidth at the typical 28.8 kilobits per second is too little to handle large streams of incoming bits.

Old, slow, nonstandard browsers. Different versions of browsers offer different functionality for viewing pages, which means that users with old browsers or who do not have "plug-in" browser enhancers (e.g., for audio, video, or virtual reality) cannot view some of the newer kinds of information.

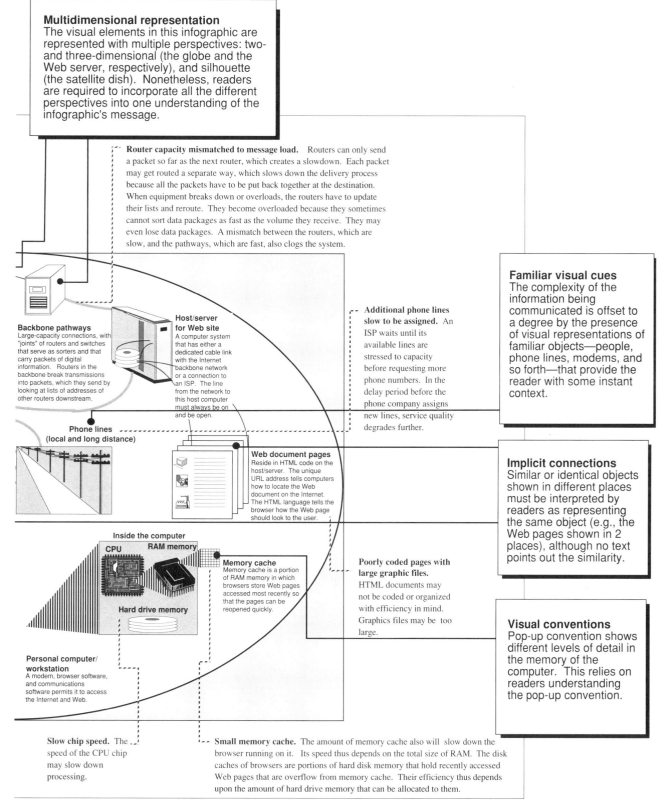

Multidimensional representation
The visual elements in this infographic are represented with multiple perspectives: two- and three-dimensional (the globe and the Web server, respectively), and silhouette (the satellite dish). Nonetheless, readers are required to incorporate all the different perspectives into one understanding of the infographic's message.

Router capacity mismatched to message load. Routers can only send a packet so far as the next router, which creates a slowdown. Each packet may get routed a separate way, which slows down the delivery process because all the packets have to be put back together at the destination. When equipment breaks down or overloads, the routers have to update their lists and reroute. They become overloaded because they sometimes cannot sort data packages as fast as the volume they receive. They may even lose data packages. A mismatch between the routers, which are slow, and the pathways, which are fast, also clogs the system.

Familiar visual cues
The complexity of the information being communicated is offset to a degree by the presence of visual representations of familiar objects—people, phone lines, modems, and so forth—that provide the reader with some instant context.

Backbone pathways
Large-capacity connections, with "joints" of routers and switches that serve as sorters and that carry packets of digital information. Routers in the backbone break transmissions into packets, which they send by looking at lists of addresses of other routers downstream.

Host/server for Web site
A computer system that has either a dedicated cable link with the Internet backbone network or a connection to an ISP. The line from the network to this host computer must always be on and be open.

Additional phone lines slow to be assigned. An ISP waits until its available lines are stressed to capacity before requesting more phone numbers. In the delay period before the phone company assigns new lines, service quality degrades further.

Phone lines (local and long distance)

Web document pages
Reside in HTML code on the host/server. The unique URL address tells computers how to locate the Web document on the Internet. The HTML language tells the browser how the Web page should look to the user.

Implicit connections
Similar or identical objects shown in different places must be interpreted by readers as representing the same object (e.g., the Web pages shown in 2 places), although no text points out the similarity.

Inside the computer
CPU
RAM memory
Hard drive memory

Memory cache
Memory cache is a portion of RAM memory in which browsers store Web pages accessed most recently so that the pages can be reopened quickly.

Poorly coded pages with large graphic files.
HTML documents may not be coded or organized with efficiency in mind. Graphics files may be too large.

Visual conventions
Pop-up convention shows different levels of detail in the memory of the computer. This relies on readers understanding the pop-up convention.

Personal computer/ workstation
A modem, browser software, and communications software permits it to access the Internet and Web.

Slow chip speed. The speed of the CPU chip may slow down processing.

Small memory cache. The amount of memory cache also will slow down the browser running on it. Its speed thus depends on the total size of RAM. The disk caches of browsers are portions of hard disk memory that hold recently accessed Web pages that are overflow from memory cache. Their efficiency thus depends upon the amount of hard drive memory that can be allocated to them.

Many Images Speak Immediately, Directly, and Emotionally—Bypassing Conscious Evaluation

One aspect of the multimodal reading process is how quickly certain parts of the reading process can take place, especially the visual reading of representative images. Although it is true that reading or hearing great poetry, stirring speeches, and moving stories can move us emotionally, none of these affects us as rapidly or directly as certain visual images can. Glancing at a scene provides a context that great writers labor long to convey. Images have the power to evoke strong, immediate feelings as well as to subtly insinuate a background climate or overall mood.

Scan the drawings on this page and consider what effects they have on you. If your experience is like that of most readers, each image on this page evokes an emotional response. This capacity, together with the property of instantaneous perception—which occurs much faster than the sequential gathering of similar information through reading text—produces a powerful communication tool.

Background and mood

In addition to foreground images (as on the facing page), background images (as in the complex landscapes on this page) may also convey an overall feeling. Thus, visual backgrounds have singular effects that are not encountered in purely prose presentations. They color interpretation and dominate mood as well as facilitate the more rapid understanding of some contexts than when a description is spelled out one word at at time.

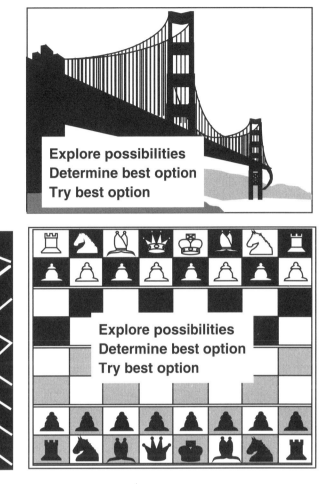

Explore possibilities
Determine best option
Try best option

Explore possibilities
Determine best option
Try best option

Explore possibilities
Determine best option
Try best option

Questions for visual language users

Major questions arise from this observation of the rapid, direct, deep ways in which humans perceive images.

- What are ethical obligations of communicators regarding the use of powerful images?
- To what extent can emotional effects be amplified or reduced by different choices of illustration and placement of text on a page?
- Are there ways in which visual language encourages superficial emotional scanning rather than careful analytical examination?

The emergence of visual language opens new fields and attracts new urgency to studies in these areas, to which very little attention has thus far been paid outside the research on advertising messages.

Visual Language Often Encourages Analysis and Synthesis

Not all visual language is instantaneously understandable. Often, information must be "figured out" by putting the verbal and visual elements together with prerequisite knowledge and skills. (For example, reading quantitative charts presupposes understanding that the data were collected in some orderly manner and were then assembled in some way, usually in a data table, before being transformed into a chart or graph.) Many people thus report that reading a visual language book is a more involving activity, and even, in some cases, is more demanding.

The theories of Jacques Bertin (1983) identify some possible sources of the difficulties that people experience in reading visual language. Bertin observed that, with many diagrams and charts, readers cannot receive information until they have understood the overall context and individual components of the diagram. His observation also applies to visual language in general. While it may make the reading process more complex and involved, it also encourages a deeper, more analytical approach.

Summary of Bertin's reading process

Stage 1. **Understand the context**

Stage 2. **Determine internal variables**

Before a graph or diagram can be understood, the reader must identify and comprehend each of its components. The reader must be able to answer the question, "What is the precise domain of this graphic?"

Next, the reader must understand which visual variable each of the components is represented by in the graph and ask the initial question.

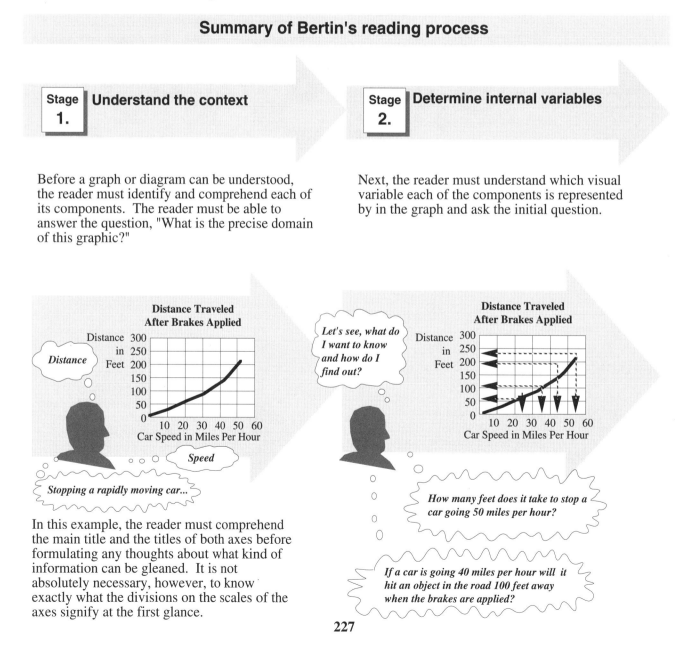

In this example, the reader must comprehend the main title and the titles of both axes before formulating any thoughts about what kind of information can be gleaned. It is not absolutely necessary, however, to know exactly what the divisions on the scales of the axes signify at the first glance.

227

Questions may be sorted by reading level

Bertin also developed a three-part classification of the levels at which a graphic may be approached.

1. Elementary level. These questions arise from focusing on a single element or component of the graphic and result in a conclusion about a single element or component. Example:

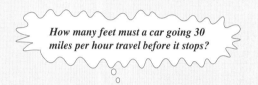

How many feet must a car going 30 miles per hour travel before it stops?

2. Intermediate level. These questions arise from focusing on groups of elements or components and result in a conclusion about the group as a whole. Example:

Is there proportionally greater distance covered when the car is traveling at 40 versus 50 miles per hour?

3. Overall or global level. These questions arise from focusing on the meaning of the overall graphic and result in a conclusion about the meaning of the whole of the information. Example:

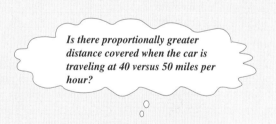

Is the relationship between speed and stopping distance generally a linear one?

| Stage 3. | **Comprehend the (new) information** |

Only after stages 1 and 2 are complete (even if they take place in a fraction of a second) can the reader perceive the new information in the graph.

This may be a Gestalt—a perception of an overall picture of the data—or it may result in detailed examination of the graph part-by-part.

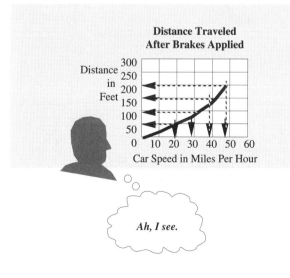

Distance Traveled After Brakes Applied

Ah, I see.

How The Eye Is Directed by Visual Language

Many people are accustomed to reading in one way only—upper left corner to lower right without skipping a word or a line. With the advent of multimedia communications and visual language, this method becomes quite limiting. We will all need a variety of new reading tactics if we are to continue to read with efficiency and full understanding.

The British art historian Michael Twyman conceived the matrix below, in which visual language units can be compared based on the type of content and the degree of directedness of viewing. The variety of different ways in which the eye must "work" to make sense of the different forms in Twyman's matrix provides us with insight into why different people have such widely variant reactions to visual language. When we encounter material that must be read in a different way than we are conditioned to read, many of us rebel and call visual language "too dense."

	Pure linear	**Linear interrupted**	**List**
Verbal/ numerical	Letter written in a continuous spiral from outside in	Poetry and most prose 	Restaurant menus, agendas, phone lists, etc. 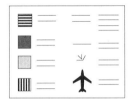
Pictorial & verbal/ numerical	Some long friezes and tapestries, some Greek vase paintings 	Comic books and other stories told in picture books 	Keys to maps, lists of pictographs and their meanings 
Pictorial	Panoramic views of city skylines and of coasts 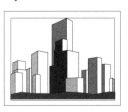	Wall paintings presented in series of discrete scenes 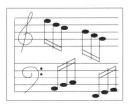	Road and airport pictorial lists of services
Schematic	Route maps and traces from EEGs and EKGs 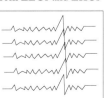	Musical notation	Lists of symbols in pictorial languages

229

Implications

The clear implication of Twyman's analysis is that the visual language communicator must become more sophisticated in understanding how the eye is directed, techniques that can be used to deliberately control eye movement, and perceptual principles that must not be violated if specific effects are to be achieved. And, of course, readers will need to become more flexible as well.

| Linear branching | Matrix | Nonlinear directed viewing | Nonlinear—most options open |

Linear branching

Family trees, organization charts

Trees with visual objects

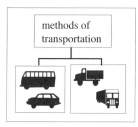

Completely pictorial branching is rare

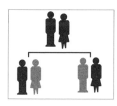

Purely schematic language trees

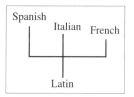

Matrix

Numerical and textual data tables

Visuals in a matrix

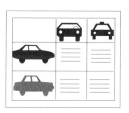

Completely pictorial matrices are rare

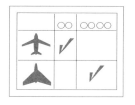

Bar charts with two-axis search strategies

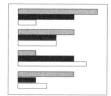

Nonlinear directed viewing

Most newspapers, some advertising

Newspapers with many pictures

The composition of most paintings and illustrations directs the eye

Network diagrams, subway maps

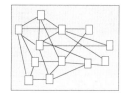

Nonlinear—most options open

Some concrete poetry, some advertising

Panoramic photos and illustrations with labels

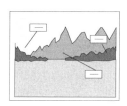

Rarely found in pure picture form, but some aerial photos are almost completely open

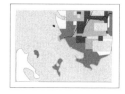

Surface maps

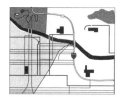

Mix of Words and Visual Elements in Different Media

In idea sketching and meetings with graphic recording, the visual elements are often more rudimentary and less developed because their function is what McKim calls "externalization of ideas" during creative problem solving. Subsequent interpretation of the visuals relies on the memory of the participants—although at the same time the visuals themselves facilitate recall.

Printed documents, projected media, and multimedia are all one-to-many broadcast media. However, they allocate different ratios of verbal to the audio or visual channel. Print documents typically contain all the relevant words on the page, whereas in projected media and multimedia, what would be printed is often allocated to a sound channel.

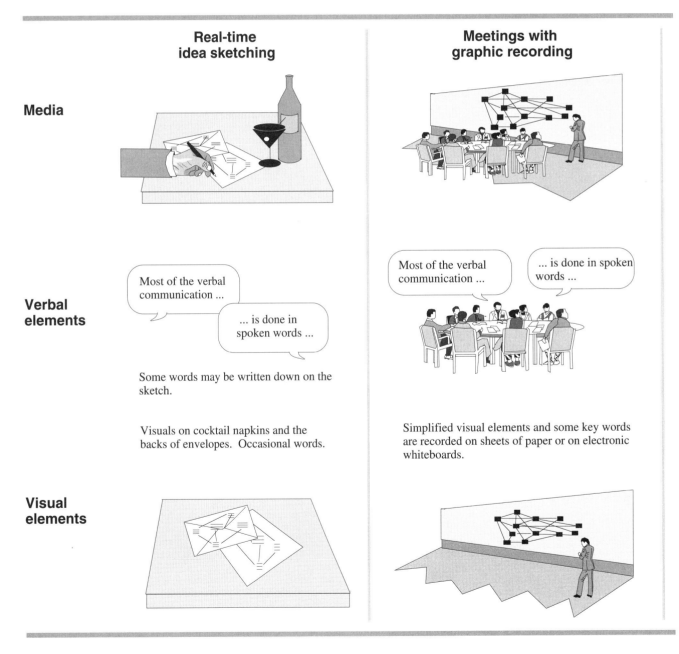

Real-time idea sketching

Meetings with graphic recording

Media

Verbal elements

Most of the verbal communication ...

... is done in spoken words ...

Some words may be written down on the sketch.

Visuals on cocktail napkins and the backs of envelopes. Occasional words.

Most of the verbal communication ...

... is done in spoken words ...

Simplified visual elements and some key words are recorded on sheets of paper or on electronic whiteboards.

Visual elements

Variations in how verbal and visual elements are allocated to different channels in visual language often obscure the fact that all of the situations are in fact visual language applications. Functional semantics, both that having to do with substance and that having to do with rhetoric may vary widely in these different usage situations.

For example, the function of reader guidance is much more critical in multimedia, where the reader is on her own, than in projected media, where a speaker provides guidance.

Printed documents

Words tightly integrated on the page with the visual elements.

Words tightly integrated on the page with the visual elements.

Projected media

Typically, most of the words are spoken when visual language is used in slide and overhead presentations.

Typically, all of the visual elements are projected. Only some of the words are projected (because of limited capacity to read them on screens).

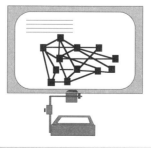

Multimedia

Multimedia presentations use a combination of printed and spoken (in the form of voice-overs) verbal elements.

Typically, all of the visual elements are presented on screen and only some of the words. A lot of words are often difficult to read for long periods on the screen.

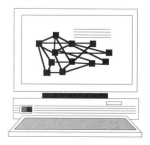

Visual Language Has a Proven Effectiveness

Basic scientific research is beginning to bear out the thesis of this book—that people find it easier and more effective to communicate by using combinations of words and images. Although visual language has yet to be subjected to a full battery of cognitive science or pragmatic tests, the few available studies support that conclusion.

Sweller, Chandler, and colleagues

The results summarized here are typical of recent studies comparing how fast and accurately high-school students and industrial workers understood a visual language version of documents (in which the text and diagrams were tightly integrated) as opposed to conventional texts (in which the diagrams were separate from the text).

In other similar experiments, John Sweller and his colleagues found from 10 to 150 percent greater speed in understanding of visual language documents and from 20 to 50 percent fewer errors (or better learning scores).

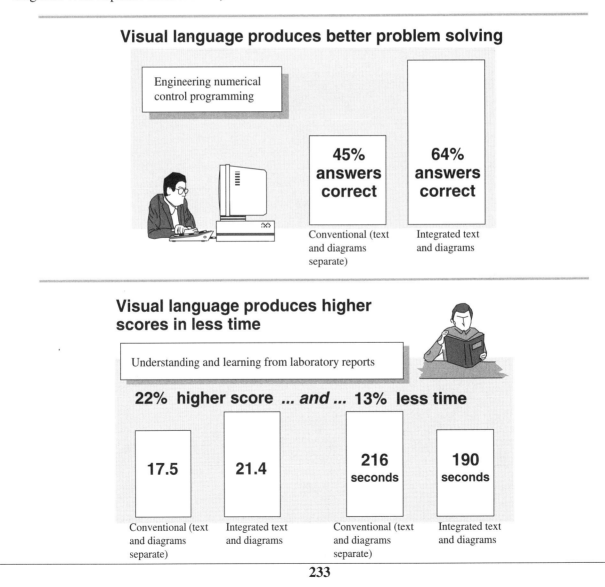

Visual language produces better problem solving

Engineering numerical control programming

45% answers correct
Conventional (text and diagrams separate)

64% answers correct
Integrated text and diagrams

Visual language produces higher scores in less time

Understanding and learning from laboratory reports

22% higher score ... *and* ... 13% less time

17.5
Conventional (text and diagrams separate)

21.4
Integrated text and diagrams

216 seconds
Conventional (text and diagrams separate)

190 seconds
Integrated text and diagrams

Visual language in business environments

A major study done at the Wharton School of Business focused on the effectiveness of visual language in presentations.

The striking results, summarized below, show that visual language in business settings encourages well-informed decision making, concensus building, and efficiency.

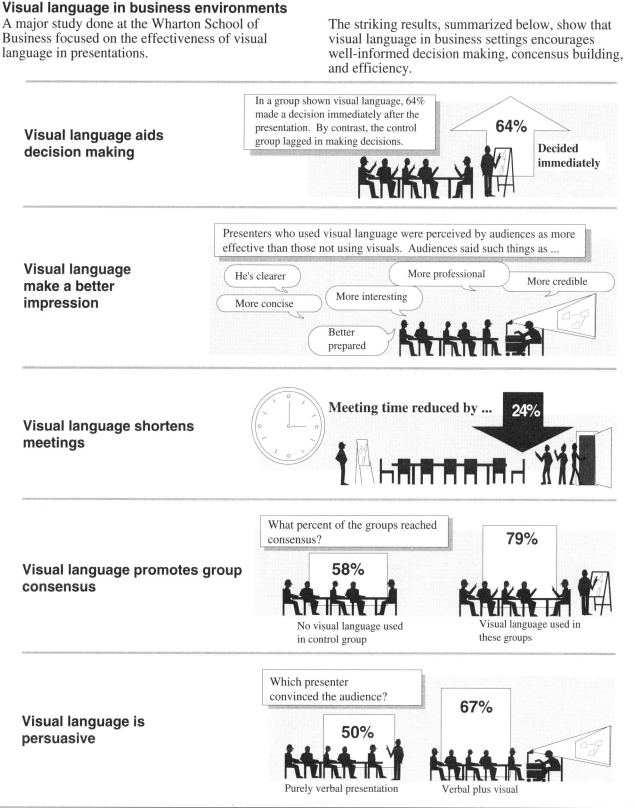

Visual language aids decision making

In a group shown visual language, 64% made a decision immediately after the presentation. By contrast, the control group lagged in making decisions.

64%

Decided immediately

Visual language make a better impression

Presenters who used visual language were perceived by audiences as more effective than those not using visuals. Audiences said such things as ...

He's clearer

More concise

More interesting

Better prepared

More professional

More credible

Visual language shortens meetings

Meeting time reduced by ... **24%**

Visual language promotes group consensus

What percent of the groups reached consensus?

58%

79%

No visual language used in control group

Visual language used in these groups

Visual language is persuasive

Which presenter convinced the audience?

50%

67%

Purely verbal presentation

Verbal plus visual

Evolving Criteria for Good Practice

Because visual language is so effective, it is important that standards and criteria develop for its use. These criteria need to be based on principles that come from both cognitive science and design. Criteria for good practice will evolve both from the evidence of careful empirical studies that compare different visual methods of expressing a similar message and from the reflective judgments of practitioners. Out of such judgments come the models, the criteria, and the aesthetic factors that together make a message effective, efficient, and attractive. We have clearly entered a period of exciting dialogue and development of these ideas.

William Cleveland and Edward Tufte are 2 major contributors to the evolving criteria for well-constructed visual language. Each approaches the field from a different perspective. Cleveland is an empiricist with an interest in the relative effectiveness of different quantitative displays. Tufte's reflective analyses of visual displays of information are quickly becoming required reading for anyone practicing information design.

Empirical data about graphical perception tasks

William Cleveland has conducted a long series of experiments over many years examining the effectiveness of different characteristics of charts and graphs. One of his many major contributions to our understanding of human perception of quantitative information regards the efficiency of various methods of representation.

In performing elementary graphical perception tasks to decode and compare information from different types of graphs, some types of graphs enable most people to perform faster and with fewer errors than others. In part, the performance differences are based on our perceptual capacities. Cleveland developed the following scale that arranges various ways of representing data in a hierarchy ranging from most understandable to least understandable. For optimum clarity, data should be displayed on a type of graph that exists as near to the top of this scale as possible.

Cleveland's scale tells us, for example, that making percentage comparisons (e.g., how much bigger is A than D?) between data expressed as areas of circles (#5 on the scale)

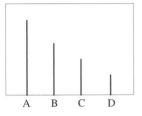

is much more difficult a task than making the same percentage comparisons when the data are expressed as positions along a line (#1 on the scale).

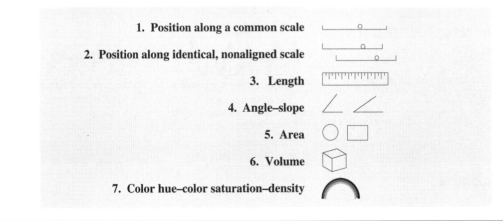

1. **Position along a common scale**
2. **Position along identical, nonaligned scale**
3. **Length**
4. **Angle–slope**
5. **Area**
6. **Volume**
7. **Color hue–color saturation–density**

A combined aesthetic-pragmatic critique

American political scientist and information designer Edward R. Tufte has written several seminal books on the analysis of communication factors in visual displays, especially of quantitative information.

Tufte's insights, 3 of which are summarized here, and the aesthetic presentations of his own books have increased the recognition in the general culture of the effectiveness and beauty of visual language.

Cannons of excellence

"Excellence in statistics graphics consists of complex ideas communicated with clarity, precision, and efficiency. Graphical displays should
- show the data
- induce the viewer to think about the substance rather than about methodology, graphic design, the technology of graphic production, or something else
- avoid distorting what the data have to say

- present many numbers in a small space
- make large data sets coherent
- encourage the eye to compare different pieces of data
- reveal the data at several levels of detail, from a broad overview to the fine structure
- serve a reasonably clear purpose: description, exploration, tabulation, or decoration
- be closely integrated with the statistical and verbal descriptions of a data set."

Chartjunk

Among other concepts, Tufte has given us chartjunk—the use of unnecessary ink on charts. He lists optical moiré effects and the overzealous use of grids among the worst chartjunk, which are charts whose designs actually impede understanding.

Clashing optical effects

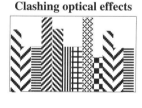

Unintended moiré effects

Excess ticks

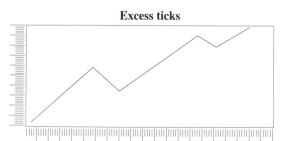

Data–Ink ratio

One of Tufte's aesthetic canons suggests that the greatest proportion of ink used in the creation of a graphical display should be used to actually present the data, or information, as opposed to the structure on which the data appear. He criticizes the use of excessive graphic elements that do not add information, and that may actually confuse or impede readers. He calls this aesthetic the data–ink ratio and expresses it with the following formula, which is read as: The data–ink ratio is the proportion of a graphic's ink devoted to the nonredundant display of data information.

$$\text{Data–ink ratio} = \frac{\text{data ink}}{\text{total ink used to print the graphic}}$$

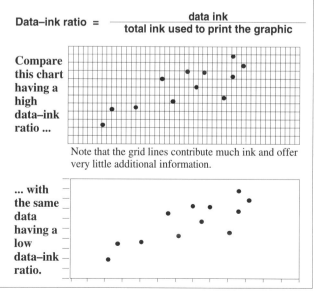

Compare this chart having a high data–ink ratio ...

Note that the grid lines contribute much ink and offer very little additional information.

... with the same data having a low data–ink ratio.

Information Design: An Emerging Profession

in • for • ma • tion   de • sign */n/*
The art and science of preparing information so that it can be used by human beings with efficiency and effectiveness. Its primary products appear as documents or slides and as presentations on computer screens. It often includes the design of forms and interactive media as well as the preparation of documents, exhibits, and presentations.

Although this section's investigations into how to obtain the optimum effectiveness with visual language should be of interest to everyone who intends to use it as a communications tool, they are of particular importance to an emerging profession that calls itself information design.

Information designers are directly involved in managing the massive complexity of modern life. The information design process attempts to systematize and reduce as much error as possible in the visual language communication process. To accomplish those purposes, the profession needs to make use of all the science and art available.

Primary objectives

The primary objectives of information design are:
1. Develop documents that are comprehensible, rapidly and accurately retrievable, and easy to translate into effective action.
2. Design interactions with equipment that is easy, natural, and as pleasant as possible. This involves solving many of the problems in the design of the human–computer interface.
3. Enable people to find their way around in three-dimensional space (especially urban, but also recently virtual) with comfort and ease.

The values that distinguish information design from other kinds of design are efficiency and effectiveness in accomplishing the communicative purpose.

Cognitive science must play a key role

For information design to reach its primary objectives, it is imperative that its practioners understand the principles of cognitive science that underlie human perception, including the Gestalt principles (➔75–76) and the limits of short-term memory.

Limits of short-term memory

George Miller's work on humans' short-term memory capacity helps us understand its limits. Miller's work also illustrates how the limits of short-term memory are pervasively influential in our learning and thinking life. By extension, then, they must also be in our information design principles and practice. We can introduce this idea with a familiar example.

You look up a phone number ...

... a little interruption and you've forgotten the number.

Where did you put the coffee, dear?

Why are such short-term memory problems so common? The answer is that humans' short-term memory capacity has severe limitations.

Two estimates of the size of short-term memory

Every thought process that requires what we call "attention" has to be held in short-term memory, and human beings can hold only a small number of "chunks" of information in short-term memory. Miller, an outstanding communications psychologist, suggested in 1956 that the number of chunks that can be held in short-term memory is 7 (plus or minus 2).

Research by Herbert Simon, the Nobel prize–winning economist and information scientist, suggests the number is smaller—around 4 to possibly 9 chunks. Whatever the size, all agree that the number of chunks is very small.

Information design principle: Organize thought so as to stay within memory limits "We must," Herbert Simon says, "organize our thought processes so they do not require us to hold more information than 4 to 7 chunks in short-term memory simultaneously."

Thou shalt pre-chunk thine information

An example: Metaphorical graphics

The metaphorical graphics of William Cole exemplify the promise of the emerging information design profession. His theories for graphical representation of information take advantage of principles of both cognitive science and good design.

Cole has criticized the use of universal or arbitrary data-display techniques (such as standard statistics presentations in time lines, pie charts, and bar graphs) as being inadequate for some important applications, such as medicine. His developing theory of metaphorical graphics is based on the human capacity to digest analogical data more readily than digital data. He says: "Metaphor graphs look like the underlying data but not in a literal way. For example, red circles that get larger as blood pressure get higher would be metaphors for blood pressure. This would not be an arbitrary graph because blood pressure would look quite different from an auto sale, nor would it be a literal graph, as it would not look literally like blood pressure, which has no obvious physical appearance."

Compared with alternative displays, usually tables of data, Cole's representation method has been shown to greatly improve rapid understanding of the data, particularly when long time periods are involved.

Example of metaphorical graphic
One of Cole's metaphorical graphics is the volume rectangle, which is used to show what is happening with a patient on a respirator.

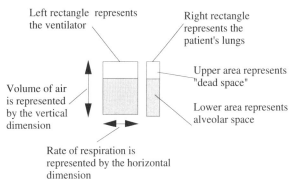

Using this method of data display, a 5-minute representation of respirator-assisted breathing might look like the following:

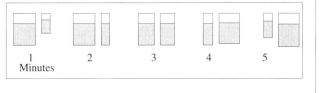

Information design is not yet a fully integrated profession. Many people in distinct disiplines currently find themselves practicing information design without calling it by that name. Although it is no doubt true that these practitioners have information design concerns specific to their particular disciplines, many of their core concerns and practices are similar. Their different names for what they do simply indicate that information design is still characterized by relatively isolated groups. Yet there is a visibly increasing tendency for such people to march under the banner of information design.

I think the profession may well develop in the same way that medicine has, where training in the foundational sciences combines with internships, residencies, and practice to produce effective training of professionals.

If the information design profession can become more unified and if it can understand its multifaceted foundations, which encompass both creative design and rigorous research, it will continue to make major contributions to the solutions of human communication problems.

Chapter 8
Conclusions and Challenges

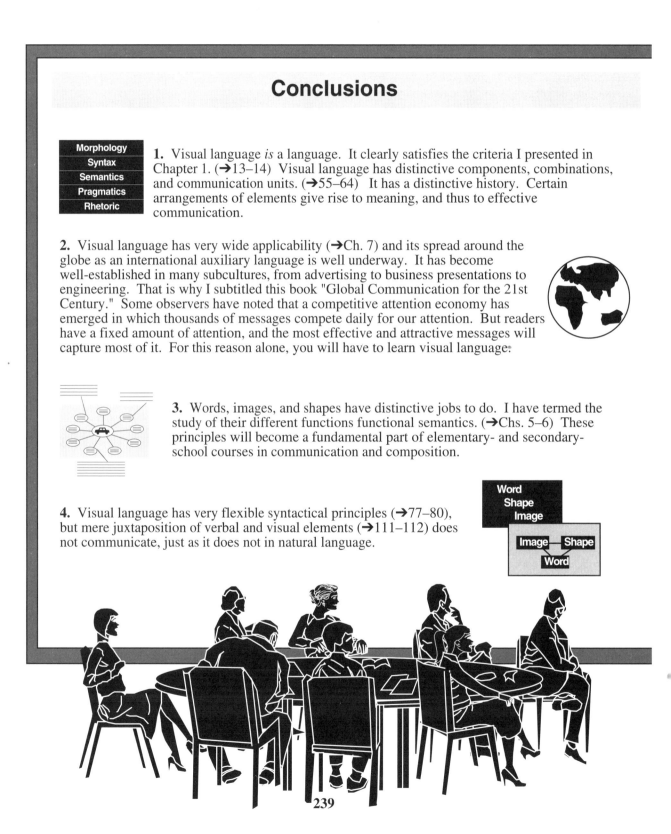

Conclusions

| Morphology |
| Syntax |
| Semantics |
| Pragmatics |
| Rhetoric |

1. Visual language *is* a language. It clearly satisfies the criteria I presented in Chapter 1. (➔13–14) Visual language has distinctive components, combinations, and communication units. (➔55–64) It has a distinctive history. Certain arrangements of elements give rise to meaning, and thus to effective communication.

2. Visual language has very wide applicability (➔Ch. 7) and its spread around the globe as an international auxiliary language is well underway. It has become well-established in many subcultures, from advertising to business presentations to engineering. That is why I subtitled this book "Global Communication for the 21st Century." Some observers have noted that a competitive attention economy has emerged in which thousands of messages compete daily for our attention. But readers have a fixed amount of attention, and the most effective and attractive messages will capture most of it. For this reason alone, you will have to learn visual language.

3. Words, images, and shapes have distinctive jobs to do. I have termed the study of their different functions functional semantics. (➔Chs. 5–6) These principles will become a fundamental part of elementary- and secondary-school courses in communication and composition.

| Word |
| Shape |
| Image |

| Image — Shape |
| Word |

4. Visual language has very flexible syntactical principles (➔77–80), but mere juxtaposition of verbal and visual elements (➔111–112) does not communicate, just as it does not in natural language.

5. Visual language requires new and different ways of reading based on percept–concept integration. (➜95–96) Many adult readers will have to engage in the exciting—and sometimes uncomfortable—process of overcoming old reading habits and learning new ones.

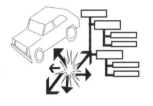

6. The language is still emerging but already has some relatively stable configurations and sufficient regularities to be used with ease. We need reference tools—visual language dictionaries and thesauri—to help us use the new language effectively.

7. Integration of verbal and visual elements has distinct but sometimes overlapping ways of operating; that is, several things can be accomplished at once with visual–verbal combinations. (➜186, 200) This elegant and efficient capacity encourages its own distinctive aesthetics and will generate whole new genres of art and functional communications.

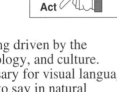

8. The ongoing creation of visual language is being driven by the increasing complexity of business, science, technology, and culture. (➜15–16) New innovations continue to be necessary for visual language to say what is difficult, or sometimes impossible, to say in natural language. This emergent phase of visual language will require ongoing attention and study as the new forms, structures, and templates are created.

9. We are just at the beginning of another communications revolution—the modern equivalent of the one that Gutenberg sparked. (➜245–246) The visual language revolution is taking place alongside other communications revolutions— the World Wide Web, animation, three-dimensional virtual reality, and intelligent and interactive visual elements. (➜243–244) The new mix of technologies and techniques will irreversibly alter communications in the 21st century.

These 9 points sum up where I think we are with visual language. We must get beyond our either/or attitude about visuals and words. And unless we continue to adopt visual language around the globe as our international auxiliary language, we run the risk of not being able to handle the demands of an increasingly complex future.

What follows in this chapter is more speculative and a little more exuberant than the previous chapters. It is an invitation to consider some of the possible implications of what we might call the visual language revolution.

Visual Language Transcends the Constraining Effects of the Alphabet

John Culkin, one of Marshal McLuhan's major interpreters, has written, "The alphabet is a funnel. All sense data must henceforth be squeezed into and through the narrow passage of print. The audible, the pictorial, the tactile, the olfactory—all get translated into the visual and the abstract. ... Reality is squeezed through the funnel of the alphabet."

"Reality comes out one drop at a time; it is segmented; sequential; it is fragmented along a straight line; it is analytic; it is abridged; it is reduced to one sense; it becomes susceptible to perspective and point of view; it becomes uniform and repeatable."

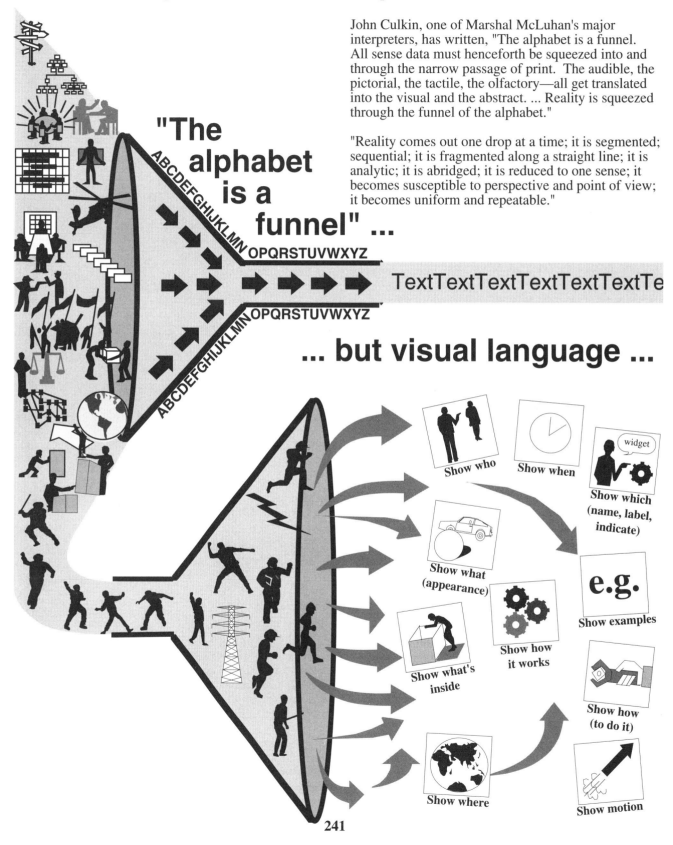

"The alphabet is a funnel" ...

ABCDEFGHIJKLMN OPQRSTUVWXYZ

TextTextTextTextTextTextTe

OPQRSTUVWXYZ
ABCDEFGHIJKLMN

... but visual language ...

Show who

Show when

widget
Show which
(name, label, indicate)

Show what
(appearance)

e.g.
Show examples

Show what's inside

Show how it works

Show how
(to do it)

Show where

Show motion

241

Visual language loosens the tremendous restrictiveness of the alphabet and prose. With visual language, the funnel can be circumnavigated. Reality and understanding can be poured back into our midst. It does not avoid the human condition of always filtering data. Of course, human perception systems in themselves act as filters: We must translate all data received through the senses and conceptual systems. Visual language, however, opens wider the gates of communication. It lets more data through, with greater complexity, accuracy, and nuance.

xtTextTextTextTextTextTextTextTextTextTextTextTextTextTextText

unleashes the full power of communication.

Visual Language Is One of Many Simultaneous Communications Revolutions

This book has focused on visual language, without paying much attention to the multiple technological and social contexts within which it is emerging. The semantic fusion of words and visuals is, as we have seen, producing communication structures that are quite different from those that have been predominant over the course of the last 500 years. Furthermore, visual language is not emerging into a vacuum, but instead in conjunction with several other major technological and communications revolutions.

Each new technology and methodology outlined on these pages is greatly impacting how we communicate with one another. Each is creating new challenges and opportunities. Visual language is no different in that regard.

What does it mean for the future of communication that so many changes are occurring nearly simultaneously?

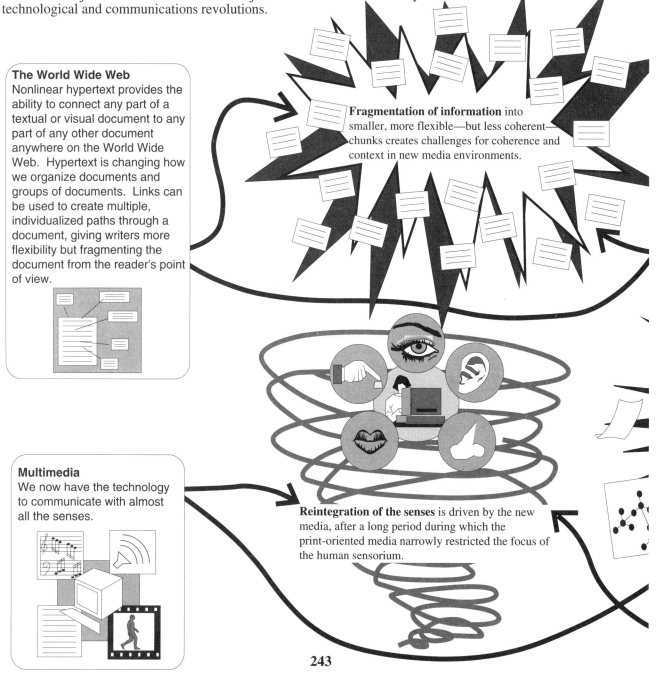

The World Wide Web
Nonlinear hypertext provides the ability to connect any part of a textual or visual document to any part of any other document anywhere on the World Wide Web. Hypertext is changing how we organize documents and groups of documents. Links can be used to create multiple, individualized paths through a document, giving writers more flexibility but fragmenting the document from the reader's point of view.

Fragmentation of information into smaller, more flexible—but less coherent—chunks creates challenges for coherence and context in new media environments.

Multimedia
We now have the technology to communicate with almost all the senses.

Reintegration of the senses is driven by the new media, after a long period during which the print-oriented media narrowly restricted the focus of the human sensorium.

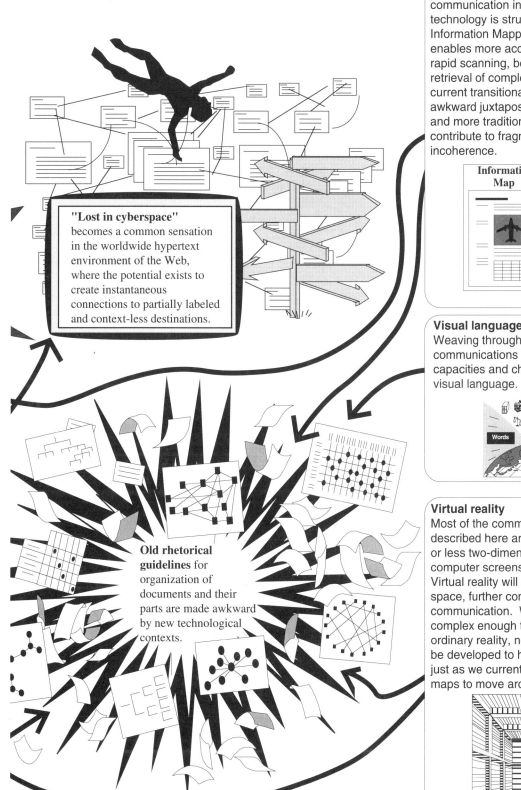

"Lost in cyberspace" becomes a common sensation in the worldwide hypertext environment of the Web, where the potential exists to create instantaneous connections to partially labeled and context-less destinations.

Old rhetorical guidelines for organization of documents and their parts are made awkward by new technological contexts.

Structured writing

One widely used modern approach to communication in business, science, and technology is structured writing and Information Mapping®. Structured writing enables more accurate analysis, more rapid scanning, better learning, and faster retrieval of complex material. During the current transitional period, however, awkward juxtapositions of structured writing and more traditional rhetorics can contribute to fragmentation and incoherence.

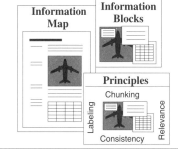

Visual language

Weaving throughout this tapestry of new communications rhetorics are all the capacities and challenges embodied in visual language.

Virtual reality

Most of the communications revolutions described here are taking place in a more or less two-dimensional world, on computer screens or on the printed page. Virtual reality will add a third dimension of space, further complicating and enriching communication. When virtual reality gets complex enough to be as interesting as ordinary reality, new rhetorics will have to be developed to help us move around in it, just as we currently need diagrams and maps to move around the natural world.

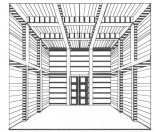

Potential Cultural Impacts

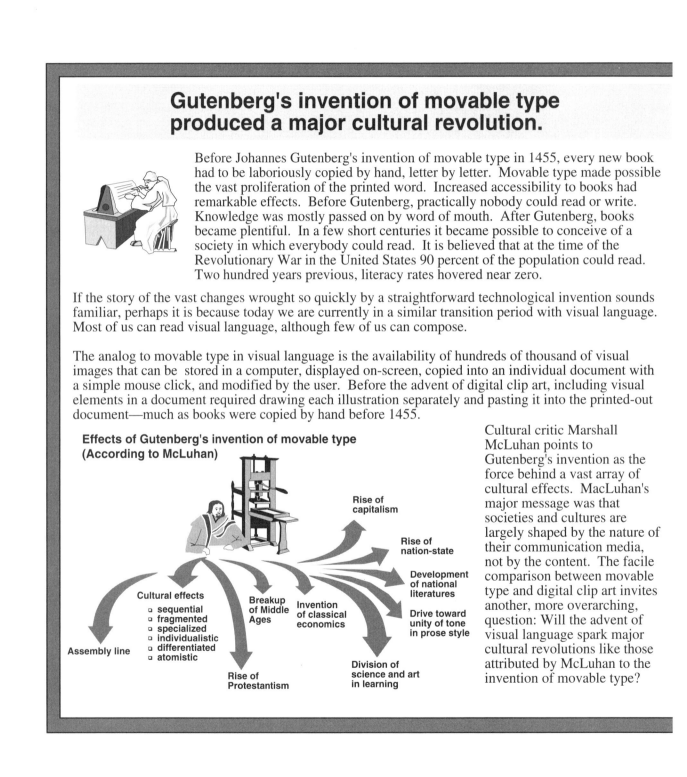

Gutenberg's invention of movable type produced a major cultural revolution.

Before Johannes Gutenberg's invention of movable type in 1455, every new book had to be laboriously copied by hand, letter by letter. Movable type made possible the vast proliferation of the printed word. Increased accessibility to books had remarkable effects. Before Gutenberg, practically nobody could read or write. Knowledge was mostly passed on by word of mouth. After Gutenberg, books became plentiful. In a few short centuries it became possible to conceive of a society in which everybody could read. It is believed that at the time of the Revolutionary War in the United States 90 percent of the population could read. Two hundred years previous, literacy rates hovered near zero.

If the story of the vast changes wrought so quickly by a straightforward technological invention sounds familiar, perhaps it is because today we are currently in a similar transition period with visual language. Most of us can read visual language, although few of us can compose.

The analog to movable type in visual language is the availability of hundreds of thousand of visual images that can be stored in a computer, displayed on-screen, copied into an individual document with a simple mouse click, and modified by the user. Before the advent of digital clip art, including visual elements in a document required drawing each illustration separately and pasting it into the printed-out document—much as books were copied by hand before 1455.

Effects of Gutenberg's invention of movable type (According to McLuhan)

Rise of capitalism

Rise of nation-state

Development of national literatures

Drive toward unity of tone in prose style

Cultural effects
- sequential
- fragmented
- specialized
- individualistic
- differentiated
- atomistic

Breakup of Middle Ages

Invention of classical economics

Assembly line

Division of science and art in learning

Rise of Protestantism

Cultural critic Marshall McLuhan points to Gutenberg's invention as the force behind a vast array of cultural effects. MacLuhan's major message was that societies and cultures are largely shaped by the nature of their communication media, not by the content. The facile comparison between movable type and digital clip art invites another, more overarching, question: Will the advent of visual language spark major cultural revolutions like those attributed by McLuhan to the invention of movable type?

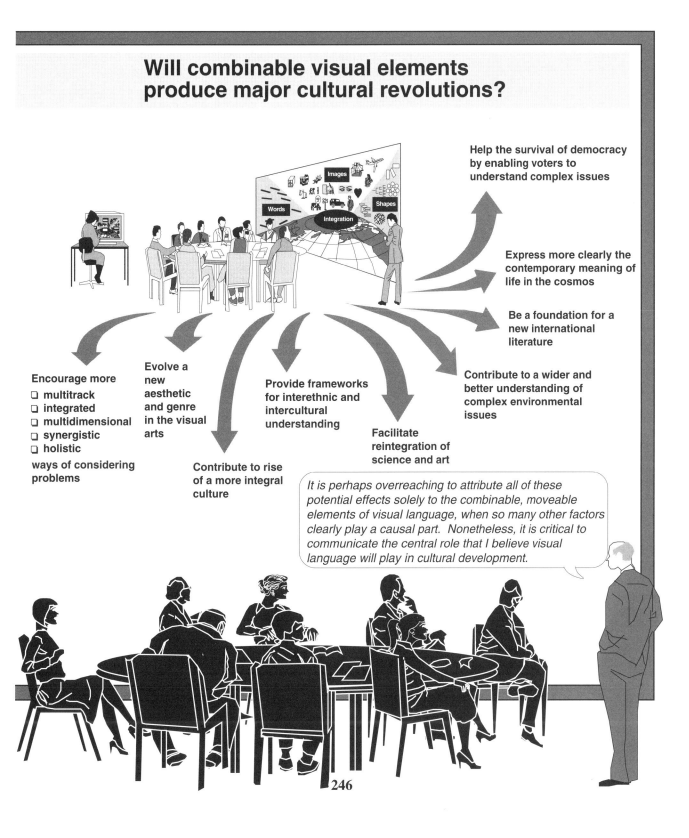

Will combinable visual elements produce major cultural revolutions?

Help the survival of democracy by enabling voters to understand complex issues

Express more clearly the contemporary meaning of life in the cosmos

Be a foundation for a new international literature

Contribute to a wider and better understanding of complex environmental issues

Facilitate reintegration of science and art

Provide frameworks for interethnic and intercultural understanding

Contribute to rise of a more integral culture

Evolve a new aesthetic and genre in the visual arts

Encourage more
❑ multitrack
❑ integrated
❑ multidimensional
❑ synergistic
❑ holistic
ways of considering problems

It is perhaps overreaching to attribute all of these potential effects solely to the combinable, moveable elements of visual language, when so many other factors clearly play a causal part. Nonetheless, it is critical to communicate the central role that I believe visual language will play in cultural development.

246

Visual Language will be a Boon to Education

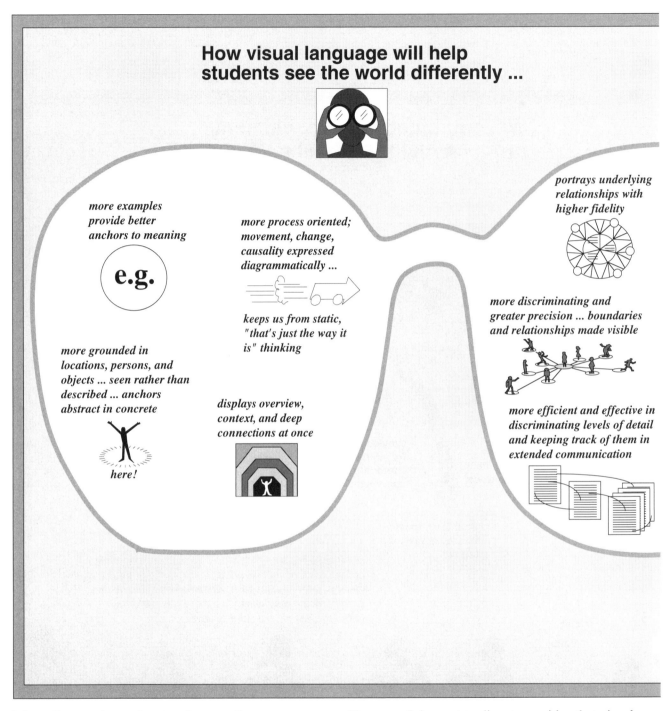

How visual language will help students see the world differently ...

more examples provide better anchors to meaning

e.g.

more grounded in locations, persons, and objects ... seen rather than described ... anchors abstract in concrete

here!

more process oriented; movement, change, causality expressed diagrammatically ...

keeps us from static, "that's just the way it is" thinking

displays overview, context, and deep connections at once

portrays underlying relationships with higher fidelity

more discriminating and greater precision ... boundaries and relationships made visible

more efficient and effective in discriminating levels of detail and keeping track of them in extended communication

Most often, we hear educators bemoan the pervasiveness of the visual culture. They attribute to it the decline in reading ability, the decrease in analytic ability, and students' poor writing skills. I do not want to dispute these data; I agree that the sheer weight of the time that students spend immersed in television, computer games, and other visual distractions keeps them from other educational activities.

However, I do want to dispute any idea that visual language as I am describing it contributes in a negative way to education. On the contrary, integrating visual language into the schools will enable students to think in more complex ways and to make better decisions through more skillful analysis. Visual language may very well improve writing ability as well; when there are fewer words on a page, each one must be scrutinized more carefully.

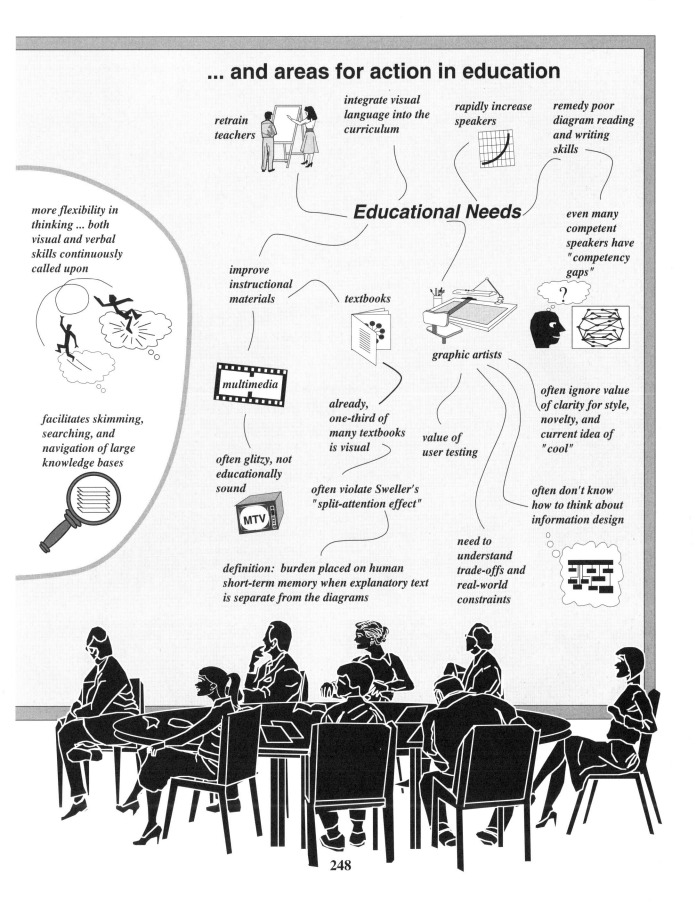

... and areas for action in education

retrain teachers

integrate visual language into the curriculum

rapidly increase speakers

remedy poor diagram reading and writing skills

Educational Needs

even many competent speakers have "competency gaps"

more flexibility in thinking ... both visual and verbal skills continuously called upon

facilitates skimming, searching, and navigation of large knowledge bases

improve instructional materials

textbooks

graphic artists

often ignore value of clarity for style, novelty, and current idea of "cool"

multimedia

already, one-third of many textbooks is visual

value of user testing

often glitzy, not educationally sound

MTV

often violate Sweller's "split-attention effect"

often don't know how to think about information design

definition: burden placed on human short-term memory when explanatory text is separate from the diagrams

need to understand trade-offs and real-world constraints

248

Visual Language is already Having Global Impacts

The widespread global use of visual language

increases learning speed

decreases learning errors

contextualizes interpretations

allows for more complex expression

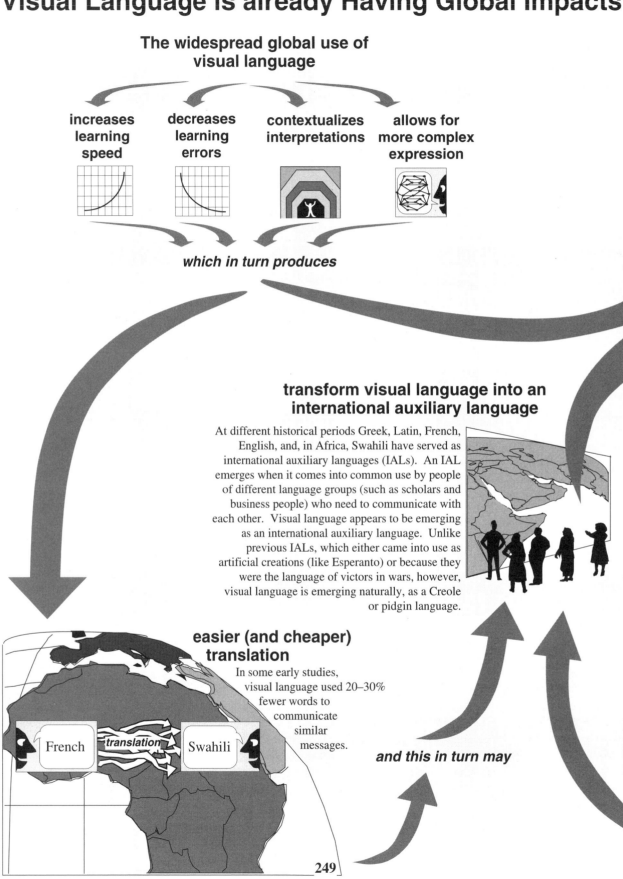

which in turn produces

transform visual language into an international auxiliary language

At different historical periods Greek, Latin, French, English, and, in Africa, Swahili have served as international auxiliary languages (IALs). An IAL emerges when it comes into common use by people of different language groups (such as scholars and business people) who need to communicate with each other. Visual language appears to be emerging as an international auxiliary language. Unlike previous IALs, which either came into use as artificial creations (like Esperanto) or because they were the language of victors in wars, however, visual language is emerging naturally, as a Creole or pidgin language.

easier (and cheaper) translation

In some early studies, visual language used 20–30% fewer words to communicate similar messages.

French *translation* Swahili

and this in turn may

249

easier communication for people speaking a second language

Much of the communication in companies and organizations around the world is done by people speaking, not their 1st learned languages, but 2nd or 3rd languages. Visual language will facilitate such communication.

which may help us resolve some of our complex global issues

Diminishing fresh water

Rights for minorities and women

Disruptive and facilitating effects of information technology

Emerging diseases

which in turn produces

Steady decrease in biodiversity

Doubling of world population in 40–50 years

Potential for rapid climate change

Decrease in cheap oil

Continuing rainforest destruction

Rapid increase in toxic wastes

Widening gap between rich and poor

Nuclear waste disposal

Ozone depletion

Rapid increase in groundwater pollution

Nuclear proliferation

Immune microorganisms

Soil erosion

Religious, ethnic, and racial hostilities

improved communication, distance learning, and teleconferencing in cross-ethnic teams

which may well lead to

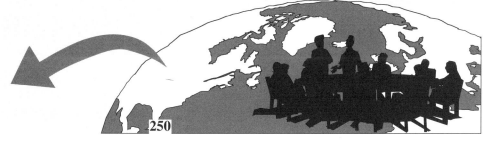

250

The Dialogue Has Begun

The 20th century has witnessed a long dialogue among linguists and philosophers about the degree to which natural language both limits and facilitates expression.

We are lucky to be living in an era in which the emergence of visual language will create new possibilities for human creativity and communication.

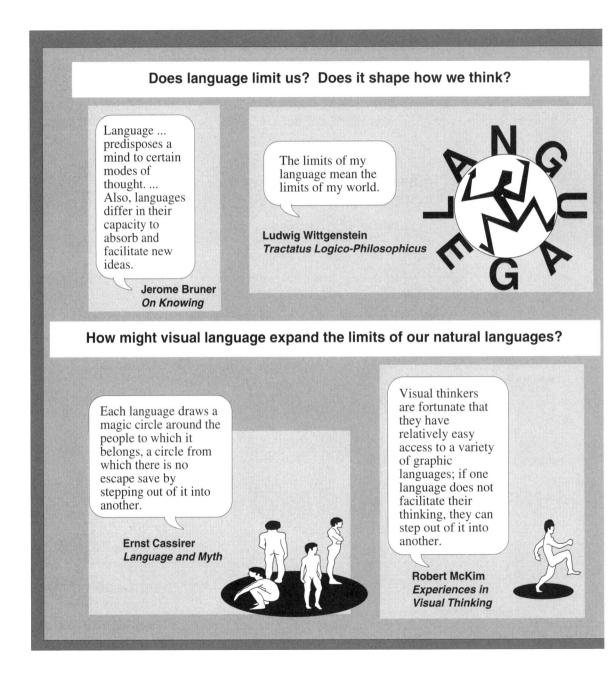

Does language limit us? Does it shape how we think?

Language ... predisposes a mind to certain modes of thought. ... Also, languages differ in their capacity to absorb and facilitate new ideas.

Jerome Bruner
On Knowing

The limits of my language mean the limits of my world.

Ludwig Wittgenstein
Tractatus Logico-Philosophicus

How might visual language expand the limits of our natural languages?

Each language draws a magic circle around the people to which it belongs, a circle from which there is no escape save by stepping out of it into another.

Ernst Cassirer
Language and Myth

Visual thinkers are fortunate that they have relatively easy access to a variety of graphic languages; if one language does not facilitate their thinking, they can step out of it into another.

Robert McKim
Experiences in Visual Thinking

Visual language has already enabled a number of people worldwide to jump out of the restrictive circle that Cassirer describes. It holds the same potential for all of us.

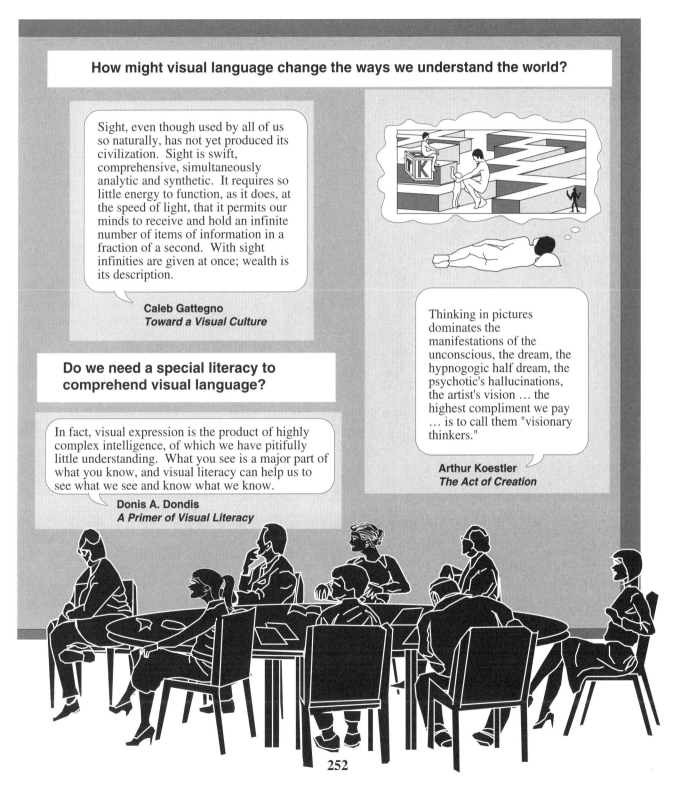

How might visual language change the ways we understand the world?

Sight, even though used by all of us so naturally, has not yet produced its civilization. Sight is swift, comprehensive, simultaneously analytic and synthetic. It requires so little energy to function, as it does, at the speed of light, that it permits our minds to receive and hold an infinite number of items of information in a fraction of a second. With sight infinities are given at once; wealth is its description.

Caleb Gattegno
Toward a Visual Culture

Do we need a special literacy to comprehend visual language?

In fact, visual expression is the product of highly complex intelligence, of which we have pitifully little understanding. What you see is a major part of what you know, and visual literacy can help us to see what we see and know what we know.

Donis A. Dondis
A Primer of Visual Literacy

Thinking in pictures dominates the manifestations of the unconscious, the dream, the hypnogogic half dream, the psychotic's hallucinations, the artist's vision … the highest compliment we pay … is to call them "visionary thinkers."

Arthur Koestler
The Act of Creation

252

The Challenges and Possibilities Are Extraordinary

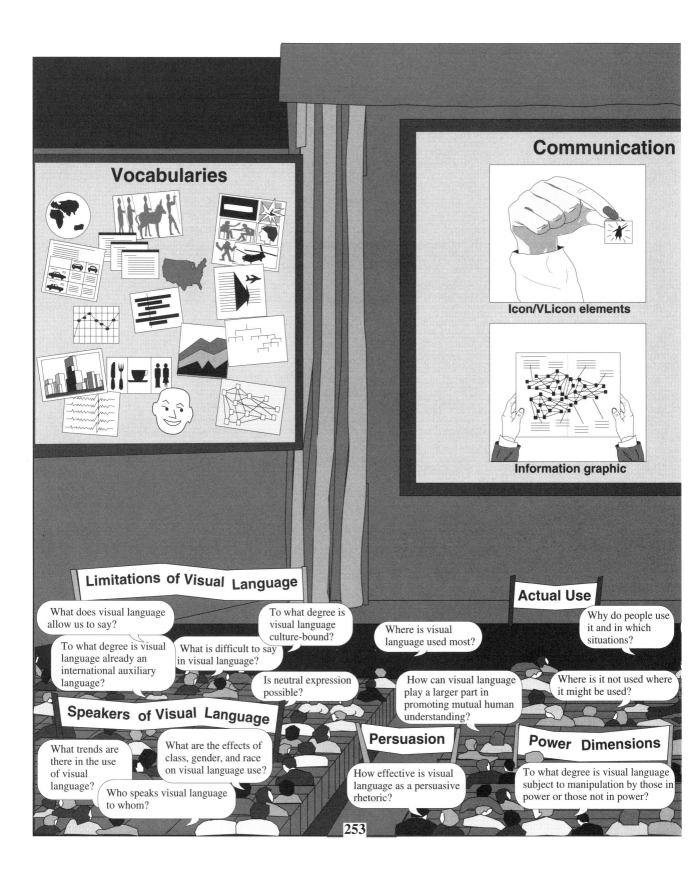

Notes

Chapter 1. A New Language Emerges

4 Quotes from Dondis (1973) and Gattegno (1969), respectively.

13–14 Why Is Visual Language a Language? Morris (1955, p. 100); Saussure (1916).

15–16 What is Driving the Emergence? Internet: 3rd quarter 1998 report from Computer Industry Forecasts (Cloverdale, CA), p. 51. PC sales: Estimate by Morgan Stanley Technology Research quoted in "U.S. Investment Research" (New York, May 1997). CD-ROMs: "Optical Publishing Industry Assessment, 9th Ed." (Woodstock, VT: InfoTech, Inc., 1998). Printers: Estimate by Morgan Stanley Technology Research quoted in "U.S. Investment Research" (New York, May 1997). Videoconferencing: "A High-Tech Way to Save Time and Money," *Nation's Business,* June 1998, p. 14. Advertising: *Statistical Abstracts of the United States,* 1996. Comic books: *Statistical Abstracts,* 1996.

21–22 Do you see what I mean? National Science Foundation (1987).

Chapter 2. A Brief History of Innovations

The publishers have striven to obtain permissions from copyright holders of the photographs reproduced in this chapter. If publishers have unwittingly infringed copyright they will gladly pay an appropriate fee upon being satisfied as to the owner's title.

23–24 Time Line: From Prehistoric Through Classical Age: Data recording: Sless (1994); White (1989); Marshack (1972). Carved bone from the Abri Lartet in the Gorge d'Enfer. ©Photo RMN.
Artwork: Windels (1949). Photo of caves of Lascaux, the Hall of Bulls. Photo by Montignac (MH 215613). ©Arch. Phot./CNMHS, Paris.
Map: Beniger and Robyn (1978); Thrower (1972); Neal (1970). Photo courtesy of the Semitic Museum, Harvard University, SM#4172.
Lists: Diringer (1953); Vervliet (1972); Twyman (1986); Neugebauer (1955). I would also like to thank 2 scholars at Univ. of California, Berkeley: Katie Keller, an Egyptologist, and Ann Kilmer, a Sumerian and Akkadian specialist. Photo shows a list of astronomical data from 104–112 BCE. ©Bildarchiv Preussischer Kulturbesitz, Berlin, Staatliche Museen zu Berlin, 1998.
Pictographic writing: Gaur (1984, p. 49).
Coordinate system: Beniger and Robyn (1978).
City plan: Thrower (1972). Photo courtesy of Friedrich Schiller Universitat, Jena, Germany.
Phonetic alphabet: Gaur (1984); Crystal (1987, p. 202).
Idea of earth as globe: Beniger and Robyn (1978); Ferris (1988). Photo by the Soprintendenza Archaeologica della Provincia Napoli e Caserta, Naples.
Information murals: Hare (1998).
Geometry manual: Beniger and Robyn (1978).
Chinese: Gaur (1984, p. 81), Crystal (1987).
Music notation: Vervliet (1972).
Euclid: Beniger and Robyn (1978).

25–26 Ancient Egyptian Language: I would like to thank Tom Hare, Stanford University, for his very useful tutoring of me in ancient Egyptian. p. 25, 1st col.: "Even the most strongly iconic use of hieroglyphs still usually requires the convention of a single supplementary stroke below or to the side of the glyph in question which as it were points to it and indicates that it is intended to represent the object it appears to be" (Hare, 1998, p. 19). p. 26, 3rd col.: Jan Assman, "Ancient Egypt and the Materiality of the Sign," in *Materialities of Communication,* quoted in Hare. The photo depicts a wall in the Temple of Seti.

27–28 Time Line: From Hellenistic Period Through Middle Ages: Invention of paper: Berry and Poole (1966). Curves on a time grid: Funkhauser (1938). Photo: Bayerische Staats-Bibliothek, München.
Graphic branching structures: Funkhauser (1938); Twyman (1986); Evans (1980). Photo: The College of Arms (MS. Muniment Room 20/5).
Tables: Twyman (1986). Photo of Ptolemy's *The Almagest* from Bibliotheque Nationale de France, Paris.
Codex: Gaur (1984).
Branching structures in diagrams: Evans (1980). Photo by permission of the British Library (Shelfmark: Roy IBX folio 5v).
Schematic diagrams: Evans (1980). Photo by permission of the British Library (Shelfmark: Roy IBX folio 6).
Bar graph: Beniger and Robyn (1978). Graph reproduced by permission of The Huntington Library, San Marino, CA.
Perspective: Edgerton (1975).
Spaces between words: Twyman (1986); Lupton and Miller (1996).
Extensive tabular information: Twyman (1986); Sullivan (1987); Diringer (1967). Photo: IV–30. Ratisbon School: Henry II Gospels (Vatican Library, *Ott. Lat. 74*), folio 9r.
Gutenberg: Gaur (1984). Bringhurst (1992) reminds us: "Printing from movable type was first invented not in Germany in the 1450s, as Europeans often claim, but in China in the 1040s. In preference to Gutenberg, we should honor a scholarly engineer by the name of Bí Sheng. The earliest surviving works printed in Asia from movable type seem to date from the 13th century, but there is a clear account of the typesetting process, and Bí Sheng's role in its development, by the 11th-century essayist Shen Kuo." Photo of Gutenberg Bible page courtesy of the Bancroft Library, Univ. of California, Berkeley.
First illustrated technical book: Clair (1969). Photo: Elmer Belt Library of Vinciana, Univ. of California, Los Angeles.
Page numbers: Gaur (1984). I would like to thank Anthony Bliss, a rare-books collector at the Bancroft Library (Univ. of California, Berkeley) for insightful information regarding initial use of indexes, routine use of page numbers, and the transition from scrolls to printed books.

29–30 Time Line: 16th Through 18th Centuries: Rectilinear tree structures: Beniger and Robyn (1978). Photo shows pedigree of family of Hesketh of Rufford, c. 1615. Photo by permission of the British Library (Shelfmark: Add 44026 Folios 7v-8).
Tables of empirical data: Beniger and Robyn (1978); Twyman (1986); Fischer and Kunz (1991).
Coordinate system: Beniger and Robyn (1978).
Leonardo da Vinci: McLanathan (1966).
Woodblock carving: Ivins (1969). This carving, "La grant danse macabre des hommes hystoriee," was made in 1499, and depicts a printing shop. Photo courtesy of Bancroft Library, Univ. of California, Berkeley.
Automatic recording device: Hoff and Geddes (1962); Beniger and Robyn (1978); Wren (1750). Photo: British Architectural Library, RIBA, London.
Data mapping: Beniger and Robyn (1978); Thrower (1981). Photo from *A new and correct chart shewing the variations of the compass in the Western and Southern oceans in the year 1700,*

William Andrews Clark Memorial Library, Univ. of California, Los Angeles.
Biographical time line: Twyman (1986, p. 216).
Coordinate paper: Beniger and Robyn (1978).
Bar chart: Beniger and Robyn (1978); Funkhauser (1936).
Descriptive geometry: Booker (1963). Photo from Monge (1798; reprint, 1922).

31–32 Priestley: Twyman (1986, p. 216). The chart on this page is from Priestley (1786). Reproduction of chart courtesy of University Research Library Special Collections, Univ. of California, Los Angeles.

33–34 Playfair: Beniger and Robyn (1978); Funkhauser (1938). Pie chart: From Playfair's translation of D. F. Donnant, *Statistical Account of the United States of America* (1805). Photo by permission of British Library (Shelfmark: 10411 f 27). Circle graph: From Playfair *The Statistical Breviary: Showing the resources of every state and kingdom in Europe.* (1801). Photo courtesy of Baker Library, Harvard Business School. Bar graph and time series are from Playfair, *Commercial and Political Atlas* (1801). Photo by permission of the British Library (Imports and Exports of Scotland [Shelfmark: LR 111 a 18], and Chart of National Debt, [Shelfmark: 8247.d.e.2.].).

35–36 Time Line: 19th and Early 20th Centuries:
Subdivided bar graph: Beniger and Robyn (1978). Photo: Alexander von Humboldt, Mexico-Atlas (Quellen und Forschungen zur Geschichte der Geographie und der Reisen Nr. 6), Stuttgart (Brockhaus/Antiquarium), 1969.
Cumulative frequency graph: Beniger and Robyn (1978).
Curve-fitting to scatterplot: Beniger and Robyn (1978).
Map with statistical diagrams: Tufte (1983); Funkhauser (1938). Photo from Marey (1885, p. 73).
Circle graph: Beniger and Robyn (1978); Funkhauser (1938).
Pie chart: Beniger and Robyn (1978).
Histogram: Beniger and Robyn (1978). Photo: Goldsmith's Library of Economic Literature, Univ. of London Library.
Visual storytelling techniques: Twyman (1990); Gombrich (1960); Couperie et al. (1968). Photo from Töpffer (1860, plates 52–53).
Polar area diagram: Cohen (1984); Funkhauser (1936).
Stereogram: Beniger and Robyn (1978).
Work Flow Charts: Gilbreth (1919). Photo from Gilbreth (1919).
ISOTYPE: Neurath (1974); Twyman (1986); Lupton (1989).
Computer flow charts: Goldstine and von Neumann (1948; reprint, 1963). Photo from von Neumann (1963, p. 161).
Pictograms: Neurath (1974); Twyman (1976); Lupton (1989); Beniger and Robyn (1978). Photo from Mulhall (1892, plate 5).
Gantt: Clark (1942). Photo from Gantt (1919).
First college course in graphical methods in statistics: Beniger and Robyn (1978).
First comparative study between pie and subdivided bar charts: Beniger and Robyn (1978); Eells (1926).

37 Töpffer: Twyman (1990); Gombrich (1960); Couperie et al. (1968). The drawings on this page are from Töpffer (1860, plates 52–53).

38 Nightingale: Cohen (1984); Funkhauser (1938). [Chart from Nightingale, *Notes on Matters Affecting the Health, Efficiency and Hospital Administration of the British Army* (1858), an 800-page report on her experiences in the Crimean War. Photo courtesy of Bancroft Library, Univ. of California, Berkeley.

39 Mulhall: Neurath (1974); Twyman (1976); Lupton (1989); Beniger and Robyn (1978). The cow diagram is from Mulhall (1892, plate 5). The boat diagram is from Mulhall (1885, facing page 35).

40 Neurath: Neurath (1974); Twyman (1976); Lupton (1989).

41–42 Gantt: Clark (1942). The charts are reproduced from Gantt (1919, 1913).

43 von Neumann: Goldstine and von Neumann (1948). Photo from von Neumann (1963, p. 161).

44 Kavanagh: Cantrell et al. (1961); Schmidt and Kavanagh (1964); Kavanagh (1960); Grad (1961). Quotations are from Schmidt and Kavanagh (1964) and Kavanagh (1960), respectively.

45–46 PERT/CPM Charts: Starr (1964). Photos from Malcolm, Rosebloom, Clark, and Fazar (1959, p. 665) and from Niemann and Learn (1960), respectively.

47–48 Time Line: Late 20th Century: PERT/CPM charts: Starr (1964); Martin and McClure (1985). Photo from Niemann and Learn (1960).
Graphic computer software: Sutherland (1963, 1965). Photo courtesy of Ivan E. Sutherland.
Decision tables: Cantrell et al. (1961); Kavanagh (1960); Schmidt and Kavanagh (1964); Grad (1961). Table redrawn courtesy of Association for Computing Machinery.
Theory of verbal/visual rhetoric: Bonsiepe (1966).
Surface rendering: Sutherland et al. (1972).
Graphical user interface and desktop metaphor: Sutherland (1965, 1963).
Theory of linear and nonlinear reading: Twyman (1979).
Theory of externalizing ideas in problem solving: McKim (1972).
World Wide Web: Holloway (1997)
Virtual reality: Ivan Sutherland, personal communication with author, 1998. Photo coutesy of Ivan E. Sutherland.
Making group process visible: Sibbet (1981).
Volume rendering: Information comes from interviews with Jim Blinn, Alvy Ray Smith, and Loren Carpenter. Photo courtesy of Loren Carpenter, Pixar Corporation.
Theory of semiotics of graphics: Bertin (1983).
Excellence in quantitative presentation: Tufte (1983).

Chapter 3. Communication Units, Morphology, and Syntax

53–54 Overview of Linguistic Analysis: Pinker (1994, pp. 149–150) is the source for the estimate of the number of English-language words and numbers that are recognizable to high-school graduates.

56 Visual Language Communication Units: For use of concept diagrams in architecture, see Duerk (1993).

57–58 Icon and VLicon Elements: "Meaning not always clearly recognizable": Easterby and Graydon (1981), as summarized by Sless (1986).

63–64 Information Murals: This infomural originally appeared in Horn (1989). Reprinted by permission.

65–66 Morphology—The Study of Visual Primitives: Bertin (1983); Saint-Martin (1987).

67–68 Three-Dimensional Components as Morphological Primitives of Perception: Biederman (1987).

69–70 Morphological Units in Visual Language:
Goldsmith's unity approach (1979) is also supported by perceptual research like Biederman's (1987), and by Evelyn Rosch's research on basic-level concept formation. Rosch's work in cognitive psychology suggests that we organize the world conceptually at a basic level that is defined by (1) the perception in Gestalts of shapes of a size easily visible to the eye, (2) a capacity to form mental images, and (3) psychomotor interactions with objects (Rosch, 1978). This is a level of size and organization that enables humans to conceptualize "discontinuities in nature that matter most for our everyday functioning" (Johnson, 1987, p. 208).

75–76 Syntax and Gestalt Theory: Quotes on p. 75 are from Haber and Hershenson (1973, p. 183–184); quotes on p. 76 are from Rock (1984, p. 116).

87–88 Same Syntax, Different Syntactical Topologies: I relied on Thiagarajan (1990) and many graphic design texts for this idea.

Chapter 4. The Emerging Semantics of Visual Language

93 The Emerging Semantics of Visual Language: Morris (1955).

99–100 Semantic Investigations: The ideas on this page were stimulated by Bonsiepe (1966) and Marcus (1983).

101–104 Types of Semantic Tight Integration: Gui Bonsiepe, whose investigation of tight integration (though not by that name) stimulated the analysis on these pages. He noted that it is difficult to propose useful explanations if we start either from prior verbal or visual descriptive systems. He proposed that a "visual/verbal rhetorical figure is a combination of two types of signs whose effectiveness in communication depends on the tension between their semantic characteristics. The signs do not simply add up, but rather operate in cumulative reciprocal relations" (Bonsiepe, 1966). Bonsiepe showed that some of the classical rhetorical devices found in text and speech can also be found in verbal-visual union. In order to understand his approach I present some of his comments on specific rhetorical devices. Bonsiepe focused his analysis on advertising. It's not surprising that the earliest attempts to understand visual language were focused on advertising messages. Many of the innovations in tight integration of verbal and visual elements were first made there. The field attracted some of the best artists and writers and has a tradition of close collaboration to produce a unified communication unit.

113–122 This section relies heavily on the ideas of George Lakoff, from lectures and in personal conversations. Also, see Lakoff and Johnson (1980).

113 Metaphors in Visual Language: As the cognitive scientist George Lakoff has pointed out, our culture has a strong widespread metaphor that tells us that "more is up and less is down." The source domain "upness," or verticality, is a fundamental way we understand the world because we walk in an upright position and feel gravity. The experience of gravity is a fundamental condition of human functioning as a body–mind. Moreover, as Lakoff says, "[There is a] structured correlation in

our daily experience that motivates every detail in this particular metaphorical mapping. Whenever we add more of a substance—say, water to a glass—the level goes up. When we add more object to a pile, the level rises. Remove objects from the pile or water from the glass, and the level goes down ... MORE correlates with UP; LESS correlates with DOWN" (Lakoff, 1987).

123–124 Diagram Vocabulary: Simon and Larkin (1989). Also, see Mayer and Gallini (1990).

131–132 Types of Highly Standardized Diagrams: Martin and McClure (1984, 1985).

133 When Vocabularies Intersect: The *Science* magazine article from which the diagram is adapted is Steller (1995, fig. 1). Steller adapted the diagram from Ellis et al. (1991, fig. 1). It is adapted here with permission from *Annual Review of Cell Biology*.

135–142 This section relies on McCloud (1993).

139–140 Emotional Expression and Faces: Erkman (1997).

145–146 Compositional Distinctions: The taxonomy is from Dondis (1973).

147–148 Associative Interpretation of Lines: These associations are garnered from 3 books, one by filmmaker Herbert Zettl (1973), one by architect Omar Faruque (1984), and one by cartoonist Scott McCloud (1993).
Horizontal: Vast open space, suggesting lakes, oceans, open fields (Faruque); passive, timeless (McCloud); earthy, satisfying (Faruque); calmness, tranquility, rest, stability (Zettl).
Vertical: Gravity, stability, stately, noble (Faruque); 2 vertical lines "together oppose each other," proud, strong (McCloud); exciting, extra energy, dynamic (Zettl).
Radial: Light, energy, petals of a flower, center to fringe, central concentration of energy, vitality at center received by fringe (Faruque).
Diverging: Expanding, increasing, reaching out, progressive separation (Faruque); earth defying, adventurous, dynamism (Zettl).
Converging: Reducing, decreasing, focusing, spatial depth, illusion of perspective and distance (Faruque).
Progression: Waves advance and recede, progression, direction (Faruque).
Retreat: Concave, retreat (Faruque).
Concave: Recessed, cut in, molded, sense of containment, inviting, protecting, shelter-giving (Faruque); warm, gentle (McCloud).
Convex: Expanding, pressing, repelling (Faruque).
Rising: Mountain peaks, tall buildings, rising, tapering upward (Faruque); dynamic, changing (McCloud); improvement, attainment, success, optimism, progress, hope (Faruque).
Falling: Converging downward, falling, sinking, degeneration, defeat, pessimism (Faruque).
Smooth, refined: Undisturbed dunes, seascapes, spotless, smooth, details evoke refinement, delicate mood (Faruque).
Rough, brutal: Irregular lines, sharp points, roughness, cracks, breaks, animal teeth, hard brutal continuous directional changes, jagged, hardness, brutality (Faruque); unwelcoming, severe (McCloud); exciting, energetic (Zettl).

Active, dynamic: Motion, quick changes of direction, fast movement, sharp, acute angles, lightning, electricity, forceful curvilinear movements (Faruque).

Static, fixed: Point at center of square or circle, uniform space around, focus, stability, bilateral symmetry, no tension, no imbalance, static emotion (Faruque).

Structural stability: Stability, strength, structure, solidity (Faruque); rational, conservative (McCloud).

Rolling, wavering, meandering: Wind, air, water, snow, sweeping, rolling curves, swelling, sliding, fluidity, casual, relaxed, interesting (Faruque).

Irregular wavering: Uncertainty, weakness, lacks confidence (Faruque).

151 Image Constancy and Slices of Space–Time: Quotes are from McCloud (1993, p. 67) and Rock (1984).

153–154 Transitions in Space–Time: These 2 pages rely heavily on the taxonomy of McCloud (1993, p. 70), whose explication of transition of comics is an excellent demonstration of both analytic ability and visual language skill. Illustrations are mine.

157–158 Chapter Summary: The central illustration is from Horn (1989). Reprinted with permission.

Chapter 5. Functional Semantics of Content

171 Show Motion: For more on "squash and stretch," see Thomas and Johnston (1981, pp. 47–51)

173 Show Which (Name, Label, and Indicate): Supercockpit is from Wright Patterson Air Force Base archives.

174 Show Which (Definitions): Tort example from Carroll (1974). For discussion, see Rowntree (1981).

176 Show Examples: Example is from Horn (1989).

Chapter 6. Functional Semantics of Rhetoric

187–188 Cluster Visual and Verbal Elements: In my book *Mapping Hypertext* (1989), I present in considerable detail some of the research that isolates the chunking function, including the classic research papers of George Miller and Herbert Simon.

194 Provide Lightness, Humor, and Irony: "There are no lazy veteran lion hunters" (Augustine's Law No. III; reprint, 1983).

Chapter 7. Pragmatics of Visual Language

201 Pragmatics of Visual Language: Crystal (1987, p. 120).

203–204 Social Context: Where has Visual Language Become a Basic Communication Tool?
Technical writers: Each of 53,000 technical writers (*Statistical Abstracts of the United States,* 1996) produces 4 pages per working day, 1 in 20 of which is estimated to contain visual language. There are 243 working days in the year.
Presenters: 70 percent of employees in the following categories are estimated to make at least 1 presentation with 10 slides annually: public officials and administrators; financial managers; personnel and labor relations managers; marketing, advertising, and public relations managers; educational administrators; architects; aerospace, civil, electrical, electronic, industrial, and mechanical engineers; operations and systems researchers and analysts; natural scientists; social scientists and urban planners; sales supervisors and proprietors; sales representatives, finance and business services; and commodities sales representatives. Total employees in these categories are 14,625,000 (*Statistical Abstracts,* 1996).
Instructors, course developers: Of the 5.4 million teachers and professors in the United States (*Statistical Abstracts,* 1996), an estimated 1 in 4 use visual language on a semiregular basis.
Engineers and drafting technicians: Sales of presentation graphics, drawings/paintings, desktop publishing, and other graphics software packages totaled $1,320,000 in 1995 (*Statistical Abstracts,* 1996). Average cost of drawing software is estimated at $250.
World Wide Web teams: An estimated 70 percent of World Wide Web sites are composed with visual language. As of January 16, 1997, Netree's Internet Statistics [http:\\www.netree.com\netbin\ internetstats] counted 1.6 million WWW sites.
Scientists and statisticians: Tufte (1983, introduction).
Cartoonists and comic book artists: *Statistical Abstracts* (1996) reports 71,428,571 comic books sold.
Advertising and graphic designers: *Statistical Abstracts* (1996) reports $8.5 billion total revenue in magazine advertising and reports 556,000 designers; 663,000 marketing, advertising, and public relations managers; and 142,000 public relations specialists.
Multimedia and animation makers: Revenue from interactive digital media was $2.4 million in 1994 (*Statistical Abstracts,* 1996).
Team managers: Estimated number of meetings adapted from a 1997 presentation made by Intel Corporation at DVC '97 quoting statistics provided by Dataquest.
Greeting cards: Estimates based on an average price per card of $1, and on the revenue and market share reports of the *New York Times* ("Wish You Weren't Here," Nov. 20, 1997). Hallmark's revenues were $3.6 billion, with 42 percent of the market; American Greetings' revenues were $2.2 billion, with 35 percent of the market.
Newspaper and magazine artists and designers: The 800 members of the Society for Newspaper Designers (as of mid-1997) create an average of 3 infographics per week.
Report and proposal writers: 70 percent of employees in the following categories are estimated to write at least one presentation annually: public officials and administrators; financial managers; personnel and labor relations managers; marketing, advertising, and public relations managers; educational administrators; architects; aerospace, civil, electrical, electronic, industrial, and mechanical engineers; operations and systems researchers and analysts; natural scientists; social scientists and urban planners; sales supervisors and proprietors; sales representatives, finance and business services; and commodities sales representatives. Total employees in these categories are 14,625,000 (*Statistical Abstracts,* 1996). At least one page of every other report is estimated to include visual language.
Architects: *Statistical Abstracts* (1996) reports 163,000 architects and 62,000 surveying and mapping technicians in 1995.
Television: Nielsen Media Research (1997).

205–206 Visability and Accessibility of Complex Issues: Infomural reproduced from a MacroVU, Inc. project.

207–208 Illumination of Cross-Boundary Issues: I would like to thank Don Michael for engaging with me in many incisive discussions of these issues.

209–210 Exploring Deeper Connections and Feelings: I would like to express my thanks to the fellows of the Meridian International Institute, San Francisco, for the benefit of many discussions that I facilitated with visual language. The drawing on this page is a partial record of one of those discussions.

211–212 Displaying Problem Analysis: These pages owe a debt to the thinking of Laseau (1986).

213 Creative Problem Solving: Quotes are from McKim (1972).

215–216 Making Group Process Visible: The framework and detail for these pages are from David Sibbet's lectures and from his 1981 book, *I See What You Mean*. I would like to express appreciation for many wonderful conversations with David.

217–218 Presenting Multiple Points of View: The example is from Horn et al. (1998).

219–220 Facilitating Cross-Cultural Communication: The examples are from Schein (1996). I am grateful to Ed Schein for illuminating dicussions of the problems of this kind of communication.

221–222 Facilitating International Communication: The tight integration of diagrams and text reduces the amount of text by a minimum of 20 to 30 percent. That estiamte is based on a few such comparisons made by MacroVU, Inc., particularly with information graphics. The list of global problems is excerpted from a 1997 United Nations report, "1997 State of the Future."

227–228 Visual Language Often Encourages Analysis and Synthesis: These pages summarize Bertin (1983, pp. 140–141).

229–230 How the Eye is Directed by Visual Language: The framework for these pages is from Twyman (1979). Illustrations are my own.

231–232 Mix of Words and Visual Elements in Different Media: Externalization of ideas is discussed in McKim.

233 Visual Language Has a Proven Effectiveness: Chandler and Sweller (1992).

234 Oppenheim et al. (1981).

235–236 Evolving Criteria for Good Practice: The quotes are from William Cleveland (1985). Stephen Kosslyn (1994) has also provided an important collection of empirically based guidelines. See also my description (1998) of information design as an emerging field. Discussions of metaphorical graphics may be found in W. G. Cole and J. G. Stewart (1993). The idea of the limits of short-term memory was introduced by Miller (1956). Also, see Simon (1979).

235–236 Evolving Criteria for Good Practice: The ideas and quotes on this page are from Tufte (1983). Visual examples are original.

237 Information Design: An Emerging Profession: See Horn (1998), Miller (1956), Simon (1979), Cole and Stewart (1993).

Chapter 8. Conclusions and Challenges

241–242 Visual Language Transcends the Constraining Effects of the Alphabet: Culkin (1967, p. 42–43).

243–246 Good discussions of these issues can be found in Lanham (1993), Bolter (1991), and Wurman (1989).

245 Potential Cultural Impacts: McLuhan (1964).

248 Visual Language will be a Boon to Education: For more on the split-attention effect, see Sweller and Chandler 1994).

249–250 Visual Language is already having Global Impacts: For an excellent discussion of international auxiliary languages, see Eco (1995).

251–252 The Dialogue has Begun: Quotations are from Wittgenstein (1922); Bruner (1962); Cassirer (1946); McKim (1972); Koestler, quoted in Dondis (1973); Dondis (1973); Gattegno (1969).

References

Augustine, N. R. 1983. Augustine's laws. Rev. and enl. ed. New York: America Institute of Aeronautics and Astronautics.

Baker, S. 1961. *Visual persuasion.* New York: McGraw-Hill.

Barker, J. 1980. *ABC for book collectors.* 6th ed. London: Granada.

Beniger, J. R., and D. L. Robyn. 1978. Quantitative graphics in statistics: A brief history. *American Statistician* 32 (1): 1–11.

Berry, W. T., and H. E. Poole. 1966. *Annals of printing: A chronological encyclopaedia from the earliest times to 1950.* Toronto: Univ. of Toronto Press.

Bertin, J. 1983. *Semiology of graphics: Diagrams, networks, and maps.* Madison, WI: Univ. of Wisconsin Press.

Biederman, I. 1987. Recognition-by-components: A theory of human image understanding. *Psychological Review* 94 (2): 115–147.

Bliss, E. K. 1965. *Semantography.* 2d ed. Sydney, Australia: Semantography.

Bolter, J. D. 1991. *Writing space: The computer, hypertext, and the history of writing.* Hillsdale, NJ: Lawrence Erlbaum.

Bonsiepe, G. 1966. Visual/verbal rhetoric. *Dot Zero* 2.

Booker, P. J. 1963. *A History of Engineering Drawing.* Linden: Chatto and Windus.

Bowman, W. J. 1968. *Graphic communication.* New York: Wiley.

Bringhurst, R. 1992. *The elements of typographic style.* Point Roberts, WA: Hartley and Marks.

Bruner, J. S. 1962. *On knowing: Essays for the left hand.* Cambridge, MA: Harvard Univ. Press.

Cantrell, H. N., J. King, and F. E. H. King. 1961. Logic-structure tables. *Communications of the ACM* 4 (June): 272–75.

Carroll, J. B. 1974. Words, meanings, and concepts. *Harvard Educational Review.* 34:178–202.

Cassirer, E. 1946. *Language and myth,* trans. S. K. Langer. New York: Dover.

Chandler, P., and J. Sweller. 1992. The split-attention effect as a factor in the design of instruction. *British Jounral of Educational Psychology* 62:233–246.

Clair, C. 1969. *A chronology of printing.* New York: Praeger.

Clark, W. 1942. *The Gantt chart: A working tool of management.* 2d ed. London: Sir Isaac Pitman & Sons.

Cleveland, W. S. 1985. *The elements of graphing data.* Pacific Grove, CA: Wadsworth.

Cohen, I. B. 1984. Florence Nightingale. *Scientific American,* March, 128–37.

Cole, W. G., and J. G. Stewart. 1993. Metaphor graphics to support integrated decision making with respiratory data. *International Journal of Clinical Monitoring and Computing.* 10:91–100.

Corel Corporation. 1994. *Corel GALLERY clipart catalog.* Ottawa, Canada: Corel.

Coupiere, P., M. C. Horn, P. Destefanis, E. François, C. Moliterni, and G. Gassiot-Talabot. 1968. *A history of the comic strip,* trans. E. B. Hennessy. New York: Crown.

Crystal, D., ed. 1987. *The Cambridge encyclopedia of language.* New York: Cambridge Univ. Press.

Culkin, J. 1967. Each culture develops its own sense-ratio to meet the demands of its environment. In *McLuhan: Hot and Cool,* ed. G. E. Stearn, 42–43. New York: Dial.

Diringer, D. 1953. *The hand-produced book.* London: Hutchinson's.

Diringer, D. 1967. *The illuminated book.* London: Faber and Faber.

Dondis, D. A. 1973. *A primer of visual literacy.* Cambridge, MA: MIT Press.

Dovas, G. 1898. *Souvenir of Egypt: Monuments, temples, mosques, and scenes from everyday life.* Cairo: N.p.

Dreyfuss, H. 1972. *Symbol sourcebook: An authoritative guide to international graphic symbols.* New York: McGraw-Hill. Reprint, 1984. New York: Van Nostrand Reinhold.

Duerk, D. P. 1993. *Architectural programming.* New York: Van Nostrand Reinhold.

Easterby, R. S., and I. R. Graydon. 1981. Comprehension/recognition tests. *AP Report* 100, (Univ. of Aston, Birmingham, United Kingdom, January 1981).

Eco, U. 1995. *The search for the perfect language.* Oxford: Blackwell.

Edgerton, S. Y., Jr. 1975. *The Renaissance rediscovery of linear perspective.* New York: Basic.

Eells, W. C. 1926. The relative merits of circles and bars for representing component parts. *Journal of the American Statistical Association* 21 (154): 119–32.

Eisner, W. 1985. *Comics and sequential art.* Tamarac, FL: Poorhouse.

Ekman, P. 1997. *What the face reveals: Basic and applied studies of spontaneous expression using the facial action coding system FACS.* New York: Oxford Univ. Press.

Ellis, R. E., J. Yuan, and H. R. Horwitz. 1991. Mechanisms/functions of cell death. *Annual Review of Cell Biology* 7:665–672.

Evans, H. 1974. *Handling newspaper text.* London: William Heinemann.

Evans, M. 1980. The geometry of the mind. *Architectural Association Quarterly* 12 (4): 32–55.

Faruque, O. 1984. *Graphic communication as a design tool.* New York: Van Nostrand Reinhold.

Ferris, T. 1988. *Coming of age in the milky way.* New York: Doubleday.

Fischer, W. and A. Kunz. 1991. *Grundlagen der Historischen Statistik von Deutschland.* Opladen, Germany: Westdeutscher Verlag.

Fleming, M., and W. H. Levie, eds. 1993. *Instructional message design: Principles from the behavioral and cognitive sciences.* 2d ed. Englewood Cliffs, NJ: Educational Technology.

Funkhauser, H. G. 1938. Historical development of the graphical representation of statistical data. *Osiris* (Bruges, Belgium) 3:269–404.

Gattegno, C. 1969. *Toward a visual culture: Educating through television.* New York: Onterbridge and Dienstfrey.

Gantt, H. L. 1913. *Work, wages, and profits.* 2nd ed. New York: Engineering Magazine Co.

Gantt, H. L. 1919. *Organizing for work.* New York: Harcourt, Brace, and Howe.

Gaur, A. 1984. *A history of writing.* London: Cross River.

Gilbreth, F. 1919. *Frank B. Gilbreth report.* New York: California Loading Co.

Glover, G. 1994. *Clip art: Image enhancement and integration.* New York: Windcrest/McGraw-Hill.

Goldstine, H. H., and J. von Neumann. [1948] 1963. Planning and coding problems for an electronic computing instrument. In *John von Neumann: Collected Works,* ed. A. H. Taub, 5:80–214. Oxford and New York: Pergamon.

Goldsmith, E. 1979. Comprehensibility of illustration: An analytical model. *Information Design Journal* 1:204–213.

Goldsmith, E. 1984. *Research into illustration: An approach and a review.* Cambridge, England: Cambridge Univ. Press.

Gombrich, E. H. 1960. *Art and illusion.* New York: Pantheon.

Grad, B. 1961. Tabular form in decision logic. *Datamation* 7 (July): 22–26.

Haber, R. N., and M. Hershenson. 1973. *The psychology of visual perception.* New York: Holt, Rinehart and Winston.

Halley, E. 1981. *The three voyages of Edmond Halley in the Paramore,* ed. N. J. W. Thrower. London: Hakluyt Society.

Hare, T. 1998. Remembering Osiris: Number, gender, and the word in Egyptian representational systems. Stanford, CA: Stanford Univ. Press.

Harley, J. B., and D. Woodward, eds. 1979. *The history of cartography.* Vol. 1, *Cartography in prehistoric, ancient, and medieval Europe and the Mediterranean.* Chicago: Univ. of Chicago Press.

Harris, R. L. 1996. *Information graphics: A comprehensive illustrated reference.* Atlanta: Management Graphics.

Hoff, H. E., and L. A. Geddes. 1962. The beginnings of graphic recording. *Isis* 53 (pt. 3, no. 173): 287–324.

Holloway, M. 1997. Molding the Web: Its inventor, Tim Berners-Lee, says the World Wide Web hasn't nearly reached its potential. *Scientific American,* December, 34–36.

Holmes, N. 1984. *Designer's guide to creating charts and diagrams.* New York: Watson-Guptill.

Holmes, N. 1991. *Pictorial maps.* New York: Watson-Guptill.

Holmes, N. 1993. *The best in diagrammatic graphics.* Mies, Switzerland: Rotovision.

Holmes, N., and R. DeNeve. 1985. *Designing pictorial symbols.* New York: Watson-Guptill.

Horn, R. E. 1989. *Mapping hypertext: Analysis, linkage, and display of knowledge for the next generation of on-line text and graphics.* Lexington, MA: Lexington Institute. Distributed by Information Mapping, Inc., Waltham, MA.

Horn, R. E. 1992a. Clarifying two controversies about Information Mapping's Method. *Educational and Training Technology International* 29 (2): 109–17.

Horn, R. E. 1992b. *How high can it fly? Examining the evidence on Information Mapping's method of high performance communication.* Lexington, MA: Lexington Institute. Distributed by Information Mapping, Inc., Waltham, MA.

Horn, R. E. 1993. Structured writing at twenty-five. *Performance and Instruction* 32 (February): 11–17.

Horn, R. E. 1997. Structured writing as a paradigm. In *Instructional development paradigms,* ed. C. Dills and A. Romiszowski. Englewood Cliffs, NJ: Educational Technology.

Horn, R. E. 1998. Information design: Emergence of a new profession. In *Information design,* ed. R. Jacobson. Cambridge, MA: MIT Press.

Horn, R. E., J. Yoshimi, R. McBride, and M. Deering. 1998. *Mapping great debates: Can computers think?* A series of 7 argumentation maps (36 x 48 in.). Bainbridge Island, WA: MacroVU, Inc.

Horton, W. 1991. *Illustrating computer documentation: The art of presenting information graphically on paper and online.* New York: Wiley.

Horton, W. 1994. *The icon book: Visual symbols for computer systems and documentation.* New York: Wiley.

Ivanov, V. V. 1992. Reconstructing the past. *Intercom* 15 (1): 1–4.

Ivins, W. 1969. *Prints and visual communication*. New York: Da Capo Press.

Johnson, M. 1987. *The body in the mind: The bodily basis of meaning, imagination, and reason*. Chicago: Univ. of Chicago Press.

Johnson, M. 1993. *Moral imagination: Implications of cognitive science for ethics*. Chicago: Univ. of Chicago Press.

Kandinsky, W. [1926] 1979. *Point and line to plane*. New York: Dover.

Karsten, K. G. 1923. *Charts and graphs: An introduction to graphic methods in the control and analysis of statistics*. New York: Prentice-Hall.

Kavanagh, T. F. 1960. TABSOL: A fundamental concept for systems-oriented language. *Proceedings of the Eastern Joint Computer Conference* 18.

Koestler, A. 1964. *The act of creation*. London: Hutchinson.

Kosslyn, S. M. 1989. Understanding charts and graphs. *Applied Cognitive Psychology* 3:185–226.

Kosslyn, S. M. 1994. *Elements of graph design*. New York: W. H. Freeman.

Lakoff, G. 1987. *Women, fire, and dangerous things*. Chicago: Univ. of Chicago Press.

Lakoff, G., and M. Johnson. 1980. *Metaphors we live by*. Chicago: Univ. of Chicago Press.

Lanham, R. A. 1993. *The electronic word: Democracy, technology, and the arts*. Chicago: Univ. of Chicago Press.

Laseau, P. 1986. *Graphic problem-solving for architects and designers*. New York: Van Nostrand Reinhold.

Lupton, E. 1989. Reading isotype. In *Design discourse: History/theory/criticism,* ed. V. Margolin. Chicago: Univ. of Chicago Press.

Lupton, E., and J. A. Miller. 1996. *Design writing research: Writing on graphic design*. New York: Princeton Architectural Press.

Macaulay, D. 1988. *The way things work*. Boston: Houghton Mifflin.

Malcolm, D. G., J. H. Rosebloom, C. E. Clark, and W. Fazar. 1959. Application of a technique for research and development program evaluation. *Operations Research*. 7 (5): 646–669.

Marcus, A. 1983. Visual rhetoric in a pictographic-ideographic narrative. In *Semiotics unfolding: Proceedings of the second congress of the International Association for Semiotic Studies, Vienna, July 1979*. Berlin: Monton.

Marey, E. J. 1885. *La Méthode graphique dans les sciences expérimentales et particuliérement en physiologie et en médecine*. Paris: Librarie de l'académie de Médecine.

Marshack, A. 1972. *Roots of civilization*. London: Weidenfeld and Nicolson.

Martin, J., and C. McClure. 1984. *Diagramming techniques for analysts and programmers*. Englewood Cliffs, NJ: Prentice-Hall.

Martin, J. and C. McClure. 1985. *Action diagrams*. Englewood Cliffs, NJ: Prentice Hall.

Mayer, R. E., and J. K. Gallini. 1990. When is an illustration worth ten thousand words*? Journal of Educational Psychology*. 82 (4): 715–726.

McCloud, S. 1993. *Understanding comics: The invisible art*. Northampton, MA: Kitchen Sink.

McKim, R. 1972. *Experiences in visual thinking*. Monterey, CA: Brooks/Cole.

McKim, R. 1980. *Thinking visually: A strategy for problem solving*. Belmont, CA: Lifetime Learning.

McLanathan, R. 1966. *Images of the universe: Leonardo DaVinci: The artist as scientist*. Garden City, NY: Doubleday.

McLuhan, M. 1964. *Understanding media: The extensions of man*. New York: McGraw-Hill.

McNaught, A. B., and R. Callander. 1972. *Illustrated physiology*. Edinburgh, Scotland: Churchill Livingstone.

Miller, G. A. 1956. The magical number seven, plus or minus two: Some limits on our capacity for processing information. *Psychology Review*. 63 (2): 81–96.

Modley, R., and D. Lowenstein. 1952. *Pictographs and graphs: How to make and use them*. New York: Harper.

Monge, G. [1798] 1922. *Géométrie descriptive*. Paris: Gauthier-Villars.

Morris, C. 1955. *Signs, language, and behavior*. New York: G. Braziller.

Mulhall, M. 1892. *Dictionary of statistics*. London: Routledge and Sons.

Mulhall, M. 1885. *A history of prices since the year 1850*. London: Longman, Green, and Co.

National Science Foundation. 1987. *Visualization in scientific computing*. Washington, DC: National Science Foundation.

Neal, H. E. 1970. *Of maps and men*. New York: Funk & Wagnalls.

Niemann, R. A., and R. N. Learn. 1960. Mechanization of the PERT system on NORC. Technical Memorandum No. K-19/59, U. S. Naval Weapons Laboratory. Washington, DC: GPO.

Neugebauer, O. 1955. *Astronomical cuneiform texts III*. London: Published for the Institute for Advanced Study, Princeton, NJ: Lund Humphries.

Neurath, M. 1974. Isotype. *Instructural Science* 3:127–150.

Neurath, O. 1973. *Empiricism and sociology,* trans. P. Foulkes and M. Neurath. Dordrecht, Netherlands: Reidel.

Oppenheim, L., C. Kydd, V. P. Carroll, and G. Carroll. 1981. A study of the effects of the use of overhead transparencies on business meetings. Unpublished paper. Wharton Applied Research Center and School of Medicine, Univ. of Pennsylvania.

Pettersson, R. 1989. *Visuals for information: Research and practice.* Englewood Cliffs, NJ: Educational Technology.

Pinker, S. 1994. *The language instinct: How the mind creates language.* New York: William Morrow.

Playfair, W., trans. 1805. *Statistical account of the United States of America,* by D. Donnant. London: Greenland and Norris.

Playfair, W. 1801. *Commercial and political atlas.* London: Corry.

Playfair, W. 1801. *The statistical breviary.* London: T. Bensley.

Playfair, W. 1786. *The commercial and political atlas.* London.

Priestley, J. 1786. *A description of a chart of biography.* London: Warrington.

Rock, I. 1984. *Perception.* New York: Scientific American Library.

Rock, I., and S. Palmer. 1990. The legacy of Gestalt psychology. *Scientific American,* December, 84–90.

Rosch, Eleanor. 1978. *Principles of Categorization.* Cognition and Categorization, ed. E. Rosch and B. B. Lloyd, 27–48. Hillsdale, NJ: Lawrence Erlbaum.

Rowntree, D. 1981. *Developing courses for students.* Maidenhead, England: McGraw-Hill.

Saint-Martin, F. 1987. *Semiotics of visual language.* Bloomington, IN: Indiana Univ. Press.

de Saussure, F. [1916] 1986. *Course in general linguistics,* trans. and annotated by R. Harris. La Salle, IL: Open Court.

Schein, E. H. 1996. Three Cultures of Management: The Key to Organizational Learning. *Sloan Management Review* 38 (1):9–20.

Schmid, C. F. 1978. The role of standards in graphic presentation. In *Graphic presentation of statistical information: Papers presented at the 136th annual meeting of the American Statistical Association.* Washington DC: U.S. Department of Commerce, Bureau of the Census.

Schmidt, D. T., and T. F. Kavanagh. 1964. Using decision structure tables. Part one: Principles and preparation. *Datamation,* February, 42–52.

Schmidt, D. T., and T. F. Kavanagh. 1964. Using decision structure tables. Part two: Manufacturing applications. *Datamation,* March, 48–54.

Shneiderman, B. 1992. *Designing the user interface: Strategies for effective human-computer interaction.* 2d ed. Reading, MA: Addison-Wesley.

Sibbet, D. 1981. *I see what you mean!* A workbook guide to Group Graphics. San Francisco: Sibbet & Associates.

Simon, H. 1979. How big is a chunk? In *Models of thought,* 50–61. 2 vols. New Haven, CT: Yale Univ. Press.

Simon, H., and Larkin, J. 1989. Why a diagram is (sometimes) worth 10,000 words. In *Models of thought,* 2:413–438.

Sless, D. 1986. *In search of semiotics.* London: Croom Helm.

Sless, D. 1994. What is information design? In *Designing information for people: Proceedings from the symposium.* Hackett, Australia: Communication Research.

Smith, S. L. and J. N. Mosier. 1986. *Guidelines for designing user interface software.* Bedford, MA: Mitre.

Starr, M. K. 1964. *Production management: Systems and synthesis.* Englewood Cliffs, NJ: Prentice-Hall.

Steller, H. 1995. Mechanisms and genes of cellular suicide. *Science* 277 (March 10): 1445–49.

Sullivan, P. 1987. *Newspaper graphics.* Darmstadt, Germany: IFRA.

Sutherland, I. 1963. Sketchpad: A man–machine graphical communication system. In *Proceedings of the Spring Joint Computer Conference:* AFIPS, May, 329–508.

Sutherland, I. 1965. The ultimate display. In vol. 2 of *Proceedings of IFIP Congress 65.* Washington, DC: Spartan.

Sutherland, I., R. F. Sproull, and R. A. Schumacker. 1972. A characterization of ten hidden-surface algorithms. Unpublished manuscript.

Sweller, J., and P. Chandler. 1994. Why some material is difficult to learn. *Cognition and Instruction* 12 (3): 185–233.

Thiagarajan, S. 1990. Presenting hierarchical information and ensampler. *Performance and Instruction,* April, 23–25.

Thomas, F., and O. Johnston. 1981. *Disney animation: The illusion of life.* New York: Abbeville Press.

Thompson, P., and P. Davenport. 1980. *The dictionary of graphic images.* New York: St. Martin's Press.

Thrower, N. J. W. 1972. *Maps and man: An examination of cartography in relation to culture and civilization.* Englewood Cliffs, NJ: Prentice-Hall.

Thrower, N. J. W. 1972. *Maps and civilization: Cartography in culture and society.* Chicago: Univ. of Chicago Press.

Thrower, N. J. W., ed. 1981. *The three voyages of Edmund Halley in the Paramore 1698–1701.* London: Hakluyt Society.

Tinker, M. A. 1963. *Legibility of print.* Ames, IA: Iowa State Univ. Press.

Töpffer, R. [1860] 1996. *Monsieur Crepin; Monsieur Pencil: Deux egarements de la science.* Vol. 2. Paris: Seuil.

Tufte, E. 1983. *The visual display of quantitative information.* Cheshire, CT: Graphics.

Tufte, E. 1990. *Envisioning information.* Cheshire, CT: Graphics.

Tufte, E. 1997. *Visual explanations: Images and quantities, evidence, and narrative.* Chesire, CT: Graphics Press.

Twyman, M. 1976. The significance of isotype. *Icographic* 10:2–10.

Twyman, M. 1979. Schema for the study of graphic language. In *Processing of visible language,* ed. P. A. Kolers, M. E. Wrolstad, and H. Bouma. New York: Plenum.

Twyman, M. 1986. Articulating graphic language: A historical perspective. In *Toward a new understanding of literacy*, ed. M. E. Wrolstad and D. F. Fisher. New York: Praeger.

Twyman, M. 1990. *Early lithographed books.* London: Farrand.

U. S. National Bureau of Standards. 1967. *Legibility of alphanumeric characters and other symbols.* Vol. 2, *A reference handbook.* Washington, DC: U. S. Department of Commerce.

Vervliet, H. D. L., ed. 1972. *The book through 5000 years.* London: Phaidon.

Volk, T. 1995. *Metapatterns across space, time, and mind.* New York: Columbia Univ. Press.

von Neumann, J. 1963. *Collected works,* ed. A. H. Taub. Oxford: Pergamon Press.

White, R. 1989. Visual thinking in the Ice Age. *Scientific American,* July, 92–99.

Windels, F. 1949. *Chapelle Sixtine de la prehistoire.* Montignac-sur-Veserre: Centre d'etudes et de documentation prehistoriques.

Winn, W. 1982. Design principles for diagrams and charts. In *The technology of text.* Englewood Cliffs, NJ: Educational Technology.

Winn, W. 1990. Encoding and retrieval of information in maps and diagrams. *IEEE Transactions on Professional Communication* 33 (3): 103–7.

Wittgenstein, L. [1922] 1981. *Tractatus logico-philosophicus.* London: Routledge & Kegan Paul.

Wren, C. 1750. *Parentalia, or, memoirs of the family of Wrens.* London: T. Osborn.

Wurman, R. S. 1989. *Information anxiety.* New York: Doubleday.

Wurman, R. S. 1992. *Follow the yellow brick road: Learning to give, take and use instructions.* New York: Bantam.

Zelazny, G. 1991. *Say it with charts.* Homewood, IL: Business One Irwin.

Zettl, H. 1973. *Sight, sound, motion: Applied media aesthetics.* Belmont, CA: Wadworth.

Index

268